CLASSIC MENU DESIGN

FROM *THE COLLECTION OF*

THE NEW YORK PUBLIC LIBRARY

BY REYNALDO ALEJANDRO

PBC INTERNATIONAL, INC.

PBC INTERNATIONAL, INC.
One School Street,
Glen Cove, NY 11542

Distributor to the book trade in the United States and
Canada:
Rizzoli International Publications Inc.
597 Fifth Avenue
New York, NY 10017

Distributor to the art trade in the United States:
Letraset USA
40 Eisenhower Drive
Paramus, NJ 07653

Distributor to the art trade in Canada:
Letraset Canada Limited
555 Alden Road
Markham, Ontario L3R 3L5, Canada

Distributed throughout the rest of the world by:
Hearst Books International
105 Madison Avenue
New York, NY 10016

Library of Congress Cataloging-in-Publication Data

Alejandro, Reynaldo G.
Classic menu design.

Bibliography: p.
Includes index.
1. Menus—Catalogs.   2. Menus—New York, (N.Y.)—
Catalogs.   3. New York Public Library—Catalogs.
I. New York Public Library.   II. Title.
NC1002.M4A44   1988   741.67   87-43304
ISBN 0-86636-064-6

Color separtion, printing, and binding by
Toppan Printing Co. (H.K.) Ltd. Hong Kong
Typography by RMP Publication Services
Photography by Justin Chu

Printed in Hong Kong
10 9 8 7 6 5 4 3 2 1

Staff

Managing Director	*Penny Sibal-Samonte*
Creative Director	*Richard Liu*
Associate Art Director	*Daniel Kouw*
Editorial/Production Director	*Kevin Clark*
Project Editor	*Peter Venezia*
Artists	*Kim McCormick*
	Donna Patterson
	Bill Mack
	Allison Butlien
Comptroller	*Pamela McCormick*

CONTENTS

Acknowledgements

 would like to thank the many people who made this book possible—from PBC International, Inc.: Penny Sibal-Samonte, my inspired Muse; Richard Liu; Daniel Kouw; and the ever helpful editor who also edited my first cookbook, Kevin Clark. From The New York Public Library Publications Office: the untiring Richard Newman, Lawrence Murphy, and William Coakley. From the Volunteers Office of N.Y.P.L.: Myrna Martin, Pauline Blech, Marc Meyer, Jeanne Lessem, the late Eunice Miller, and especially Tina Marra who had been with me since the beginning of the menu accessioning project. The entire staff of Science and Technology Research Center, Elizabeth Bentley, Gloria Rohmann, Elizabeth Fish, Lynne Fortunato, Edomond Robinson, Christopher McKee, Bruce Slutzky, Moritia Fredericks, Barbara List, and Nancy Heredia. The staff of Rare Books and Manuscripts Division and Oriental Division. For assistance in various areas of research I am very much indebted to Molly C. Totoro, Marie Luarca Reyes, Miguel Angel Martinez Alonso, Laura Stephan-Corio, and Cesar Bernardo. I want to thank most of all Will Coakley for his unending support in the early stages of the project in 1985, who with Mr. Bruce Manzer, former Chief of Science and Technology Research Center and Rizzoli's Richard Papale gave me inspiration during the formative stages and, above all to the late Herb and Cora Taylor who saw the viability of the project, may they rest in peace!

Introduction

Classic Menus of The New York Public Library

One of the strengths of The New York Public Library is its devotion to aspects of human experience that may have been neglected by other large research libraries. It should be no surprise, then, that we have one of the largest collections in America of material relating to food and wine. The Culinary Collection consists of some 80,000 items—cookbooks, periodicals, rare books, prints, manuscripts, and menus; it is housed in several divisions of the Library, with the Science and Technology Research Center serving as its reference center.

The Library's collection of over 25,000 menus is at the heart of the Culinary Collection. This is the world's largest collection of menus. The greatest concentration is in American menus of every conceivable variety. There are bills of fare for hotels, restaurants, and steamships, as well as special menus for the banquets of clubs, fraternities, and political, educational, and religious organizations. Within the conventions of course order and layout, organizations vied with each other in thinking up the most beautiful or unusual menus for their special occasions: one would be done up in silks and ribbons, another cut into the shape of a duck, a fez, or even a gridiron. Some were printed or hand-painted in gorgeous colors, with elaborate processions or sombre ships

and statesmen displayed, or attractive ladies and pert gentlemen playing for attention. And meals fit for a king were spread out for real princesses or emperors, as well as for prosperous leaders of society, business, and the professions—or guests and travelers everywhere.

Menus reflect in sometimes curious ways people's esthetics and their diets, eating habits, and, perhaps, temperaments. They give us an insight into the social and economic classes of society as well as trends and styles of food service. They present a picture in miniature of the history of food, as well as of the social history of a people. Although menus are among the most ephemeral of printed matter, there remain today thousands of menus from long-past social, political, fraternal, and military events in all parts of the world. These menus, some from the great international hotels, tell us of the foods of many regions and centuries. While they may fill us with nostalgia for a splendid and leisurely period never to be recaptured, the hints and ideas and sheer exuberance they display should inspire us to put them to good use in our own time.

That has been the impetus for this delightful sampling of the Library's classic menus in *CLASSIC MENU DESIGN*. They have been gathered by

Reynaldo Alejandro, Librarian in charge of the Culinary Collection, who has been responsible for organizing the collection and supervising its conservation, with the support of many members of the staff, particularly those of the Science and Technology Research Center. Mr. Alejandro has also helped to communicate information about the collection to all those interested in research in food and cookery: he has co-coordinated the Library's Annual Lecture Series in Cuisine held in our Mid-Manhattan Library and directed the conference "Food for Thought: Meeting the Needs of the Research Community." The Library is grateful for all these efforts to bring the collection to the attention of a wider public.

The menus collected in *CLASSIC MENU DESIGN* whether printed, handwritten, painted, were selected to demonstrate the particular delights of imagination and originality. They show the novel, the striking, the curious, and the eccentric—in terms of design and layout, color and illustration, typeface, and all combinations of paper, cloth, and even metal. As works of art they are often fine examples of their various periods—art nouveau, art deco, modern art, and sentimental popular art. Toulouse-Lautrec was one of the turn-of-the-century (or fin-de-sie'cle)

artists who put his artistic hand to such uses. He considered cookery itself an art, practiced the art himself, and in menus he designed blended the arts of cookery and painting. But for the most part, the names of the artists of the menu are lost to history.

Any research library with such a wide-ranging mission as The New York Public Library's is dependent on the dedicated support of individuals, corporations, and foundations. For the bulk of the menu collection, that support came from generous gifts to the Library at the beginning of the century from Miss Frank E. Buttolph, Mr. John McEntee Bowman, Mr. William Sloane, and Mr. John Mulholland; and for the recent informational programs, grants from General Foods Corporation, Thomas J. Lipton, Inc., and Joseph E. Seagram & Sons, Inc., and International Media Studies Foundation, Inc. For the future, the Culinary Collection has set itself two major goals: the acquisition of new and historical materials and the preservation of this premier collection.

Vartan Gregorian
President
The New York Public Library

CHAPTER 1   Christmastide

hristmas, the anniversary of the birth of Christ, is considered to be the most important day in the Christian year. Although December 25 is the celebrated day of Jesus' birth, the exact date is still unknown. Some Egyptian theologians believed the date of His birth was May 20 while others fixed the date around April 19 or 20. The orthodox Greeks and Russians continue to celebrate Christmas on January 6.

There are many ancient customs and traditions surrounding the celebration of Christmas that have been passed down through the ages. For example, caroling through the streets on Christmas eve is an old custom that was brought over from England. In the early years it became the custom for the occupants of Beacon Hill in Boston to leave candles burning in their windows if they wished the strolling singers to stop and sing a few songs in front of their house. Today caroling is still a special tradition in America with people gathering at town halls, churches, shopping malls or on the street to sing the festive and joyful songs of Christmas.

The tradition of the Christmas tree dates back to Germany in the 1500s when it is said that Martin Luther took an evergreen home to his children and decorated it for Christmas. The first official date of a Christmas tree, however, is in 1605 when one was set up in the city of Strassbourg. Lighting the tree with candles became a tradition based on the belief that candles appeared miraculously on various trees at Christmastime.

The current custom of decorating houses with greens at Christmas dates back to the tenth century when an Arab geographer noted that it was a tradition for some trees and flowers to bloom on Christmas. This tradition was also noted in the thirteenth century regarding a thorn bush at Glastonbury Cathedral which bloomed each Christmas.

The hanging of the mistletoe is traced back to the Druids, who celebrated the winter solstice by placing this revered plant on the altar of their god as a sacrifice to him. In addition, the Druid priests would pass out sprigs of mistletoe to the people so that they may hang it up in their homes. The plant was considered a symbol of future hope and peace. Our latter day tradition of kissing under the mistletoe was derived from the Druid army practice of dropping their weapons and embracing their enemies whenever they met under the mistletoe.

The custom of exchanging gifts at Christmas can be traced back to ancient Rome where the beginning of the New Year, not Christmas, was celebrated by the exchange of presents.

The belief in Santa Claus as the bearer of Christmas gifts is brought to us from Germany, where the legend of St. Nicholas dates back to the fourth century. It is said that when St. Nicholas was told that three young women had no chance to marry because their father was too poor to give them a dowry, he decided to fill three bags with gold and throw the bags through the women's windows. Soon thereafter the young women were happily married and St. Nicholas was soon credited as being the bearer of all unexpected gifts, everywhere.

The Norsemen are acknowledged as giving us the myth of Santa Claus coming down the chimney and filling the stockings with goodies. Their legend is that the goddess Hertha appeared in the fireplaces at the winter solstice and brought happiness and good fortune for those in the home.

Dr. Clement Clarke Moore, the author of the popular poem, *Twas the Night Before Christmas*, is the one who invented the eight reindeer which pull the sleigh in which Santa Claus now travels. The vision of Santa Claus as a plump, jolly old elf, with rosy cheeks, a cherry nose and dressed in fur from head to foot, is also invented by Dr. Moore and based on the appearance of one of his employees.

The custom of sending Christmas cards originated in England in 1846, but did not become popular until around 1864 or so, when the King and Queen adopted the custom and commissioned well-known artists to paint pictures for them which were later reproduced in colors. Christmas cards were introduced in America in the late 1870s and have continued to increase in popularity ever since.

Although Christmas is a holiday based in

religion, its celebration is rooted in tradition that spans the ages and includes such basic sentiments as giving, loving and sharing with family, friends, and strangers.

NEW YEAR'S DAY

The celebration of the New Year has not always taken place on January 1. The ancient Egyptians celebrated the New Year on September 21, the date of the autumnal equinox, while the ancient Greeks celebrated it on June 21, the date of the summer solstice. The Chinese ring in the New Year sometime between January and February while the Jews celebrate their New Year, Rosh Hashana, in the latter part of September. It was not until the date December 25 had been set as the day of the nativity that the church made January 1 a religious festival celebrating the circumcision of Jesus. The Feast of the Circumcision has been celebrated in the Roman church since 487 and in the Anglican church since 1549.

In ancient Rome the first day of the new year was celebrated by offering sacrifices in honor of Janus, god of gates and doors. This seemed to have set the tone for what we currently term: ring out the old year and ring in the new.

The Romans also began a custom of giving one another gifts called "strenae," taken from Strenia, the goddess of strength. This custom began sometime around 747 B.C., when the Romans presented Tatius, the king of the Sabines, branches from the trees consecrated to Strenia as tokens of good omen. This custom of presenting gifts to the emperor was introduced in England around the time of Henry III. Later on it became the habit for all the classes to give presents to friends with the wish that the new year might be happy. Ladies received presents of gloves or pins which were sometimes accompanied by money. This practice eventually gave way to our modern term of "pin money" or "glove money."

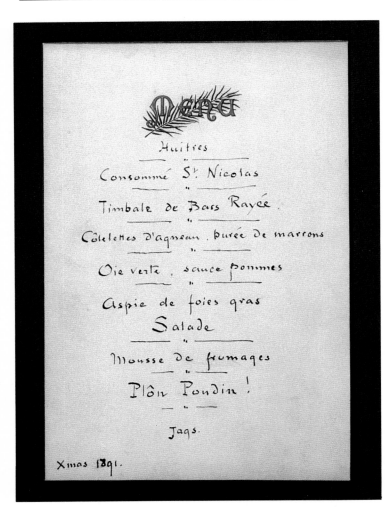

This Christmas menu of 1891 is hand inscribed in black ink upon a piece of 4 1/4"x6 1/4" cardboard. The edges are beveled and trimmed in gold, and the only decoration is the gold-and-silver embossed caption at the top.

Occasion: Christmas Dinner

Sponsor: Locke & Merrill; Proprietors

Place: Hotel Worth—Augusta, ME

Date: Christmas, 1899

This 3 1/2"x6 1/4" menu is austere compared to its contemporaries. Light green construction paper is centerfolded to accommodate a gatefold insert. The cover bears no adornment, just the name of the hotel and the holiday in green-black ink in an old English font. The insert is printed black on cream paper, and the menu is hand bound by a green silk thread.

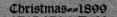

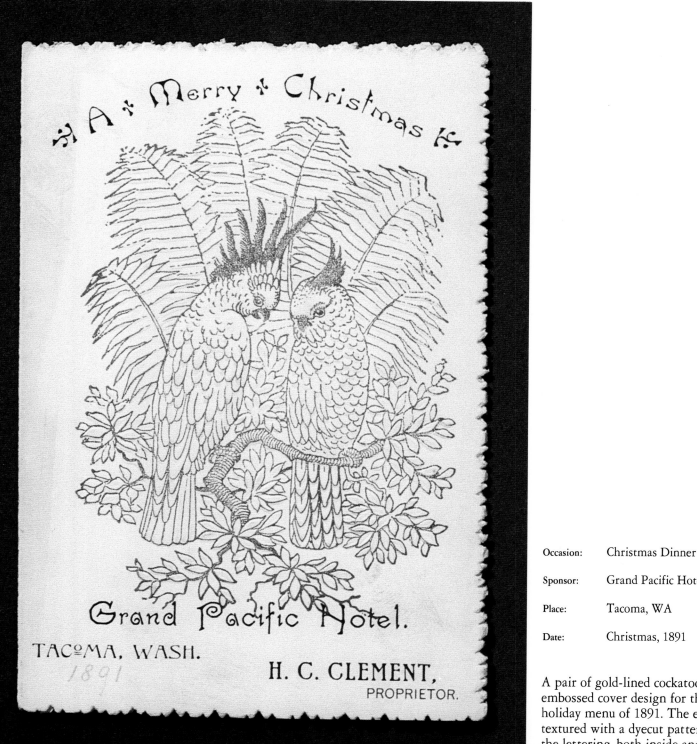

Occasion: Christmas Dinner

Sponsor: Grand Pacific Hotel

Place: Tacoma, WA

Date: Christmas, 1891

A pair of gold-lined cockatoo are the embossed cover design for this holiday menu of 1891. The edges are textured with a dyecut pattern, and the lettering, both inside and out, is in blue ink.

Occasion: Dinner Concert

Sponsor: C.A. Linsley

Place: Hotel Aberdeen, St. Paul, MN

Date: Monday, December 25, 1899

A bright-red satin ribbon binds the inner and outer sheets of this 1899 menu. Stenciled holly and silver-embossed lettering are the principals of this cover design. Inside is a one-side printed sheet in green-black ink and exclusive of decoration.

Occasion: New Year's Eve Dinner

Sponsor: Olympic Bowling Club

Place: Belvedere House, New York City, NY

Date: December 31, 1899

The Olympic Bowling Club heralded 1900 with this beautiful menu. Its simplicity is refreshing and modern. The heavily bronze embossed "Menu" is surrounded by an oblong ornate border. Green palm fronds and a lilac background accentuate the "menu" cameo. Deckled edges and simple black type further promote the "elegant" air of this centerfolded, cardboard menu.

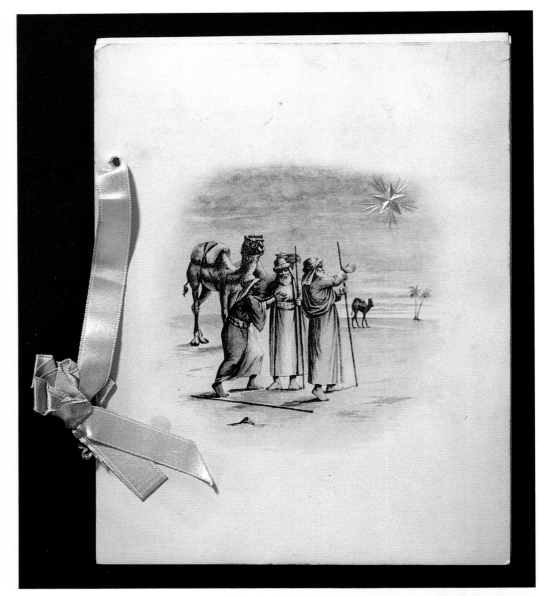

Occasion: Christmas Dinner

Sponsor: Murray Hill Hotel

Place: Park Avenue & 41st Street,
            New York City, NY

Date: December 25, 1891

This 5 1/2"x7 1/4" menu consists of three pages: the cover, in an aquatint of the Three Wise Men with silver-embossed Christmas Star; the middle page, featuring a currency-style engraving of the fashionable Murray Hill Hotel (also with silver embossing); and the last page, of the same heavy stock as the front cover, printed simply in blue ink and exclusive of decoration. A white satin bow binds the unit.

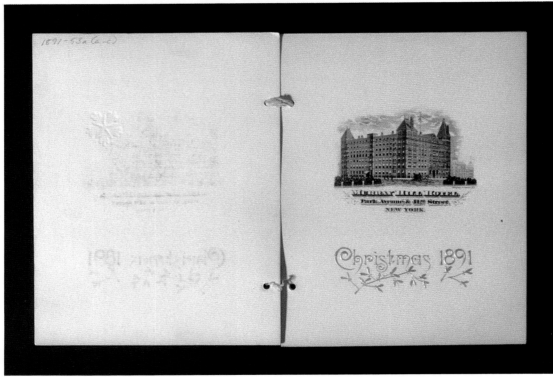

Occasion:	Christmas Dinner
Sponsor:	Hotel Schenley
Place:	Hotel Schenley, Pittsburgh, PA
Date:	Christmas, 1899

This turn-of-the-century Christmas menu hosts a splendid variety of design elements. The grey construction paper cover includes embossing in gold (the Hotel Schenley logo); in white (the holiday greeting); and in grey, green, and red (the holly branch). The woodcut design of a yuletide fireplace is hand-colored, and the binding is hand-tied white silk cord. A green mezzotint verse and illustration appears on the first inside page. The menu page is printed in deep green and is topped with a gold-embossed caption.

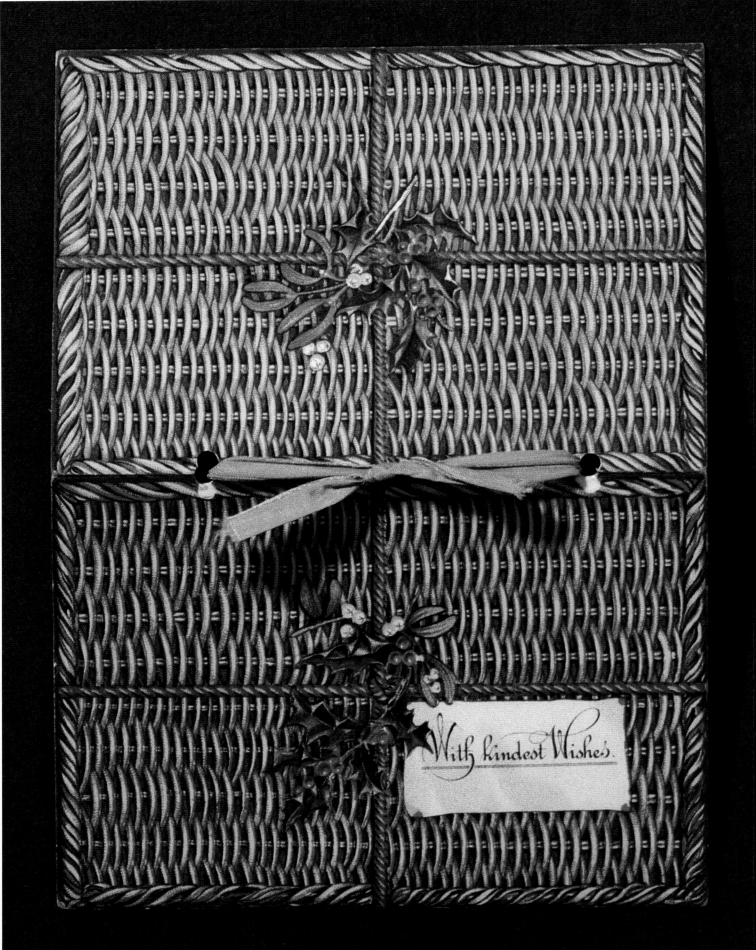

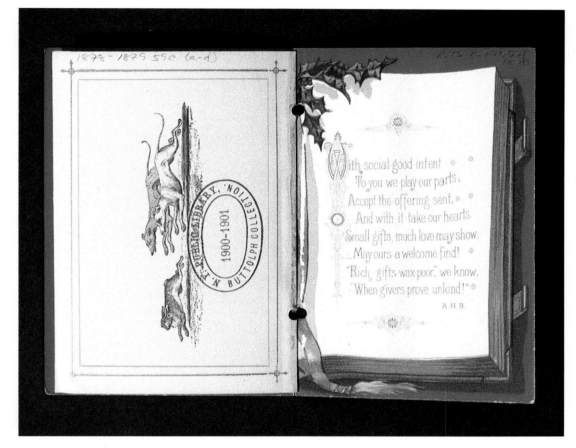

Occasion:	Dinner
Sponsor:	Lick House, George Schonewald, Mgr.
Place:	San Francisco, CA
Date:	December 25, 1879

This unique 3 1/4"x4 1/2" Christmas menu is a delightful example of Victoriana. The centerfolded cardboard covers contain a lithographed design of a wicker book cover, decorated with aqua blue handtinted cord and red and green holly leaves and berries. The cover tag reads "with kindest wishes." When the book is opened, a Christmas poem appears on the inside front cover, surrounded by a blue and red border. The single sheet, parchment paper insert is printed blue with a red and gold border. The entire menu is hand tied with a coordinating aqua blue satin ribbon.

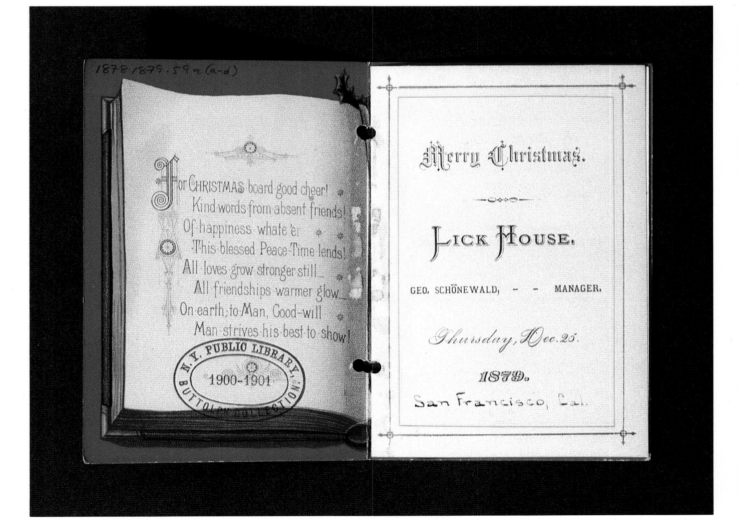

Occasion: Christmas Dinner

Sponsor: Almeria Hotel—J.C.S.
            Timberlake, Manager

Place: Tampa, FL

Date: December 25, 1899

St. Nicholas is the focal point of this Floridian menu of 1899, both inside and out. The cover, which is heavy green stock printed in gold, is decorated with a dry-embossed visage of Father Christmas surrounded by gold, green and red embossed accompaniments. The top-bound centerfold is tied with pink silk cord at the top; a matching pink satin ribbon is glued to the right. Inside, the menu sheet which is glossy coated stock, features St. Nicholas upon a snow-covered roof, about to descend the chimney with his sack of toys.

Occasion: Christmas Dinner

Sponsor: The Planters Hotel

Place: St. Louis, MO

Date: Christmas, 1896

This old Christmas menu is one of our few examples of photogravure. The silhouetted leaves are very poorly done, and the red stenciling for the berries is off register. "Christmas 1896" is blind embossed and colored red. The engraving of the hotel is surrounded by a gold embossed box and the name of the hotel is gold embossed at the bottom. A red satin ribbon unites the single sheet interior with the covers.

Occasion: New Year's Eve Dinner
             1891

Sponsor: Hamilton Johnson, Manager

Place: Royal Hawaiian Hotel,
             Honolulu, HI

Date: December 31, 1891

Raw-edged kraft paper forms the cover sheet of this centerfolded Hawaiian menu of 1892. The front cover hosts a mounted aquatint in full color, depicting an artist's image of New Year's Day in 1620. The cover is printed in red, blue and brown, and is bound decoratively with a piece of gold silk twine. The inner centerfold sheet of lighter stock is printed on both sides in red and blue ink by the "Hawaiian Gazette Printers."

Occasion:	Christmas Dinner
Sponsor:	Windsor Hotel
Place:	Jacksonville, FL
Date:	Christmas, 1899

Understated elegance is the description for this pink parchment-covered menu. The outer sheet, embossed in gold with the hotel logo, is exclusive of any other decoration, save the pink silk cord of the binding. Inside is a single sheet of thick cardboard, bevel-edged in gold leaf. Engraved border designs of holly, mistletoe, ribbon, bells, and lettering is handpainted. The menu itself is printed in black.

Occasion:	6th Annual Complimentary Dinner for the Guests of the Empire
Sponsor:	Mr. W. Johnson Quinn
Place:	Hotel Empire, Broadway & 63rd Street West, New York City, NY
Date:	Christmas, 1899

The thick, textured, aqua-colored cover of this menu is embossed with gold lettering as well as a gold frame which outlines a pasted-in 1 1/2"x2 1/4" lithograph, unseasonably titled "The Dawn of Summer." The inner sheets of the menu, which include a full calendar of the year 1900, are all printed in brown ink.

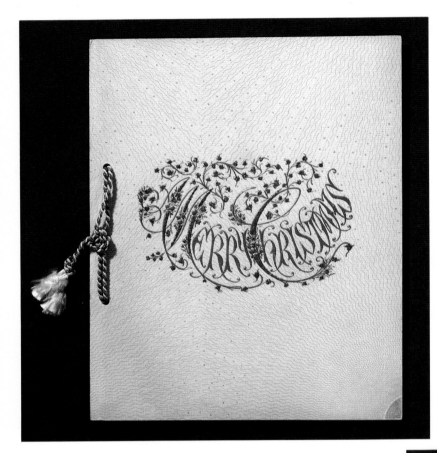

Occasion: Dinner

Sponsor: Hotel Marlborough

Place: New York City, NY

Date: December 26, 1892

Line-designed paper in a gold sunburst pattern is further decorated with a gold-embossed lettering design announcing the season's greetings. This lettering, accented with red and green glitter, is complemented with the white-and-gold silk cord used to bind the centerfolded cover to its taffeta-textured stock interior. Brown ink is used to print both the hotel logo and the menu courses of this two-sided sheet.

Occasion: Christmas Dinner

Sponsor: Hotel Chamberlin

Place: The Chamberlin, Old Point Comfort, VA

Date: Christmas, 1899

This simple Christmas menu greeted diners at the Hotel Chamberlin on Christmas, 1899. A single piece of lightweight, green cardboard is centerfolded to serve as the covers. The name of the hotel is gold embossed in the lower-right region of the cover. Two hand-painted holly branches entwine to form a "U." A deckle-edge paste on lies in the center. Note, "merrie" is spelled in true Middle English fashion. A "mock" red wax seal of the hotel and hand-tied red satin bow finish this menu.

The Fremont.

Merry Christmas,
1899.

Fremont, O.

Occasion: Christmas Dinner

Sponsor: C.J. Holloway, Proprietor

Place: The Fremont Hotel,
Fremont, OH

Date: Christmas 1899

The meaning behind the bright yellow banana embossed on this 1899 Christmas menu cover is lost forever, but the design is reflective of the Victorian influence lingering on at the end of the 19th century. A simple printing in black ink inside reveals the cuisine of the occasion.

Occasion: Christmas Dinner

Sponsor: Haddon Hotel

Place: Haddon Hall, Atlantic City, NJ

Date: Christmas, 1896

This simple menu effectively portrays the Christmas theme. A single piece of centerfolded cardboard comprises the entire unit. The menu is printed in green on the inside back cover with the word "Menu" gold embossed on a diagonal at the top. The front cover contains a fine, handtinted etching of Santa Claus making his rounds on Christmas Eve. It's interesting to point out that Santa's suit consists of a red jacket with brown slacks, and that he is on foot, not in his sled. Note the beautiful gold coloring of the church windows.

HADDON HALL
ATLANTIC CITY, N.J.

Occasion: Christmas Dinner

Sponsor: The Chelsea Hotel

Place: New York City, NY

Date: December 25, 1899

This Christmas menu is beautiful in its artistic simplicity. A single sheet of cardboard forms this centerfolded 5 1/2"x7" menu. The cover design is the elegant gold-embossed insignia for the Chelsea at its center, surrounded by a hand painted branch of holly bent to form the letter "C." This serves well as a design element—it stands for both Christmas and the Chelsea. The inside is properly plain printed in forest green ink with the single word "Menu" embossed in gold at top center.

THE CHELSEA

MERRY CHRISTMAS

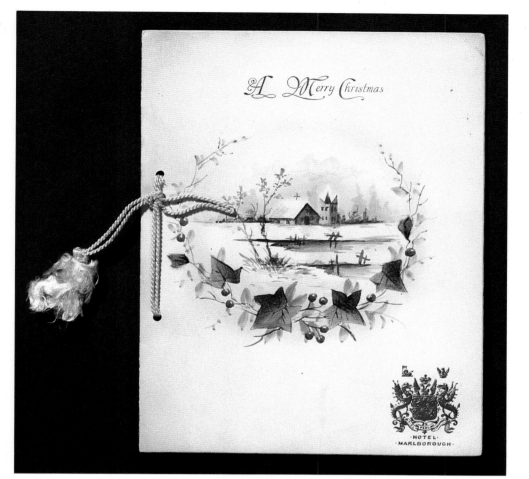

Occasion: Christmas Dinner

Sponsor: Hotel Marlborough

Place: Hotel Marlborough, New
               York City, NY

Date: December 25, 1895

The coated cardboard cover of this beautiful 1895 menu is watercolored by hand and embossed with Christmas greetings and the seal of the Hotel Marlborough of New York City. A pink silk cord with tassels binds the cover and inner sheet, which is printed in black and embossed at the top with a Victorian-lettered caption in gold.

Occasion: Christmas Dinner

Sponsor: Chas. Beermann and
               Company

Place: Kimball House, Atlanta, GA

Date: December 25, 1895

A white satin ribbon binds the two centerfolded parchment sheets of this menu. The outer sheet is coated, the front cover is gold-embossed and colored in a red and green holly design. The inner centerfold is printed one-side only in burgundy ink.

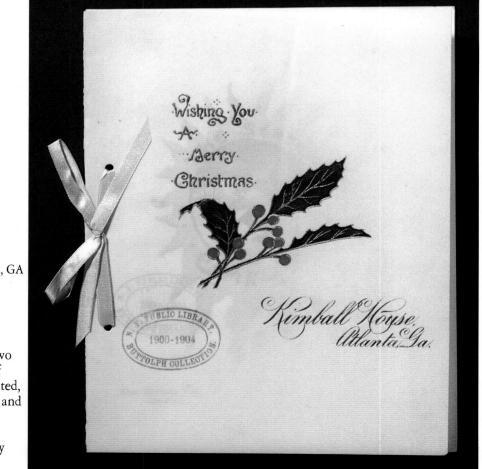

Occasion: Christmas Dinner

Sponsor: Hotel Bristol

Place: Hotel Bristol, 5th Avenue at 42nd Street, New York City, NY

Date: Christmas, 1896

Two, bevel-edged sheets of cardboard comprise the covers of this unusual Christmas menu. The front cover is completely handpainted. The focal point is a tray containing either a turkey, or some sort of roast, sitting on a table surrounded by snow and bell-laden pine branches. The insignia of the hotel is gold-embossed in the upper left hand corner. The interior consists of two sheets of lightweight stock with green-black ink for the extensive menu. The menu is bound by a white silk ribbon.

Occasion: Christmas Dinner

Sponsor: Hotel Florence

Place: San Diego, CA

Date: Christmas, 1891

Two different weights of the same flower-textured stock are used for the cover and interior sheets of this menu; both are edged in a dyecut pattern. The cover center-piece is silver-edged aquatint mount, lettered in gold. Two satin bows, one yellow and one blue, decorate the cover— the yellow ribbon also serves as binding. Both sides of the lighter stock interior sheet are printed in brown.

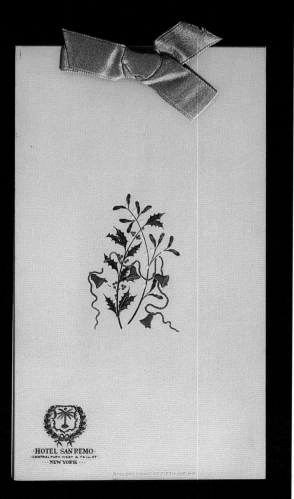

Occasion: Christmas Dinner

Sponsor: Hotel San Remo

Place: Central Park West & 75th Street, New York City, NY

Date: December 25, 1894

A fine design of embossed green-and-red holly, green-and-white mistletoe, and gold Christmas bells adorn this menu cover. The gold of the bells is repeated in the hotel's logo at bottom, left, while a beige satin bow binds the menu at the top. A single sheet within is printed in brown for the menu proper.

Occasion:	Christmas Dinner
Sponsor:	Chicago Beach Hotel
Place:	Chicago, IL
Date:	December 25, 1894

This Christmas menu of 1894 is covered in letter paper and contains one interior page of heavier stock, each printed one side only in red. The front cover is embossed in gold above and red below, with an aquatint of the Christmas Star, holly, and angels. The menu is bound with a patterned white silk ribbon.

Occasion:	Christmas Dinner
Sponsor:	Menger Hotel
Place:	San Antonio, TX
Date:	December 25, 1895

This 1895 San Antonio Christmas menu consists of a single piece of centerfolded cardboard. The fine etching, a trademark of Loughead & Co. Printers, is on the front cover. A dwarf-sized Santa in a brown suit, rests on a holly leaf. Above him, a bowl of steaming Wassail rests on a table. The only color in this illustration is the handpainted brown and the red used for the berries. Two white bows adorn the upper and lower left hand corners and are used strictly for decoration.

Occasion:	Christmas Dinner
Sponsor:	The H. C. Brown Palace Hotel
Place:	Denver, CO
Date:	December 25, 1892

Funny little manikins (sic) await the cooking of the Christmas goose on this hotel menu cover of 1892. This pen-and-ink design is surrounded by a faint wreath of aquatint cherubim. White silk grosgrain ribbon joins the cover stock to an inner sheet, which is gold-embossed and engraved with an illustration of the hotel on one side, and printed with blue ink on the other.

Occasion:	Dinner
Sponsor:	The Jefferson, Winslie and Webster, Mgr.
Place:	The Jefferson, Richmond, VA
Date:	December 25, 1895

A pencil sketch, handtinted in yellow and green watercolors is the simple decoration on the cover of this menu. The seal of the Jefferson Hotel takes prominence in the center, with a heavy gold embossing. The caption "Wishing you a Merry Christmas" is gold embossed in the lower righthand corner. A lovely white satin bow appears as if it is tied to the branch on the cover. Note, this bow serves as decoration and does not bind the menu.

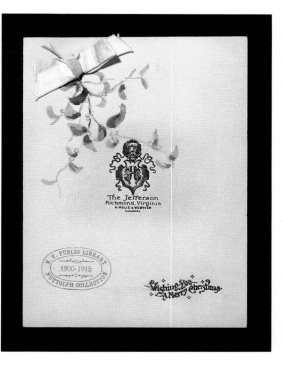

Occasion: Christmas Dinner

Sponsor: Haddon Hotel, Leeds &
              Lippincott

Place: Haddon Hall—Atlantic City,
              NJ

Date: Christmas, 1898

This 1898 Christmas menu is a prime example of turn-of-the-century Americana. Royal blue, heavy weight centerfolded textured paper forms the cover of this menu. A handpainted St. Nicholas scene (note his suit is brown, not red) adorns the cover. Embossed birds and bells, hand tinted in white further detail this menu. The Christmas greetings and the crest of the hotel are gold embossed. The single sheet centerfolded insert is printed royal blue on cream stock and the entire unit is bound with a white silk tasseled cord.

Occasion: Christmas Dinner

Sponsor: The New St. Charles Hotel

Place: New Orleans, LA

Date: Christmas, 1896

A mezzotint etching adorns the cover of this cardboard, centerfolded menu. The front cover illustration is handtinted in red, green, pink, orange and yellow. "Merry Christmas" and the hotel name are gold embossed. The menu printed on the inside back cover is a drab brown ink. It's interesting to note that the majority of these Christmas menus were printed by Loughead & Co., Philadelphia.

Occasion: New Year's Day Dinner

Sponsor: Hotel Savoy

Place: Hotel Savoy, San Francisco, CA

Date: Tuesday, January 1, 1895

A silver and bronze glitter laden trellis is the dye-cut pattern enjoyed by a central display of embossed violets on this menu cover. When opened, a translucent window is revealed behind the trellis and violets, mounted in place inside by a dyecut covering sheet of identical latticework design. The menu page is printed in blue ink and accented with a red stenciled caption. Dye-cut edges add further detailing.

Occasion: Christmas Dinner

Sponsor: Geo. H. Avery, Proprietor

Place: Hotel Castleton, Staten Island, NY

Date: December 25, 1895

Centerfolded light blue cardboard heavily embossed with Victorian embellishment in grey-green and gold serves for this menu cover. Green ink is used to print the fare listed inside the Christmas Day dinner menu of 1895.

Occasion:	Christmas Dinner
Sponsor:	Hotel Marlborough
Place:	New York City, NY
Date:	December 25, 1894

Watercolor and pen-and-ink were both applied to the cover design and lettering of this Christmas menu, and all by hand. A dancing couple of the late 19th century is depicted in brown-ink outlining and colored in green, yellow, pink, blue, brown and white. The Hotel Marlborough's coat of arms is gold-embossed at the upper left corner, and the cover card and inner menu sheet are bound in white tasseled silk cord at the left margin.

Occasion: Christmas Dinner

Sponsor: Hotel Alcazar, Jos. P.
               Greaves, Mgr.

Place: St. Augustine, FL

Date: Christmas, 1897

This Christmas menu probably contains the strangest illustration of all of our holiday menus. A fine-line etching adorns the cover of this centerfolded cardboard sheet. Santa and his reindeer are barely visible to the left of a giant holly leaf. Inside the leaf, a young maiden holds holly leaves in her apron as she stands near a roaring fire. The maiden's dress, the leaves, the hearth, and the fire are all hand tinted. The crest of the hotel and the holiday are silver embossed. The printer inadvertently left off the date, which had to be handwritten in. The interior of this menu is a single sheet of centerfolded linen paper, showcasing the menu and concert program in silver ink.

Occasion: Dinner

Sponsor: The New St. Charles Hotel

Place: The New St. Charles Hotel,
               New Orleans, LA

Date: December 25, 1899

Embossed with gold, green and red and featuring a handcolored engraving of a young woman ice skating, this New Orleans Christmas menu of 1899 is printed in brown on the interior sheet and bound with a tasseled silk cord in rich crimson.

Occasion:	Christmas Dinner	Designed to resemble a bank book of checks, this 1895 menu "delivers to the bearer" a course per check. Inside the 6 1/2"x3" leather-covered cardboard covers are 18 "checks," three front pages (one illustrated with a lithograph of The Portland Hotel), and three back pages (one of which lists the musical program in gold). The front leather cover is gold-embossed.
Sponsor:	The Portland Hotel, H. C. Bonner, Manager	
Place:	Portland, OR	
Date:	December 25, 1895	

No. 7

Portland, Or., December 25, 1895.

Chef of The Portland Hotel,

OF PORTLAND, OREGON.

Deliver to _____ *Bea*

Oregon Turkey, Roasted and Stuffed with Oysters
CRANBERRY SAUCE

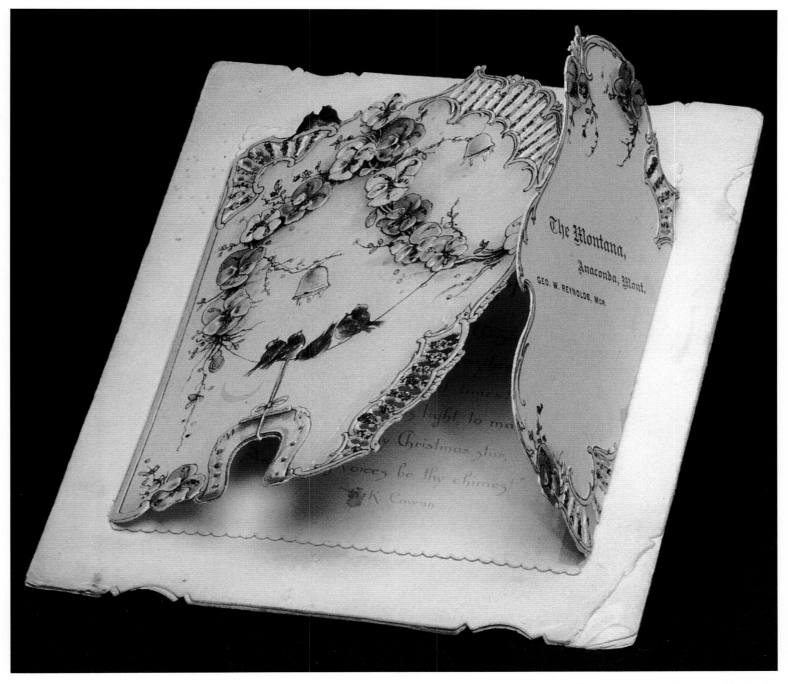

Occasion:	Christmas Dinner
Sponsor:	The Montana, George W. Reynolds, Manager
Place:	Anaconda, MT
Date:	Christmas, 1896

Dyecut paper is a feature of both the menu card foundation and of the Christmas greeting card which is mounted upon it. Inside the two-flapped greeting card portion is a verse printed in light green; the folded flaps are trimmed with embossing, multi-colored mezzotint, and glued-on glitter. The reverse side of the unit contains the printed menu in black.

Occasion: Christmas Dinner "XMAS
with the Poets"

Sponsor: Everett House, William M.
Bates and B.L.M. Bates,
Proprietors

Place: Union Square, New York
City, NY

Date: Christmas, 1895

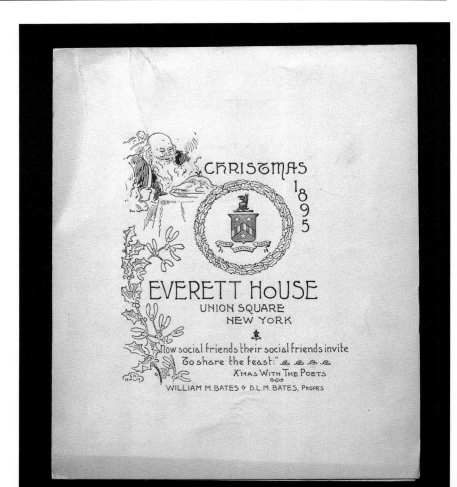

This centerfolded cardboard menu is
printed entirely in green, except for
the wine list which appears in red on
the inside front cover. The most
interesting point of this menu is the
reproduction of William Thackeray's
"The Mahogany Tree" on the inside
back cover. This poem is a tribute to
one of the most beloved Christmas
traditions—the Christmas tree. The
back cover was used for autographs.

...MENU...

Lynnhavens
Caviar   Celery
Green Sea Turtle   Consomme Princess
Queen Olives   Salted Almonds   Head Lettuce
                                          SAUTERNE
Broiled White Shad, Drawn Butter Sauce
Sliced Cucumbers   Duchesse Potatoes
Capon, Oyster Sauce

Prime Ribs Beef, Dish Gravy
Creamed Potatoes   Suckling Pig Stuffed with Chestnuts
Young Turkey, English Dressing, Cranberry Sauce
                                    Green Peas
                                          SHERRY
Larded and Braised Sweetbreads with Mushrooms
Rice   Tucked Quail, en Surprise
Spanish Souffle, Glace   Stewed Tomatoes
Maraschino Punch

Salmi of Prairie Chicken, Chasseur   CLARET
Asparagus   Roast Mallard Duck, Raspberry Jam
                                    Candied Potatoes
Lobster, Mayonaise Dressing

English Plum Pudding, Hard Sauce
Mince Pie   Pumpkin Pie
              Bisque Ice Cream
Assorted Cakes   Fruit
        Nuts   Raisins
Confectionery   Layer Figs
    Cheese   Roquefort   Edam   Cream

1900	JANUARY.	1900
MON. 1		WED. 17
TUE. 2		THR. 18
WED. 3		FRI. 19
THR. 4		SAT. 20
FRI. 5		SUN. 21
SAT. 6		MON. 22
SUN. 7		TUE. 23
MON. 8		WED. 24
TUE. 9		THR. 25
WED. 10		FRI. 26
THR. 11		SAT. 27
FRI. 12		SUN. 28
SAT. 13		MON. 29
SUN. 14		TUE. 30
MON. 15		WED. 31

Occasion: Christmas Dinner

Sponsor: Central Hotel—R. L. Lucas, Proprietor

Place: Charlotte, NC

Date: December 25, 1899

A menu with the gift of a useful one-year calendar inside, this 1899 design is comprised of six centerfolded sheets of heavy stock; the cover is light blue, the rest is off-white. On the front cover is a cut-out photographic cameo framed in white embossing; the lettering is also embossed in white. The printing inside is entirely in brown.

Occasion: New Year's Dinner

Sponsor: Palace Hotel

Place: Denver, CO

Date: January 1, 1893

Baby New Year chases Father Time on the cover of this Denver hotel's New Year's menu. This aquatint engraving is accompanied by silver-embossed lettering and a white silk grosgrain ribbon binding. This parchment paper cover wraps the thick sheet of the menu listed inside.

Occasion: Christmas Dinner

Sponsor: The Lenox

Place: San Francisco, CA

Date: December 25, 1892

Pink-tinted cardboard is centerfolded and embossed with bird, butterfly and flowers for this San Francisco holiday menu of 1892. It is printed on both sides in blue ink.

Occasion: Christmas Dinner

Sponsor: The Windsor Hotel

Place: The Windsor Hotel

Date: December 25, 1895

This 1895 Christmas menu is decorated with a combination pen-and-ink and mezzotint illustration, a handpainted holly-framed scene in which Santa and his reindeer fly across a moonlit sky. The menu also includes one-side printing in green and the gold-embossed "Merry Christmas" at top right.

Occasion: New Year's Eve Dinner

Sponsor: Cron & Mitchell

Place: The Aquarium, 244 Third Avenue, New York City, NY

Date: December 31, 1895

Happy New Year 1896 was greeted with this simple 4 1/4"x6 1/2" menu from the Aquarium. Gold embossed "Menu" serves as the main decoration, while a hand tinted strawberry is located directly beneath. White ribbon binds the centerfolded cardboard cover to the centerfolded linen paper insert. The menu is printed in dark green with strangely ornate type. To further embellish this menu, a deckled edge finishes the cover.

Occasion: New Year's Day Dinner

Sponsor: The Cameron, D.P. Smith,
            Proprietor

Place: The Cameron, La Crosse,
            WI

Date: January 1, 1898

Art Nouveau is apparent in this New Year's Day menu. Gold and Green embossed leaves surround the bronze enclosed holiday and date in roman numerals. A pink bow adorns the wreath and serves as spot color to highlight the date. The single-sheet, centerfolded interior is gold printed on a heavy cream stock. The centerfolded cardboard cover is hole punched, along with the insert to accommodate the final flourish--a white and pink silk-tasseled card.

Occasion: New Year's Dinner

Sponsor: Hotel Marlborough

Place: New York City, NY

Date: January 1, 1894

One centerfolded sheet of heavy textured stock in a silver satin finish is the cover of this New Year's menu of 1894. This Victorian beauty also employs gold embossing, handpainted flowers in pink, black and green, and a white silk cord binding at the cover. The interior sheet, of thin stock, is printed two sides in blue ink. Note that the cover design is also the New Year—1894.

Occasion: Christmas Dinner

Sponsor: Hotel Continental

Place: Philadelphia, PA

Date: December 25, 1894

A colorful Christmas cameo is created with a blue-ink cover etching of General Washington and his troops in boats upon icy waters, commemorating December 25, 1776. It seems a strange theme for a Christmas menu until one considers that the design was made for the Hotel Continental of Philadelphia, PA. This two-page menu, colored by hand on the cover and printed in blue inside, is tied with a blue-and-gold striped satin ribbon at top.

Occasion: Dinner

Sponsor: Sherman Square Hotel—Walter Lawrence, Proprietor

Place: Boulevard and West 71st Street, New York City, NY

Date: December 25, 1895

Loughead & Co. printed this delightful 1895 Christmas menu for the Sherman Square Hotel in New York City. A drunken lad sits in an empty punch bowl as he rings the bell for the new year. Two handtinted holly branches entwine and surround a glowing star. A banner reads "Right Hearty Wishes." The two pieces of cardboard making up this 6 1/2"x7 1/2" menu are center hole punched at top center and tied together with a white satin ribbon.

Occasion: New Year's Dinner

Sponsor: Hotel Marlborough

Place: New York City, NY

Date: Sunday, January 1, 1893

Late Victorian influence is clearly evident on the cover design of this 1893 New Year's dinner menu. A faux-lace backdrop is printed on thick beige paper and embossed in gold, then accented in colored glitter. A rich gold-and-crimson cord of silk ties the cover sheet to a thin inner sheet of two-tone taffeta texture; one side is beige, the other (printed) side is light blue. Both sides are printed in brown.

Occasion: Dinner to the Traveling Salesmen and Heads of Department

Sponsor: The Lockwood-Taylor Hardware Company

Place: The Hollenden Hotel, Cleveland, OH

Date: December 28, 1896

This centerfolded, 4 1/2"x6 3/4" cardboard menu is a clever design of a hinge. The menu itself is hinge-shaped, and a simple lithograph of the joint with three screw heads decorates the front cover. The screw heads are hand colored gold and the type is printed red and black. The hinge design reinforces that the sponsor of the banquet is the Lockwood-Taylor Hardware Company. The interior is a simple black printed menu with a lithograph of the company's factory in Cleveland, Ohio.

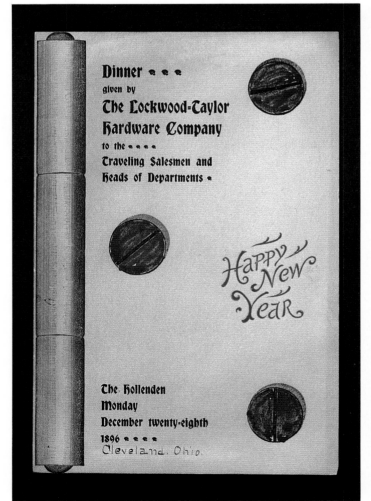

Occasion:	New Year's Dinner
Sponsor:	The Chilberg
Place:	Tacoma, WA.
Date:	January 1, 1894

Heavy textured stock is dyecut and folded twice to create a double overlap for this 1894 New Year's Dinner menu. The cover is embossed in a flowering branch design overlaid with gold, pink and yellow. The lettering of the cover, as well as of the inside, is in blue ink. The dyecut edging is gold-rubbed in places.

Occasion:	New Year's Day Dinner
Sponsor:	The Hollenden Hotel
Place:	The Hollenden Hotel, New York City, NY
Date:	January 1, 1899

Bright green silk covers and binds the cardboard foundations of this New Year's menu. Inside, two separate cards 5"x7" are printed in black: on the left is a lithograph of the Hollenden; on the right is the printed menu. Each is framed with coated white stock overmounted. The front cover is lettered in black and handpainted with flowers in purple and white.

hanksgiving is an all-American holiday that is rich in tradition. It is therefore not surprising that Thanksgiving in the 1980s is celebrated in much the same way as it was when the Pilgrims first shared their harvest with the Indians in 1621.

As most Americans know, the first Thanksgiving was established in 1621 by Governor Bradford as a day to give thanks to God for the autumn's bountiful harvest. Governor Bradford, being politically aware, also decided to extend an invitation to the local Indians to help them partake in the harvest celebration. This first Thanksgiving was a three day celebration which included grateful prayers, harvest food and sport games.

The first Thanksgiving repast was similar, though not identical, to today's traditional roasted turkey, cranberry sauce, sweet potatoes and pumpkin pie. Several types of wild fowl could be found along the shores of Cape Cod in 1621, including partridges, ducks, geese and turkeys. In all probability, several of each kind of bird was shot and brought back to the settlement to be roasted or stewed. Pumpkin was sure to be at the first Thanksgiving, although the Pilgrims were more likely to have eaten it boiled plain rather than sweetened in a pie. Cranberries, as well as other kinds of native wild berries and nuts, were also served at the meal as an accompaniment to the meat. Corn was most certainly served at the first dinner, probably in the form of "hasty pudding" which was made by kneading it into ersatz bread and fried in cakes.

Not all of the food for the first Thanksgiving was supplied by the Pilgrims. The Indians also contributed to the celebration by bringing popcorn, something which the Pilgrims had never seen. Legend has it that popcorn was discovered in the fifteenth century when a band of young Indians threw some corn cobs on the campfire and thus discovered the secret hidden within the kernels.

Although a large part of this original celebration was dedicated to thanking God for the bountiful harvest and feasting on the food which He gave, it also included recreational time for the Pilgrims and Indians to spend together. Sports were included in the celebration, such as track and field events and "stool ball," a game similar to croquet. The Pilgrims also took this opportunity to give the Indians a demonstration of their powerful English muskets.

Today Thanksgiving is marked in American calendars as a one day holiday on the last Thursday in November, but it is often observed as a four-day weekend of celebration. As with the first "three-day" celebration of Thanksgiving, our modern-day version includes gathering together all family members and close friends for one day of grateful prayers and traditional fares, and three more days of leftovers and sports, with stool ball giving way to football games.

EASTER

Easter, the celebration of the resurrection of Christ is the most revered day in the Christian calendar. It is celebrated on the first Sunday after the full moon following the spring equinox. The actual day of the Easter celebration varies from year to year and can occur anytime between March 22 and April 25.

The resurrection of Christ from the dead is synonymous with the renewal of life signified by the Spring. Therefore, the name Easter was used, which is derived from the Teutonic goddess Eostre whose festival celebrated the renewal of life in the spring.

There are many traditional symbols of Easter, such as furry rabbits, baby chicks, colored eggs, and lilies. The egg is said to be symbolic of the resurrection because it holds the seed of life. Eggs were originally associated with Easter because it was forbidden to eat them during Lent. Eggs were served on Easter Sunday, however, and dyed red to signify the blood of Christ and symbolize joyousness for sacrifice of His life for us. The ancient Greeks, Romans and Egyptians also traditionally ate brightly colored eggs at their spring feast. Today, eggs are said to be hidden by the Easter Bunny, and children search their homes and gardens for the multicolored treasures on Easter morning.

Easter is a joyous and spiritual holiday that is

not only celebrated by Christians for the resurrection of Christ but is also observed by all people as a symbol of Spring and the beginning of warm weather, sunshine and the renewal of life. Easter is a joyful holiday that is celebrated worldwide with religious services, as well as traditional songs, games and food.

ST. PATRICK'S DAY

St. Patrick's Day, March 17, honors the anniversary of the death of the patron saint of Ireland in 493. According to Roman Catholic authorities, St. Patrick was actually born in Scotland to a member of a Roman family of high rank. At the age of sixteen, Patrick was captured by the Irish and sold as a slave. After six years of slavery, Patrick escaped to Britain and decided to devote his life to religious work. In 433 the Pope commissioned him to Ireland where his first visit was to his old master. He paid the master the price of his freedom, and then, it is said, he converted the man and his family to Christianity.

There are many legends of St. Patrick. One tells of how he attempted to explain the Trinity by plucking a shamrock from the meadow and telling the people that each of the leaves represented the three persons of the Trinity and the stem represented the godhead. Another tells of how St. Patrick rid all of Ireland of snakes. He managed to banish all the snakes but one, which refused to leave. St. Patrick then made a box and asked the serpent to enter it. The serpent refused, however, saying that the box was not large enough to hold him. After a long discussion on the appropriate size of the box, the serpent entered it in order to prove to St. Patrick that it was indeed too small. As soon as the snake entered the box, St. Patrick closed its lid, locked the box, and threw it out to sea.

St. Patrick's Day has been celebrated in America since early times, but celebrations outside the Catholic church began in 1737 in Boston with the Charitable Irish Society. Through the years, more societies were established in other cities and the St. Patrick's Day celebration grew in popularity. These societies usually celebrated the day by giving a public dinner and having prominent speakers respond to toasts. Today, St. Patrick's Day is celebrated by all Americans, regardless of nationality or religious creed. Parades are marched, shamrocks are worn, boiled corn beef dinners are eaten, and lots of beer is consumed in honor of this patron saint.

Occasion:	Thanksgiving
Sponsor:	Hotel Alcazar
Place:	Hotel Alcazar, St. Augustine, FL
Date:	Thanksgiving Day, 1899

The rustic scene of this 1899 Thanksgiving Day menu was created with a woodcut and hand-rubbed brown ink. Stipple is also used to enhance shaded areas. Measuring 6 1/2"x9 1/2", the thick paper of this menu is deckled at the edges for a finishing touch of informal antiquity. The signature "BBB" in the lower right corner probably refers to the printers Bailey, Banks & Biddle of Philadelphia.

Occasion:	Thanksgiving Dinner
Sponsor:	City Council of Huntington, WV
Place:	Florentine Hotel, Huntington, WV
Date:	November 30, 1899

A rather large piece of cardboard, 6 3/4"x10 3/4", with hand-beveled and hand-colored edges in dark brown was used for this Thanksgiving Dinner menu. Pen-and-ink lithography is combined with mezzotint and hand-applied watercolors to create a fanciful border at the top. Directly beneath the border is the silver embossed word "dinner," which shares its argent glow with the prongs of the fork and the blade of the knife above it. Likewise, the glowing orange hue of the border's pumpkin is repeated in the orange-red ink used to print beverages, a nice accent to the food items which are printed in black. This attention to chromatic detail in only one of the fine points of this menu's design. Its composition of text is also handsome and well thought out.

Occasion:	Thanksgiving Day Banquet
Sponsor:	The American Society
Place:	London, England
Date:	Thanksgiving Day, November 30, 1899

Excepting the few curlicue uppercase letters on its cover, this menu design is notable in its general lack of Victorian intricacy. A pen-and-ink lithograph depicting a corn and wheat theme form the caramel-colored backdrop for dark brown intaglio lettering. A rectangular embossed frame furnishes the cover's border. Inside the centerfolded cardboard, two thin-lined boxes enclose text: On the left, the all-French menu, and on the right, the toast list, both composed in simple serifed font printed in tuxedo-style black on white.

Occasion: Thanksgiving Dinner

Sponsor: The Russell House

Place: The Russell House, Detroit, MI

Date: November 30, 1899

The front cover of this 1899 Thanksgiving dinner menu is decorated with a hand-colored lithograph of a brown eagle. The bird is yoked with the "Thanksgiving" caption and is situated over a curious sort of condensed global map, which shows Cuba and Puerto Rico (in pink, blue and yellow) to the west, the Philippine Islands (in pastel green) to the south, and the Sandwich (Hawaiian) Islands (in pastel peach) to the east. The centerfolded inner sheet of the menu is printed on two sides. One page is red ink only, announcing that dinner is served from "6 to 8 P.M." The innermost pages are printed in red and green ink with gold-embossed intricately designed headings "Music" and "Menu" of Victorian influence. The back cover contains the gold-embossed insignia of the Russell House.

Occasion: Thanksgiving Day

Sponsor: The Hollenden

Place: The Hollenden, Cleveland, OH

Date: November, 1899

The 5 1/2"x5 1/2" square of this menu unfolds to a single rectangular piece of 16 1/2"x5 1/2" cardboard. The top third of the fold contains en embossed flower in metallic gold and silver, its pink and green hues applied in watercolors by hand. The bottom third, which is decorated with frolicking rabbits and the gold-embossed hotel logo, creates the front cover of the menu when folded to meet the top, and its edges are dye-cut for further style.

Occasion:	Thanksgiving Dinner
Sponsor:	The Van Nuys Hotel
Place:	The Van Nuys Hotel, Los Angeles, CA
Date:	Thanksgiving, November, 1899

The first of the three centerfolded sheets of this menu is of 10 1/2"x16" heavy-stock, eggshell-colored paper; the second is of the same size and also in eggshell, but of a lighter stock; and the third, innermost centerfolded sheet is of a thick, pink onion-skin paper. These three pieces are bound with pink silk cord drawn through two holes at the fold and tied in a one-loop bow. A thick strip of ribbon, also in pink silk, forms a decorative insert on either side of the intaglio "99," which is watercolored pink by hand and outlined in silver. The second page, right, is printed in blue, announcing the place, date, and occasion, and also sporting an intaglio design of holly leaves and berries. The inside right of the second sheet is also printed in the blue ink and features an embossed "dinner" heading. The pink onion-skin is reserved for information on the evening's entertainment, also in blue ink.

Occasion:	Thanksgiving
Sponsor:	Hotel Vendome
Place:	Hotel Vendome, New York City, NY
Date:	November, 1899

Photographic reproduction is the highlight of this menu design. On the front and back outer covers of the centerfold cardboard are (front) a photo reproduction entitled "Thanksgiving Offering" and (back) a photo reproduction of the Hotel Vendome taken from an elevated perspective, probably from a building across the street, at its location: the intersection of Broadway and 41st Street in New York City. Printed by a company in the more rural area of Elmira, New York, this menu is still very Victorian in its ornate lettering and borders, both of which are embossed and overlaid in gold on the cover. Inside is one-color printing in brown, giving the music of the occasion on the left side and the menu on the right.

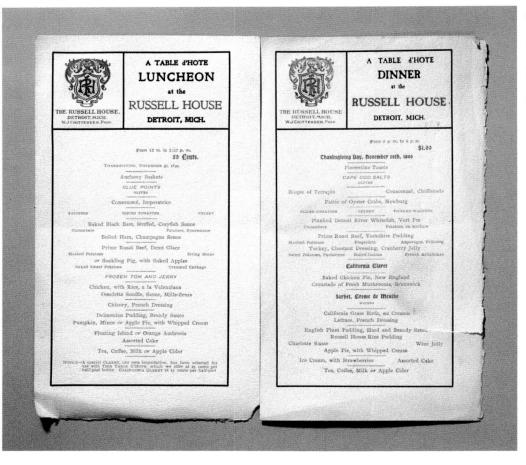

Occasion: Thanksgiving Luncheon

Sponsor: Russell House

Place: Russell House, Detroit, MI

Date: November 30, 1899

As stated on the luncheon menu, the first of the two holiday meals served by the Russell House on Thanksgiving Day was between the hours of Noon to 2:30 P.M....And for a whopping 50 cents, one could eat like American royalty. Firm borders of thick black ink enclosed print in three colors. On the lunch menu a primary use of green ink is accented in black and mauve; on the dinner menu the accents are black and red. The upper left corner of both menus contains the restaurant logo in embossed green. On each of the two menus, one edge of the textured rag paper is left raw.

Occasion: Thanksgiving Dinner

Sponsor: The Chelsea Hotel

Place: The Chelsea Hotel, 222 West 23 St., New York City, NY

Date: November, 1899

The artistic heritage of the Chelsea Hotel is reflected in the simple elegance of this 5 1/2"x7 1/2", two page menu. The cover design is a pen-and-black ink lithograph in colors of fleshtone, yellow, green, blue and red-orange. The embossed hotel insignia as well as the "Thanksgiving" caption at the bottom are in light lavender. This lavender embossing is also used inside for the "menu" heading. The menu items are set in simple small capitals in brown ink. The two pages of this menu are joined with white satin ribbons tied in bows at the top.

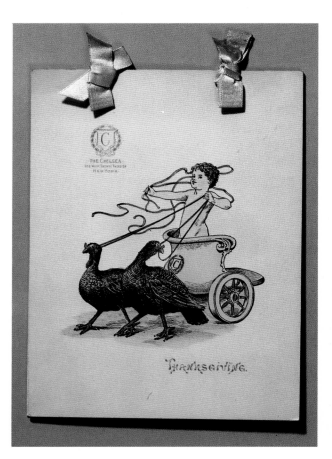

Occasion: Thanksgiving

Sponsor: The California Hotel

Place: The California Hotel, San Francisco, CA

Date: November 24, 1898

Bound at the top left corner with a metal ring, two pieces of paper form the three-side printed menu used for Thanksgiving dinner at the California Hotel in 1898. The top sheet is a dye-cut, bevel-edged piece of thick cardboard printed in blue and metallic gold. The second sheet is red construction paper printed on both sides in black ink. The most interesting feature of this menu is the advertisement for the San Rafael Golf Club found on the back side, which incidentally is of the same proprietorship as the California Hotel.

Occasion: Thanksgiving

Sponsor: Hotel Windermere

Place: Hotel Windermere, Chicago, IL @ Cornell Avenue & 56th Street

Date: November 24, 1898

Green construction paper is the mat of this 1898 holiday menu, which measures 6"x5". On the outer cover is a light-hearted pencil drawing on medium stock white paper, which has been pasted onto the centerfolded construction paper. This brown-ink drawing, signed by the artist "Metcalf, Chicago," shows a football player and young woman. The latter is peeking at the athlete from behind a garland barrier, a playful grin on her face.

Occasion:	Thanksgiving Dinner
Sponsor:	Hotel Manhattan
Place:	Hotel Manhattan, New York City, NY
Date:	Thursday, November 24, 1898

One centerfolded 12″x18″ piece of coated stock is used for this menu. The rich design of the full-color engraved cover is the result of overlaid color, and an excerpt of President McKinley's Thanksgiving Proclamation of October 28, 1898, is superimposed upon it in dark blue ink. The engraving itself is an exploration of American/Thanksgiving symbols; the American Indian, the Eagle, and variations of Stars and Stripes form a wide, colorful border for this menu. The same blue ink used on the cover is used inside to describe the holiday fare. The two sheets are tied together with one crimson satin ribbon, bowed at the left margin. This menu was printed in Paris, France.

Occasion:	Thanksgiving Dinner
Sponsor:	Hotel Manhattan
Place:	Hotel Manhattan, New York City, NY
Date:	Thursday, November 26, 1896

This is the first of two nearly identical menus featured in this book. The differences between the design used in 1898 and the one used here, in 1896, are as follows: This menu is larger, leaving an unprofessional-looking, flat, white border at the left; where President McKinley's holiday message appears on the 1898 cover is an embossed "Thanksgiving '96" in gilt; the back cover of this 1896 menu hosts an illustration of the hotel in blue ink; and, of course, the menu items printed inside are changed altogether, this earlier version of the design used by the Hotel Manhattan is less masterfully tailored in design and appearance.

Occasion: Thanksgiving Day Dinner

Sponsor: Hotel San Remo

Place: Hotel San Remo, Central Park West & 75th Street, New York City, NY

Date: November, 1898

Uncle Sam is poised with knife and fork, ready to devour the roast turkey upon his lap, in this menu's cover lithograph. The outer sheet of this four-page menu is a centerfolded piece of 10 1/2"x13" cardboard; on the front of the centerfold is the lithograph, on the back is the red-and-blue hotel insignia. The inside sheet is also centerfolded, and of the same size, printed on both sides in dark blue ink, and embossed in gold on the menu page. The pages are hole-punched and joined with a red satin ribbon.

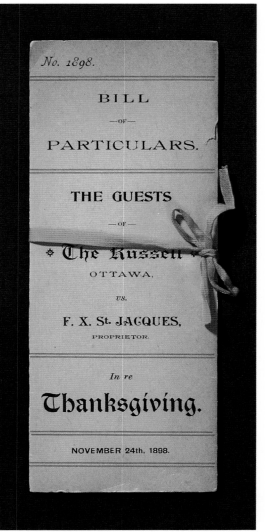

Occasion: Thanksgiving Dinner

Place: The Russell Hotel, Ottawa, Canada

Date: November 24, 1878

This menu is designed to mimic the format of a legal docket, with the outer thick, beige stock tri-folded to wrap the inner page, which is printed in black and ruled at the top and left margins in orange-red. These ink colors are repeated on the outer cover. Introduced and closed with text simulating legal jargon, the inside sheet is also "sealed" with an orange paste-on embossed in gold with the logo of the Russell. The menu is tied with a pink cotton ribbon.

Occasion:	Thanksgiving Party
Sponsor:	The Tremont
Place:	The Tremont, Oshkosh, WI
Date:	November, 1896

This delightful menu is a masterful blend of elements. On the cover are the embossed hand-watercolored turkey and embossed "Thanksgiving" in metallic silver. (The artist, however, forgot to color the turkey's feet!) The establishment's name is printed in brown ink. This brown ink is used inside and on the back cover of the menu as well. On one page are the lyrics to the song *America*; on the page facing the menu is comic verse to honor cooks, cooking, and food; then there is the menu itself, featuring its own "Tremont Mineral Spring Water" as one of the refreshments; followed by an engraving of an Indian on the backside of page 3; and, finally, an engraving of the Tremont House on the back cover.

Occasion:	Thanksgiving
Sponsor:	The Baldwin
Place:	The Baldwin, San Francisco, CA
Date:	November, 1896

Centerfolded coated card stock is used for this menu's 5 1/2"x6 1/2" covers. The front cover features two-color printing in blue and yellow-gold, and an etching of four turkeys. The blue ink of the etching lends itself to the cool grey-blue of a typical November landscape, and the embossed caption at the upper left balances the color scheme with its yellow-gold. The centerfolded inner sheet is of light-weight paper printed in black ink; on one side is the menu, and on the other is a lithograph design of the Baldwin Building.

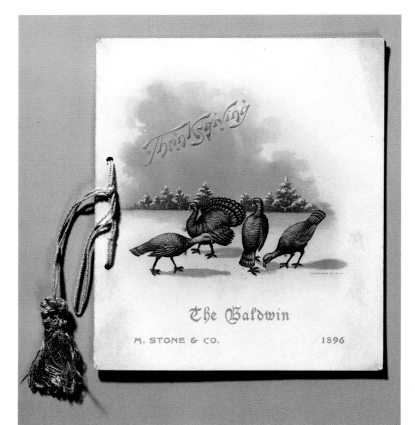

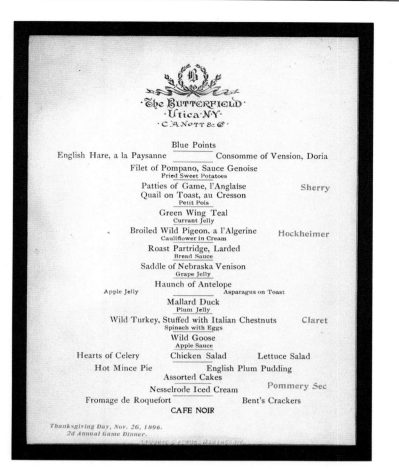

The Butterfield
Utica·N.Y.
·C·A·NOTT & C°·

Blue Points
English Hare, a la Paysanne ———— Consomme of Vension, Doria
Filet of Pompano, Sauce Genoise
Fried Sweet Potatoes
Patties of Game, l'Anglaise   Sherry
Quail on Toast, au Cresson
Petit Pois
Green Wing Teal
Currant Jelly
Broiled Wild Pigeon, a l'Algerine   Hockheimer
Cauliflower in Cream
Roast Partridge, Larded
Bread Sauce
Saddle of Nebraska Venison
Grape Jelly
Haunch of Antelope
Apple Jelly   Asparagus on Toast
Mallard Duck
Plum Jelly
Wild Turkey, Stuffed with Italian Chestnuts   Claret
Spinach with Eggs
Wild Goose
Apple Sauce
Hearts of Celery   Chicken Salad   Lettuce Salad
Hot Mince Pie   English Plum Pudding
Assorted Cakes
Nesselrode Iced Cream   Pommery Sec
Fromage de Roquefort   Bent's Crackers
CAFE NOIR

Thanksgiving Day, Nov. 26, 1896.
2d Annual Game Dinner.

Occasion:	Thanksgiving Dinner—"2nd Annual Game Dinner"
Sponsor:	The Butterfield
Place:	The Butterfield, Utica, NY
Date:	November 26, 1896

This one-side-printed beveled-edge sheet of cardboard is a holiday tribute to the game of the country; fish, fowl, deer, antelope and rabbit are all represented in the dishes served on this day in 1896. Foods are printed in blue, wines in red. The Butterfield logo is embossed in gold at top, center, on this 5"x6 1/2" menu.

Occasion:	Thanksgiving Dinner
Sponsor:	Hotel Marlborough
Place:	Hotel Marlborough, New York City, NY
Date:	November, 1896

A gracefully handpainted turkey in watercolor is the focus of this Thanksgiving dinner menu. The upper left corner carries the hotel coat of arms in gold-embossed design. Centerfolded 0.1-inch thick cardboard forms the covers of this 5 1/2"x7" menu, its edges bevel-cut, while inside is a centerfolded sheet of thick paper printed in blue ink on one side. The pages are hole-punched and are bound with white silk cord.

·HOTEL·
·MARLBOROUGH·

Occasion: Thanksgiving Dinner

Sponsor: Hotel Marinette; Lant
               Wood—Proprietor

Place: Marinette, WI

Date: November 26, 1896

The Victorian style is alive and well
on this 1896 Thanksgiving menu,
which features elaborate gold
embossing, print reproduction of the
chase of a turkey for Thanksgiving
Dinner, edging is dye cut and
beveled. A white satin ribbon is tied
in a bow at left serving as both
binding and inner/outer decoration.
The inner sheet of the menu is
printed on two sides: the prefacing
page in gold ink, the inner menu in
brown. Humorous quips are printed
between the entries of the menu, for
example, "My salad days, When I
was green in judgement." The back
cover displays the hotel insignia in
brown-ink lithography.

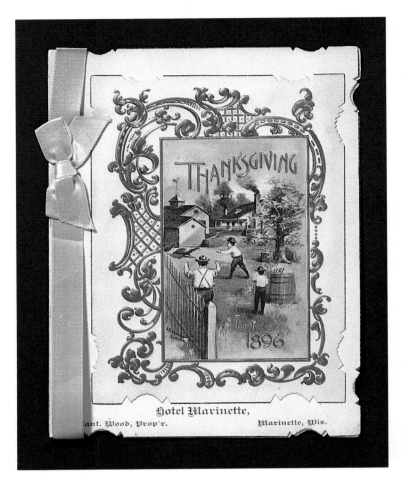

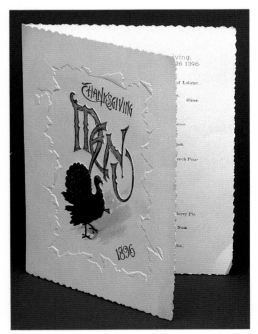

Occasion: Thanksgiving Dinner

Sponsor: The Beaumont; Henry
               Bertram, Proprietor

Place: Green Bay, WI

Date: Thursday, November 26,
               1896

Dye-cut edges echo the "torn" theme
of the embossed border, which forms
a sort of "ripped window" frame for
the gold-embossed turkey and
lettering at the center of the front
cover. "Menu" is accented in blue.
Inside is the list of holiday fare,
printed in black. Turkey was
prepared three different ways for the
feast.

Occasion:	Thanksgiving Party
Sponsor:	Hotel Iroquois
Place:	Hotel Iroquois, Buffalo, NY
Date:	November, 1896

The 6 o'clock dinner for which this menu was used was accompanied by a full musical program performed by the hotel orchestra. This 5 1/2"x7" menu is comprised of 2 centerfolded sheets: the cover in thick cardboard, the inner pages of parchment paper. The inside sheet features two-sided, two-color printing in brown and black. The front cover is embossed in gold, brown, and taupe with Victorian-style detailing; but the fine black lines of the embossed turkey at the upper left corner are sadly muted by a heavy layer of overlaid gold. The back cover is decorated with an illustrated bust of an Indian—surely the Iroquois emblem of the hotel. A fancy white silk ribbon joins the menu pages in a bow at the front.

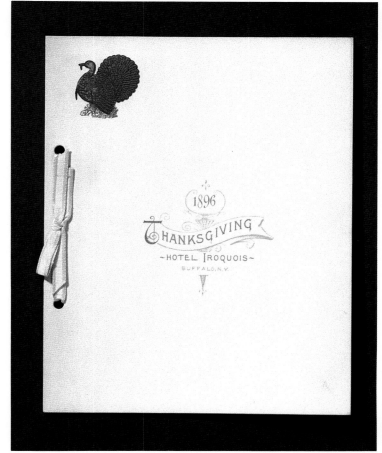

Occasion:	Thanksgiving Dinner
Sponsor:	The Windsor
Place:	The Windsor, New York City, NY
Date:	November 26, 1896

One sheet of thick parchment paper, 6 1/2"x8 1/2", is embossed in gold at the top and printed in green for this 1896 menu. At the bottom left corner is a lithography; the subject is a harmless-looking maiden who approaches her dinner bird with an unthreatening piece of ribbon. This quaint pictorial is handcolored in red and pink.

Occasion: Thanksgiving

Sponsor: Hotel Vendome

Place: Hotel Vendome, Boston, MA

Date: Thursday, November 28, 1895

Victorian design is in full bloom on the front cover of this 1895 menu. From the ornate lettering of the embossed hotel logo and Thanksgiving caption, to the hand-watercolored flowers in pink, red and orange, to the wide, silk moire binding ribbon in hues of silvery blue and peach, this menu epitomizes the artistry of the Victorian era. Cardboard book-wrapped in linen paper forms the covers; inside is a 10″x14″ sheet of linen paper centerfolded and printed one side only in golden-brown ink.

Occasion: Thanksgiving

Sponsor: The Jackson

Place: The Jackson, Chicago, IL

Date: November 28, 1895

10 1/2″x14″ cardboard is centerfolded and printed on two sides of this Thanksgiving menu. The front cover has a Halloween flavor to its orange-and-black design, in which a boy climbs a stark, leafless tree to reach an embossed white turkey silhouetted against a huge orange moon. This illustration is a pen-and-ink lithograph. The cover is embossed at the top and bottom; the top in orange for the hotel's name, the bottom announcing the occasion in plain relief of the white cardboard. The menu printed inside is in a deep salmon-colored ink.

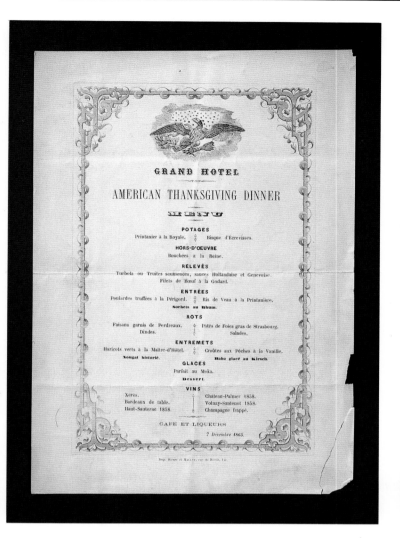

Occasion: American Thanksgiving
              Dinner in Paris, France

Sponsor: Grand Hotel

Place: Grand Hotel, 144 Rue di
              Rivoli, Paris, France

Date: December 7, 1865

Intricacy of design is evident in this menu's border, which is of many fine engraved lines in metallic gold. The top center lithograph is of the American bald eagle, complete with claw-held arrows and laurel branch, and breast-plated in stars, stripes and a ribbon that reads "*E Pluribus Unum.*" This lithograph, like the text of the menu, is printed in black ink upon 7 1/4″x10 1/2″ lightweight, coated stock.

Occasion: Thanksgiving Dinner

Sponsor: American Colony in Berlin;
              Joseph A. Wright, United
              States minister, presided

Place: Hotel de Rome, Berlin,
              Germany

Date: November 29, 1866

This simple 4″x6″ menu is printed in brown ink on one side. The lithographic American emblem at the top is the only decoration to this menu, which was sent by Captain Nathan Appleton, who attended the dinner, to "F.E.B." on his way to Russia. Joseph A. Wright, the U.S. minister in Berlin at the time, presided at the event.

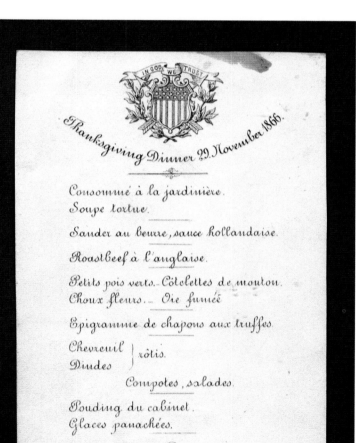

Occasion: Annual Banquet of the Hibernian Society

Sponsor: The Hibernian Society

Place: The Continental Hotel, Philadelphia, PA

Date: March 17, 1891

The embossed front cover of this Irish-American inspired menu features a clover relief pattern in a half-circle about one metallic blue-green clover and a gold embossed eagle clutching the Irish and American flags in flight. The cover also features lettering in embossed green and gold. Ribbons of green and gold (Irish flag colors) satin bind the menu cover to its inner pages, which are printed in deep green.

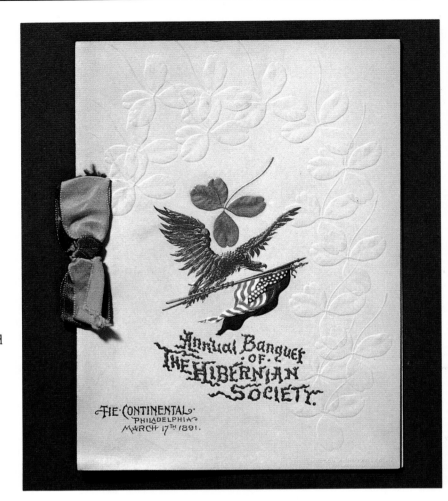

Occasion: 107th Anniversary Dinner of the Friendly Sons of St. Patrick

Sponsor: Friendly Sons of St. Patrick

Place: Delmonico's, New York City, NY

Date: Tuesday Evening, March 17, 1891

Nearly all of the six pages which comprise this St. Patrick's Day menu are decorated in some manner. The two covers, of thick white cardboard, are both embossed. The front is in gold for the bust of Moore and letterings, and the back in green foil over a bunch of clover. The front cover also features a green-ink lithographic representation of an Irish loch and the hand-painted flags of Ireland and America. The inner pages feature pen-and-ink renditions of rural Irish landscapes.

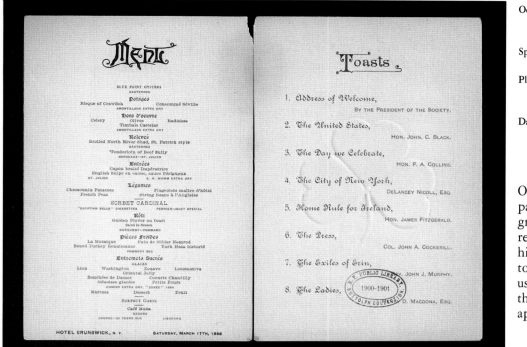

Occasion: Annual Dinner of the Knights of St. Patrick

Sponsor: Knights of St. Patrick

Place: Hotel Brunswick, New York City, NY

Date: Saturday Evening, March 17, 1888

One color dominates the thick linen paper of this St. Patrick's Day menu: green, of course. Excepting accents in red ink, which are used inside to highlight wines, tobaccos, and the toastmasters of the event, green is used for a variety of fonts and for the huge embossed clover leaf which appears on the front cover.

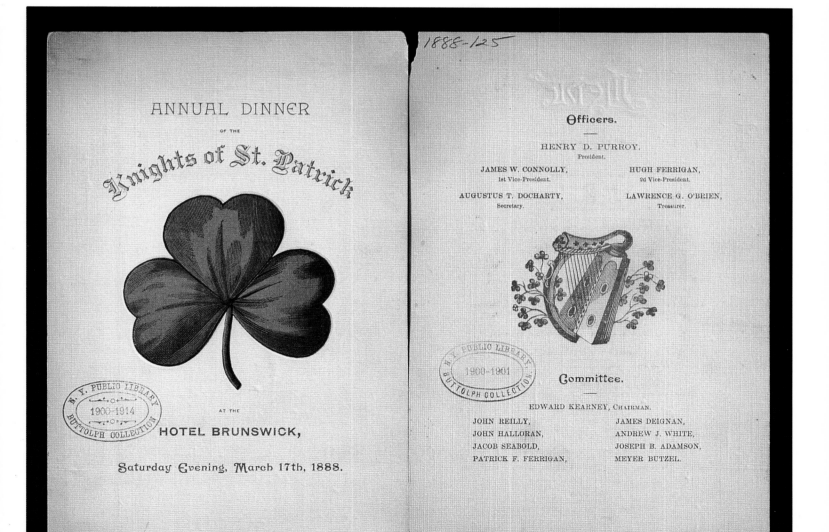

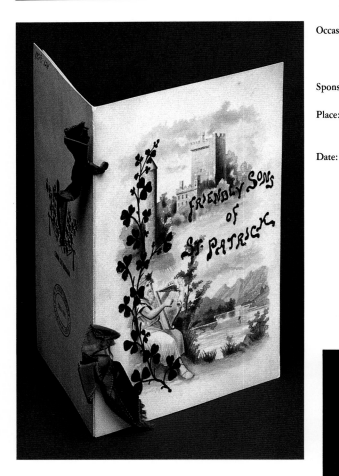

Occasion:	104th Anniversary Dinner of the Friendly Sons of St. Patrick
Sponsor:	Friendly Sons of St. Patrick
Place:	Delmonico's, New York City, NY
Date:	Saturday, March 17, 1888

This four-page menu designed for the Friendly Sons of St. Patrick is one of the many created for the New York City based club by the obviously Irish printhouse of Dempsey & Carroll. The front cover is illustrated with a lyrical engraving of Hibernian theme, while the back cover is embossed with harp, clover, ivy, and lettering in gold and two shades of green foil, respectively. The inner pages of this four-page cardboard menu are printed on one side in gold and embossed at the top in green foil.

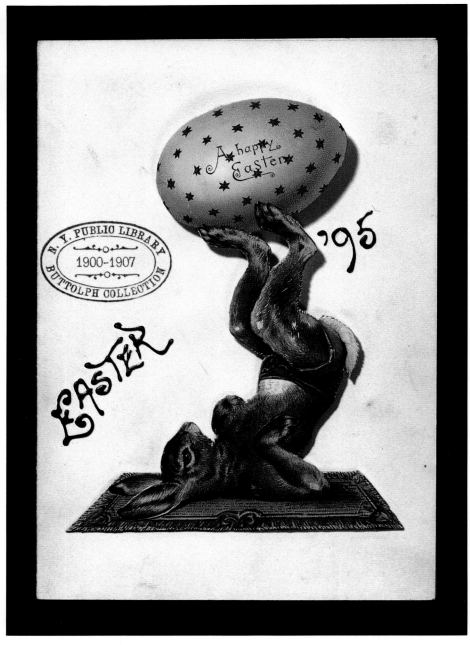

Occasion:	Easter Dinner
Sponsor:	Hotel Brunswick
Place:	New York City, NY
Date:	April 20, 1895

An acrobatic dyecut rabbit (printed in England) is pasted on the cover of this Easter menu. Easter '95 is handpainted on with gold oil paint. The interior of this 4 1/2"x6 1/2" centerfolded cardboard menu is printed in brown. The "Music Programme" appears on the back cover, also printed in brown.

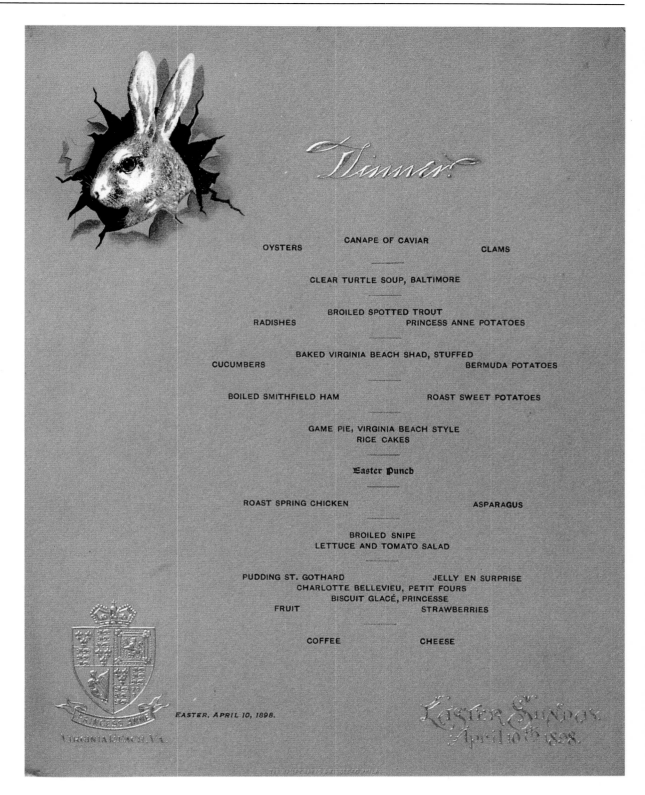

Dinner

CANAPE OF CAVIAR
OYSTERS   CLAMS
_____

CLEAR TURTLE SOUP, BALTIMORE
_____

BROILED SPOTTED TROUT
RADISHES   PRINCESS ANNE POTATOES
_____

BAKED VIRGINIA BEACH SHAD, STUFFED
CUCUMBERS   BERMUDA POTATOES
_____

BOILED SMITHFIELD HAM   ROAST SWEET POTATOES
_____

GAME PIE, VIRGINIA BEACH STYLE
RICE CAKES

Easter Punch
_____

ROAST SPRING CHICKEN   ASPARAGUS
_____

BROILED SNIPE
LETTUCE AND TOMATO SALAD
_____

PUDDING ST. GOTHARD   JELLY EN SURPRISE
CHARLOTTE BELLEVIEU, PETIT FOURS
BISCUIT GLACÉ, PRINCESSE
FRUIT   STRAWBERRIES

COFFEE   CHEESE

EASTER, APRIL 10, 1898.

Easter Sunday
April 10th 1898.

Occasion:	Easter Dinner
Sponsor:	Princess Anne Hotel
Place:	Virginia Beach, VA
Date:	April 10, 1898

The Princess Anne Hotel selected this single piece menu for its Easter 1898 dinner. The menu is printed in forest green on a spring green stock. The caption "Dinner," the holiday, and the insignia of the hotel is silver embossed. The bright spot of this ordinary menu is the realistic etching of a rabbit's head peeking through a hole in the background. The final decoration is a red glass bead insert used for the rabbit's eye.

Occasion: Easter Sunday

Sponsor: Windsor Hotel

Place: Fifth Avenue, New York
             City, NY

Date: April 18, 1897

With best Easter Wishes

The Windsor Hotel used this Bavarian-printed menu to welcome Easter 1897 in New York City. This deckle-edged, centerfolded cardboard menu showcases German ingenuity at its best. Pull the tab on the front cover and the handtinted chicken lifts her wing and shows off her newly-hatched brood of chicks. The interior of the menu is printed in gold ink in sans serif type.

Occasion: Easter Dinner

Sponsor: Hygeia Hotel

Place: Old Point Comfort, VA

Date: Easter, 1897

Two sheets of thin cardboard comprise this fine example of early Art Nouveau. A purplish mezzotint engraving of an angelic heralder is used on the cover; the name of the hotel and "Easter" greetings are silver embossed in a highly ornate typeface. A purple satin ribbon binds the two pieces together; the second sheet contains an engraving of two cherubs playing "tug o'war" with a silver-embossed flower garland. The menu is printed beneath in an unusual shade of orchid.

Occasion: Easter Dinner

Sponsor: Murray Hill Hotel

Place: New York City, NY

Date: Easter, 1895

A single piece of bevel-edged 0.3" thick cardboard was used for the Murray Hill Hotel Easter 1895 menu. The hotel name and the holiday are both silver embossed. The dinner listing is printed in a hard-to-read silver. The only decoration is a handcolored, embossed lily in the upper lefthand corner.

Occasion:	Easter Breakfast	
Sponsor:	The Windsor Hotel, Hawk & Wetherbee	
Place:	New York City, NY	
Date:	April 14, 1895	

A watercolored pencil sketch of two daffodils appears on the cover of this Easter menu. Two pieces of beveled-edged heavyweight cardboard are bound by a bright gold satin ribbon. Two inserts are bound in: the first contains the breakfast menu printed in lilac ink, while the second contains the luncheon menu also in lilac ink.

CHAPTER 3   Patriotic Events

uly 4, Independence Day, has been a joyous celebration in these United States since the Declaration was first adopted in 1776. In that year, however, the people of Philadelphia delayed the celebration until Monday, July 8, when a mass meeting was held in what is now called Independence Square. The celebration included a reading of the Declaration, a parade of the battalions, and bells and chimes which rang all day and all night.

The next year, in 1777, the people of Philadelphia celebrated July 4 in a very similar fashion to the way it is now celebrated, with bonfires in the streets and fireworks in the evening. A large dinner was held and then a parade of soldiers marched through the city. In addition, many people took to lighting candles in their windows at night.

Similar celebrations were held each July 4, with the largest celebration occurring in 1788 when the Constitution had been approved by nine states, the requisite number of states needed to ratify the document. The celebration of the Fourth of July gradually spread across the country, as new states and territories were admitted into the Union.

Today, Independence Day is a holiday celebrated all across the country, with each region contributing its own unique traditions to the celebration. Fireworks are present everywhere, signifying the gun powder of the Revolution. Picnics and parties are often held on this auspicious day, with clambakes being the traditional fare in New England and barbecues being the traditional fare of the South and West. In Missouri the annual Tom Sawyer Fence-Painting Contest is held, while Akron, Ohio celebrates America's ethnic heritage with an International Festival. Perhaps the most poignant celebration of Independence Day, however, occurs each year in Monticello, where newly naturalized citizens are sworn in and honored.

STATUE OF LIBERTY

The Statue of Liberty is considered to be our national symbol of freedom, hope, and democracy. It was presented on July 4, 1884 to the United States from France and commemorates the alliance between France and the United States during the American Revolution.

The copper statue is 152 feet high and is in the form of a woman with an uplifted arm holding a torch. It is erected upon a 150 foot concrete and granite base in the shape of an 11-pointed star. The statue was designed by Frederic Auguste Bartholdi and became a national monument in 1924.

GEORGE WASHINGTON'S BIRTHDAY

The first known celebration of George Washington's birthday outside of his immediate family occurred in 1778 when the band of the Fourth Continental Artillery marched to headquarters at Valley Forge and serenaded the General. New York, however, claims to be the first to hold a celebration, when on February 22, 1783 a group of men met at a hotel for dinner and made speeches in praise of Washington. Afterwards, they decided to meet there for an annual celebration.

During Washington's first year as President, in 1790, Congress decided to adjourn on this date in honor of the President and to extend its congratulations to him. This annual adjournment for the President's birthday continued until 1796, when the resolution was defeated and Congress remained in session.

After Washington's term of presidency, his birthday was celebrated rather sporadically. John Adams made official notice of his anniversary and encouraged its celebration, but Thomas Jefferson ignored the day. It was not until Washington's death in 1799 that Congress adopted the resolution that February 22, 1800 be observed throughout the country for the expressed purpose of showing esteem for the first President. Large celebrations were held in honor of Washington's one hundreth, one hundreth and fiftieth, and two hundreth birthdays. Today, February 22 is considered a legal U.S. holiday.

MILITARY

The United States armed forces can be broken

down into the army, navy, air force, and marines. Each of these branches has had their share of heroes and famous units throughout various conflicts in American history.

Many of these heroes and units received dinners as part of their tribute and recognition for defending the United States against her various enemies. Admiral Dewey, Commander Perry, the Third Army Corps, and many others are represented in this section.

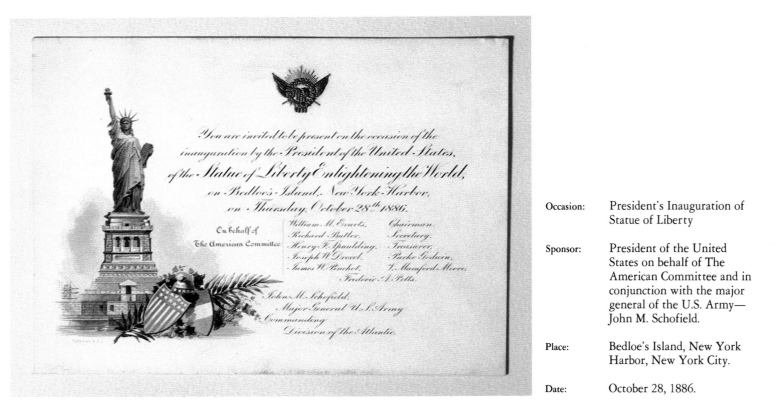

Occasion: President's Inauguration of
               Statue of Liberty

Sponsor: President of the United
               States on behalf of The
               American Committee and in
               conjunction with the major
               general of the U.S. Army—
               John M. Schofield.

Place: Bedloe's Island, New York
               Harbor, New York City.

Date: October 28, 1886.

As the official invitation of the
President of the United States, this
lithograph by Tiffany & Co. conveys
the stateliness of the occasion
marking the inauguration of France's
gift of the Statue of Liberty. The
statue is reproduced in minute detail
and a gold-embossed wreath
encircles the flags of the U.S. and
France in an historic
commemoration of their alliance and
goodwill. The recipients of this
invitation may have also had the
honor of invitation to Delmonico's
for the banquet which followed the
inauguration. The banquet invitation
and menu is featured here.

   This invitation is the *first* part of
a two-part official invitation to both
the inauguration *and* the banquet
following the inauguration.

Occasion: Statue of Liberty dinner sponsored by principals of the Windsor: Gardner Wetherbee, William S. Hawk, and Andrew R. Blakely.

Place: The Windsor, Fifth Avenue, New York City.

Date: Thursday, October 28, 1886.

While featuring both French and American cuisine, this dinner menu gives top billing to the American fare. A special soup, however, both honors the Statue's creator and combines Old and New World flavors.

Occasion: Arrival of Statue of Liberty in the U.S.

Sponsor: The Common Council of the City of New York.

Place: City Hall, New York City

Date: June 15, 1885 1:00 P.M.

Engraved in two-color (black/green) ink, this 8"x5 1/2" one-sided invitation marks the arrival of the Statue of Liberty in New York City. Note the hand-painted flags of France and the United States and the lithographic detail rendered in the decorative seal of the Statue.

Occasion: Banquet, 11th Annual
Banquet, Old Guard, Albany
Zouave Cadets

Sponsor: Albany Zouave Cadets

Place: Hotel Kenmore, Albany,
NY

Date: December 12, 1894

The cover of this four-piece menu is
a handpainted watercolor of a young
lad with a gold ribbon running
behind the portrait. The three other
pieces are printed in black ink and
list the menu, the music program,
and the members of the guard.

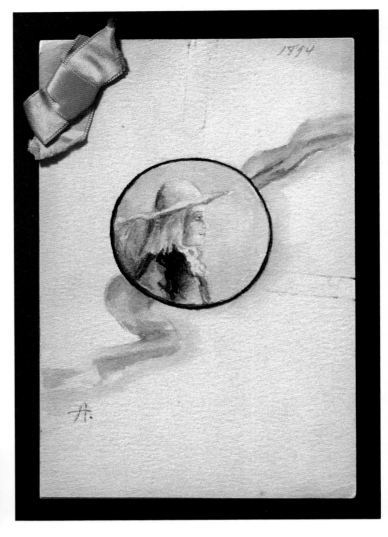

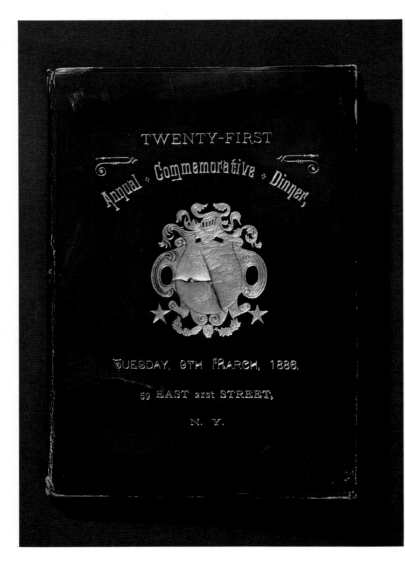

Occasion: Dinner, 20th Annual
Commemorative

Sponsor: Major General J. Watts de
Peyster

Place: 59 East 21st Street, New
York City, NY

Date: March 9, 1886

This leather covered book measures
4 3/4"x7". The cover is dyed navy
blue and has a gold embossed seal,
the inside front and back covers are
covered in gold silk. The inside front
cover contains a photogravure
portrait of Major General J. Watts
de Peyster smoking a cigar. The 60-
page book contains letters, lists of
guests at past dinners, and quotes
from various people. The book is
hand-sewn.

Occasion: Dinner, 2nd Reunion
             Blueberry War

Place: St. Paul, MN

Date: July 26, 1897

This centerfolded, cardboard 5 1/ 2″
x6 3/4″ menu, contains a single
sheet of parchment paper,
centerfolded and bound in with a
white satin ribbon. The cover
illustration is a simple lithograph in
gold with glue and green tinting.
The menu is printed in dark blue
ink. All of the desserts served at this
function used blueberries as the main
ingredient.

Occasion: Dinner, 35th Annual
             Reunion of the Third Army
             Corps Union

Place: Hotel Manhattan, New
             York City, NY

Date: May 5, 1899

This single piece, full-color
lithographed menu is interesting for
two reasons; it originally folded in
half to serve as a placecard, and the
Statue of Liberty is drawn in the
upper lefthand corner with her right
breast exposed.

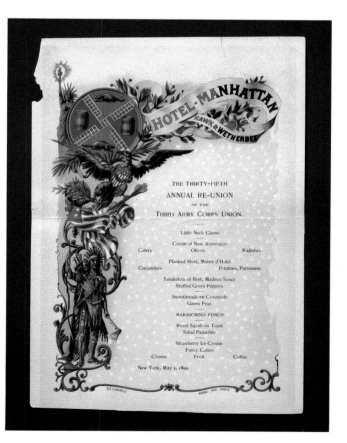

Occasion: Banquet Commemoration of Perry's Victory

Place: The Hollenden, Cleveland, OH

Date: September 10, 1896

Three pieces of 5 3/4"x7 1/2" cardboard are dye-cut in the shape of a sail in this menu. The cover contains a terrible woodcut of Admiral Perry in a gold-embossed ship's wheel. An embossed flag has been colored red and blue, and Perry's saying "We have met the enemy and they are ours" is embossed in the wheel, barely visible. White silk thread has been punched through the front cover to appear as if the sail is tied on to the lithographed mast. The menu is bound by four metal rings.

Occasion: Ladies' Banquet

Place: Salter's Hall

Date: July 25, 1894

A tri-folded piece of cardboard makes up this 3 1/2"x9" oblong menu. Bronze and dark beige inks are used throughout. The cover contains a simple design with a decorative border. When unfolded, the entire side of the menu gives the seating chart for the affair.

Occasion: 4th of July

Sponsor: Hotel Dennis

Place: Hotel Dennis, Atlantic City, NJ

Date: July 4th, 1899

Textured blue kraft paper embossed with the Hotel Dennis logo and turn-of-the-century style lettering forms the centerfolded cover of this menu. Inside is a one-side printed sheet of glossy stock folded into three sections. Two of the three sections are photogravures (not shown). One is a photogravure of a painting (the signing of the Declaration of Independence) and the other is of the room in which the Declaration was signed. The third section is the menu, and as shown, it is printed blue on white, with a red stenciled heading at the top. A red, white and blue silk cord ties the kraft cover to one fold of the inner sheet. This menu measures 5"x6 1/2": its styling suggests the seaside location of the hotel.

Occasion: Evacuation of New York by
            the British

Sponsor: Sons of the Revolution

Place: Delmonico's, New York
            City

Date: November 26, 1894

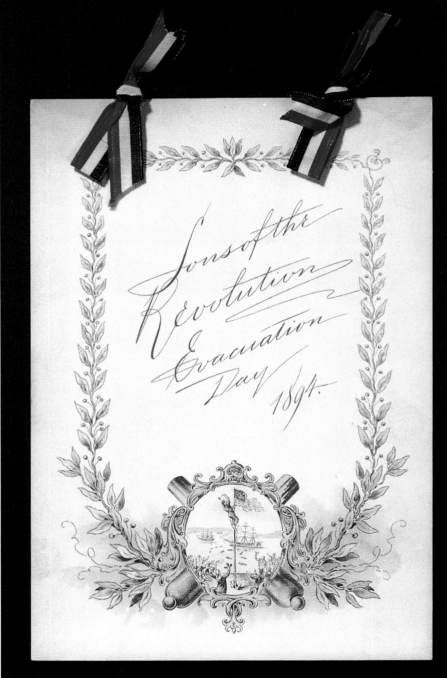

For this menu, two pieces of cardboard paper are printed one side each and bow-tied through two holes at the top with tricolored silk ribbons in red, white and blue. These 5 1/2"x8" cards combine a red, blue and red mezzotint process with lithographic ornamentation and lettering in brown ink. On the cover is a cameo of the scene in which the British departed and the new American flag was raised. Inside, the menu items are surprisingly international in name and flavor. Also, while most of the Delmonico's menus in this collection reflect an allegiance between the New York City restaurant and Tiffany & Co., this particular menu was designed and printed by J. Ottomann Lithographers Co. Consequently, it is interesting to note that the apostrophe is missing from the spelling of "Delmonico's" on this menu.

Occasion: 4th of July

Sponsor: Murray Hill Hotel, New York City

Place: Murray Hill Hotel, New York City

Date: July 4, 1892

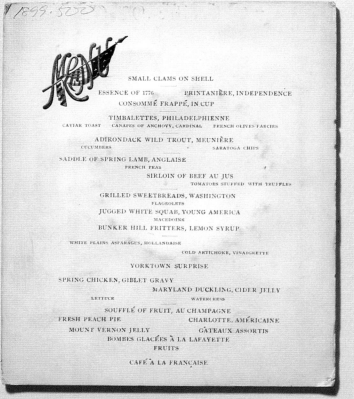

MENU

SMALL CLAMS ON SHELL

ESSENCE OF 1776   PRINTANIÈRE, INDEPENDENCE
CONSOMMÉ FRAPPÉ, IN CUP

TIMBALETTES, PHILADELPHIENNE
CAVIAR TOAST   CANAPÉS OF ANCHOVY, CARDINAL   FRENCH OLIVES FARCIES

ADIRONDACK WILD TROUT, MEUNIÈRE
CUCUMBERS   SARATOGA CHIPS

SADDLE OF SPRING LAMB, ANGLAISE
FRENCH PEAS
SIRLOIN OF BEEF AU JUS
TOMATOES STUFFED WITH TRUFFLES

GRILLED SWEETBREADS, WASHINGTON
FLAGEOLETS
JUGGED WHITE SQUAB, YOUNG AMERICA
MACEDOINE
BUNKER HILL FRITTERS, LEMON SYRUP

WHITE PLAINS ASPARAGUS, HOLLANDAISE

COLD ARTICHOKE, VINAIGRETTE

YORKTOWN SURPRISE

SPRING CHICKEN, GIBLET GRAVY
MARYLAND DUCKLING, CIDER JELLY
LETTUCE   WATERCRESS

SOUFFLÉ OF FRUIT, AU CHAMPAGNE
FRESH PEACH PIE   CHARLOTTE, AMÉRICAINE
MOUNT VERNON JELLY   GÂTEAUX ASSORTIS
BOMBES GLACÉES À LA LAFAYETTE
FRUITS

CAFÉ À LA FRANÇAISE

Located in the era's most fashionable district of New York City, the Murray Hill Hotel presented this menu of dye-cut 0.3-inch cardboard to its patrons on July 4th, 1892. The window on the front of this menu features the hotel's logo—an embossed griffin stenciled in gold and handpainted. The special foods listed on the back side reflect the occasion, in 3-color printing—red, blue, and gold. Great design consideration was given to the flag at the upper left corner over which hang the embossed letters of the word "Menu."

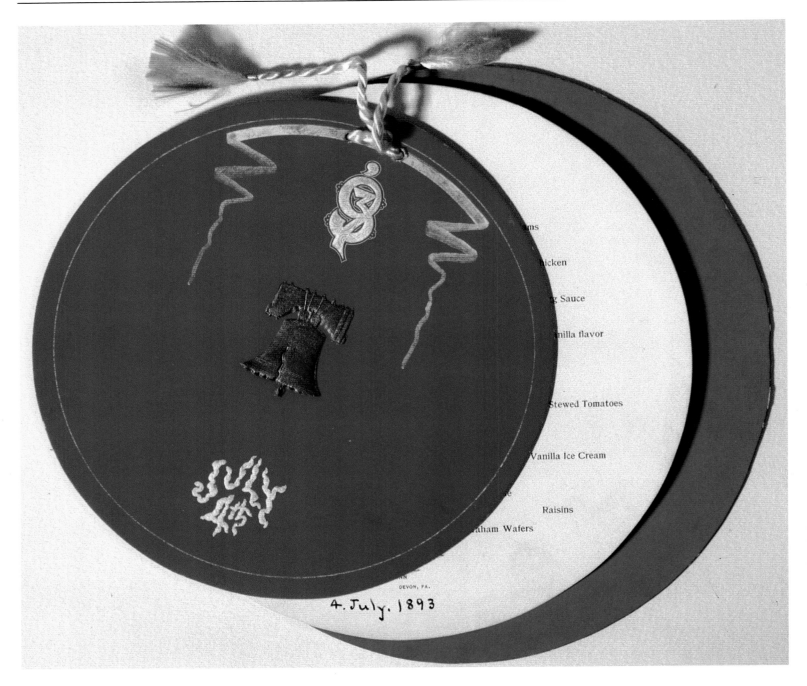

4. July. 1893

Occasion: Independence Day

Sponsor: The Devon Inn/Hotel
             Windsor

Place: Devon Inn, Devon, PA

Date: July 4, 1893

This menu sports the patriotic tricolor theme of the July 4th holiday in three circular pages joined with a white silk cord. The red cover page is embossed in three areas. At the top is an elaborately hand-painted "93," the year of the celebration; in the mid-area is a wonderful reproduction of the Liberty Bell, stenciled over in gold; and at the bottom "July 4th" is given a surprisingly abstracted embossing. The dinner menu inside tantalizes the patrons' palate with items ranging from "Little Neck Clams" and "Soft-Shell Crabs, Fried" to "Spring Lamb, Mint Sauce" and "Independence Pudding, Brandy Sauce."

BRITISH LEAVING AMERICA

BANQUET OF
THE SONS OF THE REVOLUTION
TO COMMEMORATE THE
EVACUATION OF NEW YORK
BY THE BRITISH

DELMONICO'S
Nov. 25 1895

Occasion:	Banquet to commemorate the evacuation of New York by the British
Sponsor:	Sons of the Revolution
Place:	Delmonico's, New York City
Date:	November 25, 1895

Tiffany & Co. designed and printed the pen-and-ink lithographic montage that appears on the cover sheet of this 2-page menu. The 5 1/4"x7 1/2" thick cardboard pieces are joined at the top with two satin bows, one gold, one blue; menu text, as well as the emblems, logo, and historical scenes created for this menu, is in one-color print.

Occasion: 4th of July

Sponsor: Barnum & Bailey, Ltd.

Place: Plymouth, England

Date: July 4, 1899

As is obvious from this menu of 1899, relations between the United States and England had vastly improved since the Revolutionary War. This full-color lithograph reveals that not only was this Independence Day feast held in England, it also was catered by an American food service. Naturally, the fare was North American, but the menu was produced in Leeds by the Queen's printer.

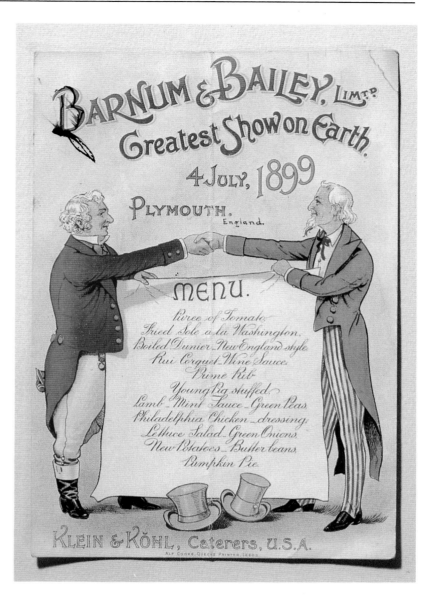

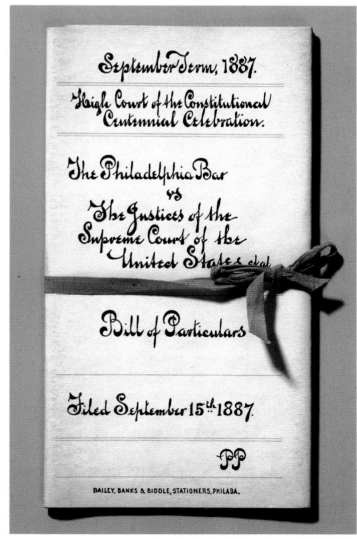

Occasion: High Court of the Constitutional Centennial Celebration

Sponsor: The Philadelphia Bar Association

Place: American Academy of Music, Philadelphia, PA

Date: September 15, 1887

This bound, three-page breakfast menu is tri-folded, punch-holed, and metal-ringed for stylistic imitation of a legal docket. Comprised of thick paper and utilizing two-color printing, this unusual menu also showcases stenciling, embossing, and a handsome engraving of John Marshall, the first Supreme Court Justice.

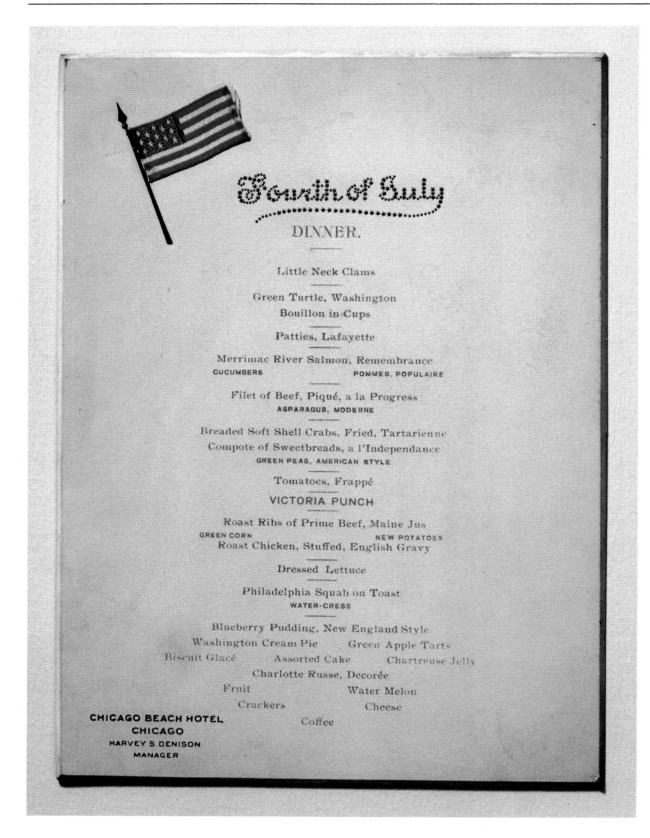

Fourth of July

DINNER.

Little Neck Clams

Green Turtle, Washington
Bouillon in Cups

Patties, Lafayette

Merrimac River Salmon, Remembrance
CUCUMBERS   POMMES, POPULAIRE

Filet of Beef, Piqué, a la Progress
ASPARAGUS, MODERNE

Breaded Soft Shell Crabs, Fried, Tartarienne
Compote of Sweetbreads, a l'Independance
GREEN PEAS, AMERICAN STYLE

Tomatoes, Frappé

VICTORIA PUNCH

Roast Ribs of Prime Beef, Maine Jus
GREEN CORN   NEW POTATOES
Roast Chicken, Stuffed, English Gravy

Dressed Lettuce

Philadelphia Squab on Toast
WATER-CRESS

Blueberry Pudding, New England Style
Washington Cream Pie   Green Apple Tarts
Biscuit Glacé   Assorted Cake   Chartreuse Jelly
Charlotte Russe, Decorée
Fruit   Water Melon
Crackers   Cheese
Coffee

CHICAGO BEACH HOTEL
CHICAGO
HARVEY S. DENISON
MANAGER

Occasion:	Fourth of July
Sponsor:	Chicago Beach Hotel
Place:	Chicago Beach Hotel, Chicago, IL
Date:	July 4, 1895.

The gold-embossed "Fourth of July" heading of this dinner menu is a script composed of stars in varying sizes. The silk flag paste-on decoration in the upper left corner adds texture as well as vibrant red, white, and blue color. Cardboard of 0.3-inch thickness was printed in a 2-color process of blue and red.

Occasion:	Dinner for the Boston City Government
Place:	Faneuil Hall, Boston, MA
Date:	July 4, 1862
Catered by:	J. B. Smith

Four runs of color through the press resulted in this dinner menu created for the Independence Day celebration of the Boston City Government. At least four sizes of typeface were handset in a process using blue, red, black and gold ink. Bordering the menu's front cover is an elaborate ribbon-and-lace design, with the engraved pattern of black printed first, followed by an overlay of gold. The thin, light stock used for this menu was centerfolded and printed on two sides. It is 5 1/4"x8".

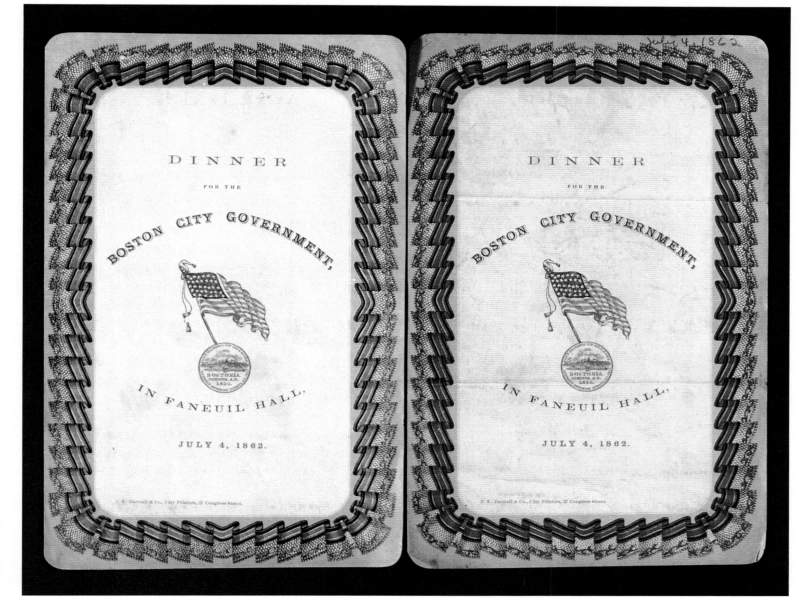

Occasion: 4th of July

Sponsor: The Bass Rock

Place: The Bass Rock, Gloucester, MA

Date: Thursday, August 30, 1888

Obviously intended as both menu and take-home memento, this 4th of July flag menu has surprisingly survived the past 100 years with hardly a hint of wear or age. This is especially incredible when one considers that it is made of crepe paper. When folded in three, the menu is 4 1/2"x6 1/2"; unfolded to its full-flag glory, the dimensions are 9"x13". One-side color printing in blue ink is used to describe the Anglo-American fare. Note the 42 stars of the flag, signifying only 42 states in the union during 1888.

Occasion: July 4th

Sponsor: Hotel Victory

Place: Hotel Victory, Bay Island, Ohio

Date: Tuesday, July 4th, 1899

Bright red and green firecrackers burn and explode on the cover of this 1899 menu. Embossed to raise the stick of each firecracker, as well as the lettering, this menu also features mezzotint shading. One-color printing is used inside to describe the menu's "heartland" cuisine of flavors and foodstuffs common to the midwest: boiled ham and cabbage, roast goose, string beans, corn on the cob, and tapioca pudding with apples and cream sauce.

Occasion: 4th of July

Sponsor: Mr. Rodman Wanamaker, president of the American Art Association of Paris

Place: New residence of the American Art Association of Paris

Date: July 4th, 1897

Instead of a torch, Lady Liberty raises a champagne glass on this center-folded menu's front cover. Created in a dark green, pen-and-ink design, both the Lady and the items listed on the menu emphasize the Franco-American flavor of the gathering. Inside is the program of toasts, addresses, and music, which is also printed in the deep green ink. A comparatively large menu, it is 8"x9 3/4" and uses heavy-stock brown kraft paper.

Occasion:	4th of July
Sponsor:	Hotel Roanoke
Place:	Hotel Roanoke, Roanoke, VA
Date:	July 4, 1895

This Independence Day menu features 4 1/2"x7" heavy stock paper of a light green color, printed one side only in one color—sienna. The embossed eagle-and-flag emblem at top-center carries the theme of this occasion in a vibrant red, white, blue and gold stencil. The total design effect of the color scheme is one of unusual harmony and elegance.

Menu.

CONSOMME CELESTINE
QUEEN OLIVES

GREEN TURTLE
CHOW CHOW

BOILED PENOBSCOT SALMON, JOINVILLE SAUCE
CAVIAR, ON TOAST   POTATOES PARISIENNE

BOILED SMITHFIELD HAM, SAUCE MADEIRA

PRIME RIBS OF PHILADELPHIA BEEF
LONG ISLAND DUCK, APPLE SAUCE
SADDLE OF LAMB, MINT SAUCE

STEWED TERRAPIN, MARYLAND STYLE
SWEETBREADS, PIQUE, CHAMPIGNONS
PEARS, A LA POMPADOUR

MASHED POTATOES   CAULIFLOWER, CREAM SAUCE
FRIED EGG PLANT   GREEN PEAS
NEW STRING BEANS

TOMATO MAYONNAISE   CHICKEN SALAD

CHAMPAGNE SORBET

BROILED SQUAB, WITH CRESSES

CHERRY PIE   LEMON MERINGUE
ITALIAN EGG KISSES   WHITE LADY CAKE
ASSORTED CAKES

CALIFORNIA PEACHES   GEORGIA WATERMELON   GOLDEN APRICOTS
HARLEQUIN ICE CREAM

EDAM AND PINEAPPLE CHEESE   NUTS AND RAISINS

CAFE NOIR

Hotel Roanoke,
Roanoke, Va.
S. R. Campbell, Manager.
Fourth of July,
1895.

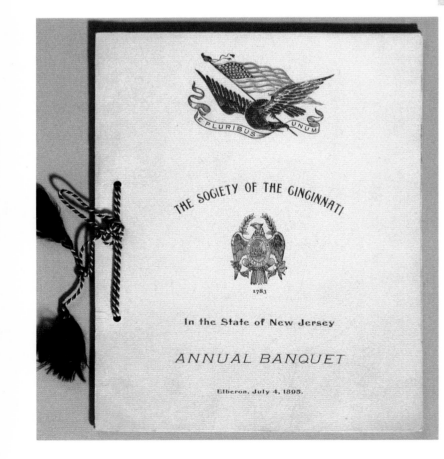

THE SOCIETY OF THE CINCINNATI

1783

In the State of New Jersey

ANNUAL BANQUET

Elberon, July 4, 1895.

Occasion:	Annual Banquet
Sponsor:	The Society of the Cincinnati in the State of New Jersey.
Place:	Elberon, NJ
Date:	July 4, 1895

A patriotic red, blue, gold and silver embossed emblem and the logo of the Society of the Cincinnati share the symbolic eagle on the cover of this 1895 banquet menu. Using a format of 5 1/4"x6 1/2" coated cardboard, this combination of souvenir and menu was printed in blue monochrome, center-folded, and bound with a tricolor cord of red, white and blue. It is printed on two sides, with an inside page designated for signatures.

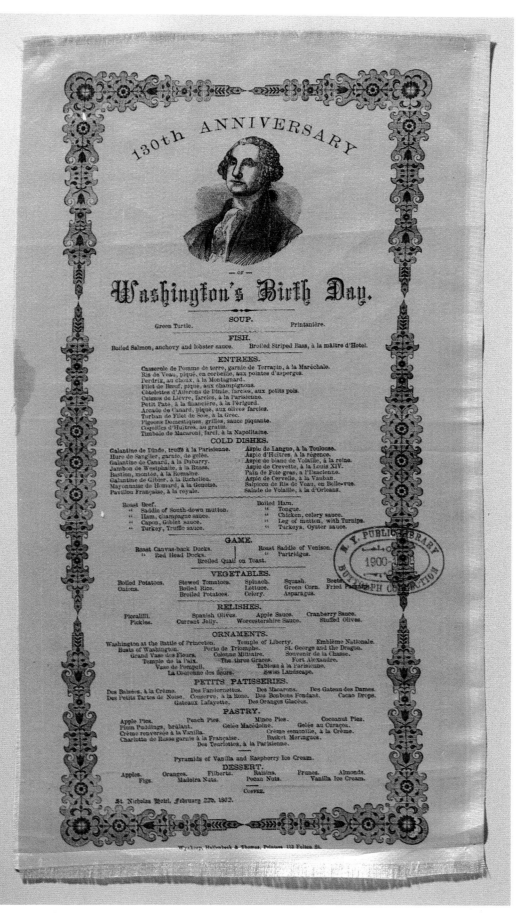

Occasion: 130th Anniversary of Washington's Birthday

Sponsor: St. Nicholas Hotel

Place: St. Nicholas Hotel, Brooklyn, NY

Date: February 22, 1862

One large (6 1/2″x12″) pink ribbon forms the print surface for this 1862 holiday menu celebrating the 130th anniversary of George Washington's birthday. A complex engraving in black ink adorns the menu surface. Victorian-style borders enclose a voluminous selection of foods, and a bust engraving of George Washington himself presides over the entries at top, center. The fabric edges at the top and bottom are thread-pulled to create a decorative fringe.

Occasion:	Washington's Birthday
Sponsor:	Sons of the American Revolution
Place:	Hotel Brunswick, New York City, NY
Date:	February 22, 1892

A number of printing methods were combined to achieve the spirited design and coloration of this menu's cover. While lines in black are the result of basic pen and ink, color and black-based areas of shading are achieved with a stipple process. These tiny dots are printed in layers of color wherein the primary shades mix to create greens, oranges and variations of the brown ink used in the lettering. Inside, a one-color printing in blue ink lists the menu items, and a black-ink border of austere design seems to foretell of the imminent, more modern style of the 20th century. The two, thick cardboard pages of this 5 1/2"x8" menu are joined with satin ribbons in New York state's colors: gold and blue.

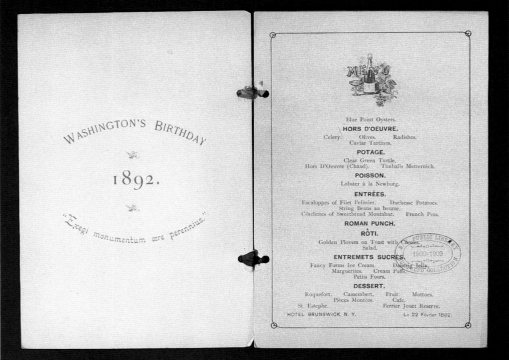

Occasion: Banquet in honor of President of the United States (Benjamin Harrison)

Sponsor: Delegates to International American Conference

Place: The Arlington, Washington, DC

Date: Wednesday, April 16, 1890

A design fit for the President of the United States (Benjamin Harrison) was required for this menu, and Tiffany & Co. rose to the occasion. The front cover is embossed with a gilt three-wreath emblem, and under the elegant script lettering is a fine engraving of banquet theme. The two-piece unit is of thick cardboard and is tied at the top with three satin ribbons in red, white, and blue. The actual menu, which is printed solely in blue ink on the back side of the second page, is uncomplicated in both design and, seemingly, in cuisine. However, while the salmon, spring lamb, cold asparagus in vinaigrette dressing, and tutti-frutti ice cream could be construed as "simple" fare, a handwritten account of the event was "one of the most elaborate (and) artistic dinners ever given...conspicuous by the number of distinguished people present."

CHAPTER 4  Organizations

pecialized groups or clubs play a major role in our lives. People with similar interests, job affiliations, ethnic backgrounds, religious beliefs, and political ties join together to form the Knights of Columbus, the Young Republicans, the Masons, the Daughters of the American Revolution, the Hibernian Society, the Philadelphia Dog Club, and the St. Louis-San Francisco Railroad Co. Employees Club, to name only a few.

These clubs usually have an annual dinner to highlight the accomplishments and events of the previous year. Many of the menus contain stylized versions of the various organizations' logos and emblems. Also, these menus served a dual purpose— at the dinner, they were used to list the varying events at the dinner, the music program, and the meal, and at the completion of the occasion they were kept as souvenirs.

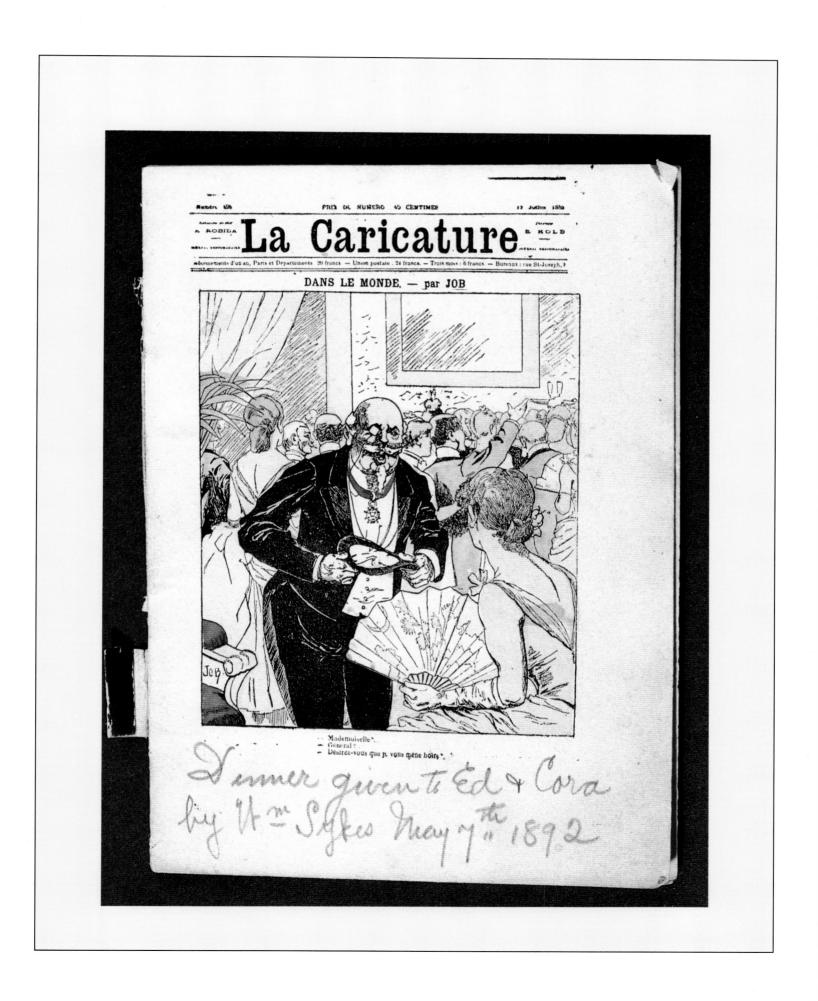

Occasion: Dinner

Sponsor: El-Kahir Temple, N.M.S.

Place: Kirkwood House, Des Moines, IA

Date: February 15, 1899

Everything from the red construction-paper "fez," to the gold-embossed logo, to the black-silk tassel of the binding on this menu cover is perfectly representative of the Shriners organization. Cut in "fez-shape" to match the covers are two inner centerfolded sheets of white paper printed in black on both sides.

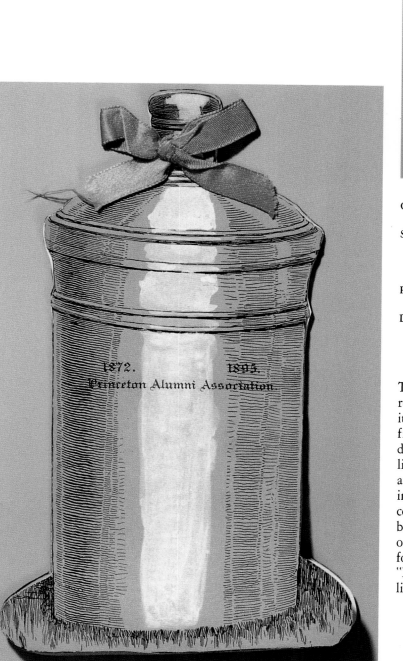

Occasion: 24th Annual Dinner

Sponsor: Princeton Alumni Association of Washington, DC

Place: Washington, DC

Date: 1895

The rather simplistic bell-like resemblance of this menu is due to its being entirely handmade; the front cover of grey coated stock decorated with a pen-and-ink lithograph and handpainted in white, and the back cover of the same stock in white, painted black on the back cover. The school's colors (gold and black) are used to print one side each of the four inside pages. Three of the four are embossed. Future President "Professor Woodrow Wilson" is listed as a guest of the occasion.

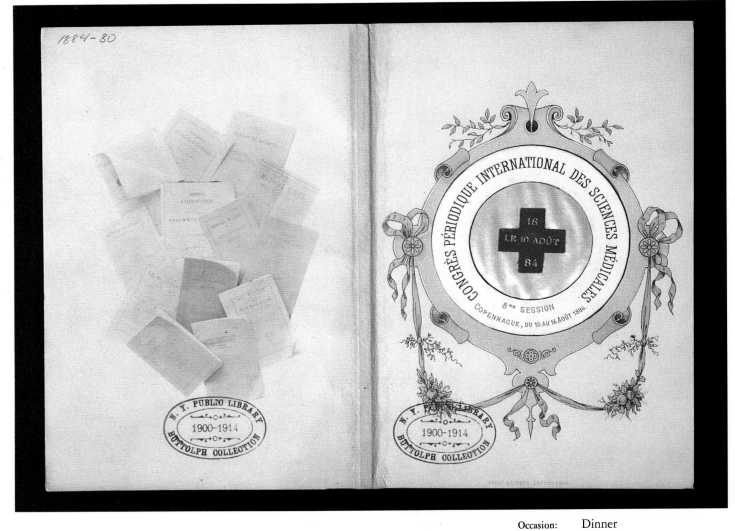

Occasion: Dinner

Sponsor: Dougres Periodique Internationale des Sciences Medicales

Place: Copenhagen, Denmark

Date: August 10 to 16, 1884

While the outside of this cardboard centerfold menu is respectful and elegant in its design presentation of the field of medicine, the "inside story" is a hilarious depiction of what is probably truer to actual daily events: in two-color (green and fleshtone) lithographic illustration, one finds a lighthearted menagerie of comical characters undergoing treatment. The front cover is an aquatint frame design surrounding a dye-cut ring printed in gold, which in turn windows a gold-printed, red-satin cross affixed to a white-satin mat. On the back cover is a photolithograph collage of medical journals.

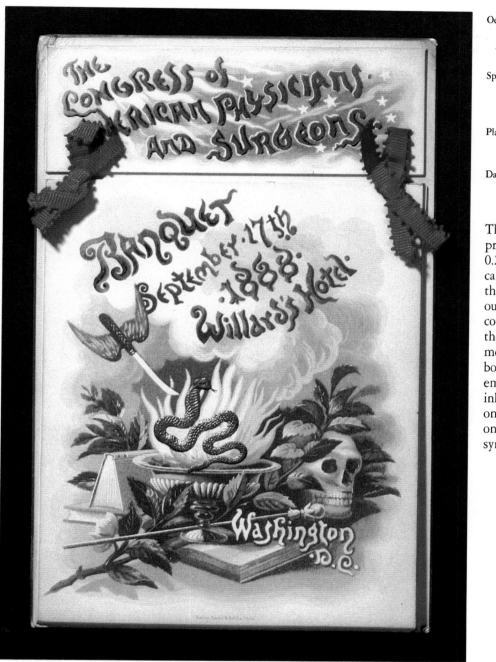

Occasion: The Congress of American Physicians and Surgeons Banquet

Sponsor: The American Physicians and Surgeons Association of Washington, DC

Place: Willard's Hotel, Washington, DC

Date: September 17, 1888

The mount foundation and the final printed page of this 1888 menu is a 0.2-inch thick piece of gilt-edged cardboard, printed in black. Two thinner pieces of cardboard, the outermost of which features the covering aquatint design, make up the smaller hinged pages of the menu. The inside page is printed on both sides; the menu side is gold-embossed and complemented in red ink. The "music" side is plain black on white. The gold-embossed snake on the cover is surrounded by other symbols of medicine and surgery.

Occasion: Dinner

Sponsor: Congres de l'Association des Chimistes de Sucrerie et de Distillerie de France & des Colonies

Place: Lille, France

Date: July 8, 9, 10, & 11, 1901

The two-color aquatint design of this 1901 Chemists Association menu seems to suggest that the profession at that time was more art than science. An elaborate feat in illustration, this 5 1/2"x9" menu is a reflection of the lasting effects of Victorian style.

Occasion: 15th Anniversary Dinner

Sponsor: Clover Club

Place: Hotel Bellevue,
Philadelphia, PA

Date: January 21, 1897

Each and every side of this dye-cut,
six-piece menu is printed. The outer
covers are both engraved designs:
the front is the green clover leaf of
the dye cutting (along with other
Clover Club emblems), the back is an
illustration of a vase and a quote of
the poet John Milton. Embossing is
included on the inside covers, and
the interior pages are printed in
blue, red, brown and sienna-colored
inks. White silk twine is looped
through the hole-punched "stalk" of
each clover leaf page and tied to bind
the entire unit.

Occasion: Banquet 100th Anniversary
                of the Husars Regiment

Place: Grand Hotel Hungaria,
                Budapest, Hungary

Date: June 8, 1898

One sheet of coated stock with rounded corners is folded into a two-flap enclosed format for this menu. The outside thus becomes a three-panel illustration in full-color lithography; inside, the lettering is in red and blue-green over a backdrop of military art lithography in blue-green and yellow. This menu was created and printed in Budapest for a military banquet held on June 8, 1898.

Occasion: 9th Annual Banquet

Sponsor: Ohio Society of New York

Place: Delmonico's, New York City, NY

Date: February 17, 1894

The Homer Lee Bank Note Company of New York was commissioned in the design of this 1894 menu, a fact that is apparent in the fine engraved lettering and art of the front cover. The embossed grape bunches used on the covers (front and back) and inner page is symbolic of the Bunch of Grapes Tavern, Boston, MA, where The Ohio Company was organized in 1786. Inks in green, black, brown, blue and gold are used, and the three pages are bow-bound with a ribbon of tan silk.

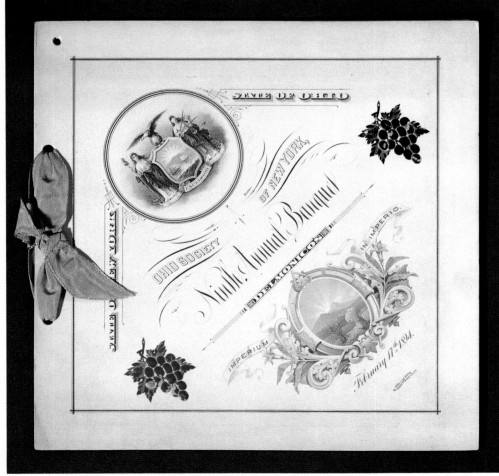

Occasion: The 12th Annual Banquet of the Young Republicans of Philadelphia

Sponsor: The Young Republicans of Philadelphia

Place: Horticultural Hall, Philadelphia, PA

Date: February 12, 1892

The cardboard covers of this menu are the primary design areas. The front is an aquatint bust of Abraham Lincoln with gold-embossed lettering below. The bow of a wide violet satin ribbon, which loops through the three inner sheets and connects these to the covers, serves as adornment at the front. Each of the inner pages are printed on one side in black and are gold embossed. The menu sheet also features red ink. The back cover is a gold-embossed emblem of the club, with a handpainted banner in rich violet.

Occasion: Dinner

Sponsor: The American Antiquarian Society

Place: Parker House, Boston, MA

Date: April 27, 1898

Two centerfolded sheets are used to form the cover and inner pages of this menu. The cover sheet is coated cardboard; the inner sheet is linen stock. Both are printed on one side only. The cover design is an embossed color lithograph of the American flag in red, blue and gold ink. In the blue area of the flag, the red and blue inks overlap to create purple creases. This enhances the windblown effect of the embossing. A red-white-blue striped cotton ribbon joins the cover to the inner sheet, which is printed in black-green.

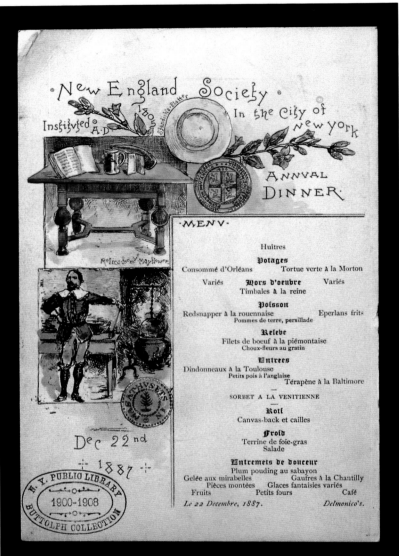

Occasion:	Annual Dinner
Sponsor:	New England Society in the City of New York
Place:	Delmonico's, New York City, NY
Date:	December 22, 1887

Pen-and-ink lithography enlivened with a variety of hues is the focal point of this menu. The menu items, printed in black, are separated from the decorative border section with a frame.

Occasion:	Banquet
Sponsor:	International League of Press Clubs
Place:	Palace Hotel, San Francisco, CA
Date:	January 18, 1892

Four 5″x9″ cards—one white, one lavender, one pale green, and one mint green—are tied top left, with a piece of hemp twine and sealed in red wax. The cover is an aquatint in green, with lettering in green-black and gold. The green-black ink is complemented with red ink headings on the inside sheets, each of which contains one-side text about the occasion and/or fare that epitomizes the rich wit and sarcasm of turn-of-the-century press editorials.

Occasion: Chicago Day Banquet

Sponsor: The Hamilton Club of Chicago, IL

Place: The Auditorium

Date: Monday, October 10, 1898

Mezzotint was used to create historic Chicago scenes on the interior of this menu's linen cardboard covering.

Thin silky stock was used for the six sheets inside, all printed one-side in black and attached with glue (at the last page) and with a tri-color silk ribbon through holes punched at the top. The first inner sheet is embossed with gold and a handpainted illustration of an eagle and flag appears at the top. "Menu" and "Toast" captions on the third and fourth pages are embossed in gold.

Occasion: 14th Annual Dinner

Sponsor: Gridiron Club

Place: Arlington Hotel,
              Washington, DC

Date: January 28, 1899

Many a famous name appears as in attendance on the inside of this Gridiron Club Annual Dinner menu: the President of the United States, William McKinley, Henry Cabot Lodge, and John Philip Sousa. The menu itself features the usual lithographic logo designs in pen-and-ink (monk with gridiron); a back cover design in brown and green isinglass; and 18 coated inner pages, printed and decoratively illustrated in black ink. The last page is also printed with two photographic honorary Gridiron Club medals. The menu pages are joined with three black and white silk ribbons tied at the top.

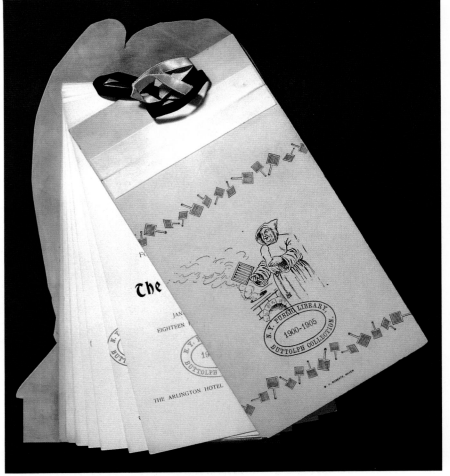

Occasion:	The Glee Dinner
Sponsor:	The Criterion, Piccadilly Circle West
Place:	London, England
Date:	Wednesday, June 22, 1887

Singing and dining were the combined activities of this 1887 affair. The menu, designed and printed in London, features blue-black ink on white cardboard for the front cover, full color on the back. The back cover, however, uses color only to frame the illustration at the center, which like the front and inside is printed in blue-black ink. Victorian borders and decorative lettering are evident.

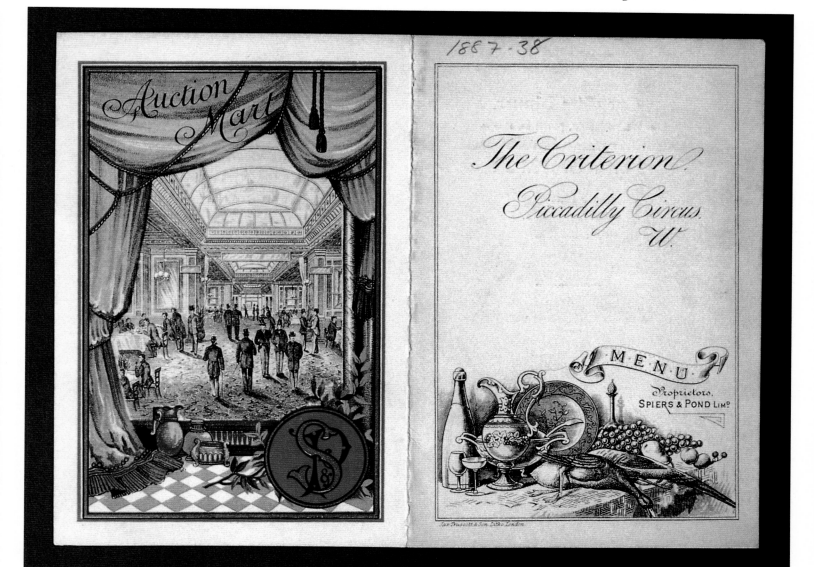

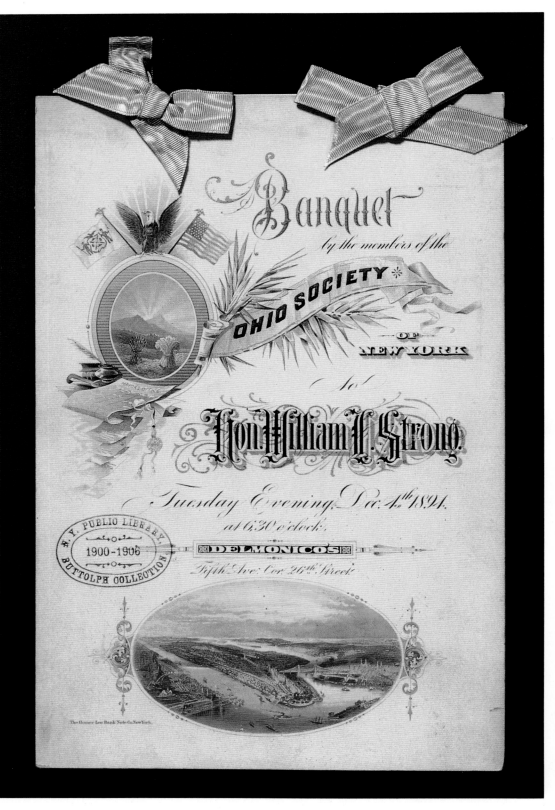

Occasion: Banquet for Hon. William J. Strong

Sponsor: Ohio Society of New York

Place: Delmonico's, Fifth Avenue, New York City, NY

Date: December 4, 1894

Perhaps the most obvious reason this menu resembles legal tender is that it was created and printed by the Homer Lee Bank Note Company of New York. A large surface, 6"x9", permits a variety of engraved design of this menu cover, printed in blue, black and sienna inks. The middle sheet of this three-page menu is textured silk stock printed in black. The third page, of the same stock as the first, is also printed only in black. Two wide, beige grosgrain ribbons tie the menu at the top.

Occasion: Dinner to Commemorate George Washington's Birthday

Sponsor: Daughters of the American Revolution

Place: Ebbitt House, Washington, DC

Date: February 22, 1894

Two woodcut cameos in burnished red ink are the centerpiece of this menu cover design. Although the occasion was George Washington's Birthday, Martha Washington is featured alongside her husband—a logical coexistence in the imagination of the Daughters of the American Revolution, who commissioned the menu. Inside, a gold-embossed hatchet tops the menu list, which is printed in black. The two 5 1/2″x7 1/4″ cardboard pages of this menu are joined with a blue grosgrain ribbon tied in a bow.

Occasion: Dinner

Sponsor: Union League Club

Place: Union League Club

Date: January 10, 1888

Gold embossing and a cameo-like crayon-and-watercolor illustration are the two major designs on this 1888 menu. Printed one-side-only in blue ink, the wines are divided from the food courses with a vertical ribbon-look rule at the right margin.

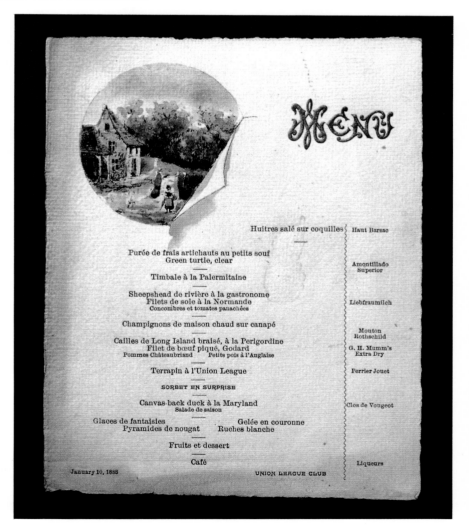

Occasion: Banquet

Sponsor: Board of Trade &
Transportation

Place: Hotel Brunswick, New York
City, NY

Date: February 20, 1886

Semicircular dyecut cardboard is
halved and bevel-edged in gold for
the inner print surface of this menu.
The two halves are both fringed in
silk, but only the front cover is
completely covered in the crimson
satin (which also serves as binding)
and printed in gold. A dry-embossed
clipper ship is the front cover's
centerpiece, but it must be said that
its glue-based mounting on the satin
as well as the gold ink were not
artistically successful. Neither the
glue nor the ink adhered properly.
The inside, however, is clean, classic
and interesting in its shape and
detail.

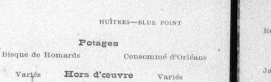

MENU

HUÎTRES—BLUE POINT

Potages

Bisque de Homards   Consommé d'Orléans

Variés   Hors d'œuvre   Variés
Timbales Morlôt

Relevés

Saumon à la Nantaise   Filet de Bœuf Balzac

Entrées

Chapon braisé à l'Ambassadrice

Côtelettes d'Agneau Castellane

Légumes

Pommes de Terre Duchesse
Flageolets maître d'hôtel
Petits Pois à la française

SORBET CONDORCET

Rôti
Red-head Duck   Bécassines sur canapé
Celery Mayonnaise

Pièces Froides
Jambon en Damier
Galantine Historiée
Langue de Bœuf Montpelier
Aspic de Filets de Sole

Entremets
Pouding Diplomate   Gelée Moscovite

GLACES FANTAISIES

Petits Fours   Gâteaux assortis

PIÈCES MONTÉES

Mottoes   Fruits & Dessert   Fromage
Café

20th February, 1886.

Occasion:	5th Annual Banquet Ale Brewer's Association
Sponsor:	Ale Brewer's Association of New York and New Jersey
Place:	Hotel Brunswick, Fifth Avenue, New York City, NY
Date:	Wednesday, February 8, 1888

The Hotel Brunswick, whose Victorian style initials appear on the last page of this menu, was the meeting place for this Association's 1888 annual banquet. New York City's Fifth Avenue was the fashionable address, and if the menu is any mirror to the event, it was grand indeed. A host of delicacies was served, each course was accompanied by fine wine, which are the only items printed in red ink while the rest of the printing is in black. The covering paper is one centerfolded piece of 12 1/2"x17" rag paper. The inner centerfold is of thin white kraft paper. Both pieces are torn at the edges for decorative purposes; the cover is handpainted in watercolors.

Occasion:	125th Annual Banquet Dinner of the Philadelphia Hibernian Society in Honor of St. Patrick's Day
Sponsor:	Hibernian Society of Philadelphia
Place:	Hotel Walton, Philadelphia, PA
Date:	Tuesday, March 17, 1896

A mezzotint harp of green is the cover theme for this St. Patrick's Day Banquet menu. Six sheets, each printed in green ink, are identically dye-cut and bound at the top and bottom with green and gold striped satin ribbons. The menu page is accented in red for tobacco and wines, the menu and toast captions gold-embossed. The interior of this menu also features engraved decorations of clover and the Hotel Walton where the banquet was held.

Occasion:	Banquet
Sponsor:	Board of Trade & Transportation
Place:	Hotel Brunswick, New York City, NY
Date:	February 22, 1884

A dyecut, embossed, full-color aquatint clipper ship is mounted upon a wreath of white silk fringe for this menu cover. The wreath is overlaid with a pink satin bow at bottom right, and the 4″x6 3/4″ cardboard cover is printed and bevel-edged in gold. The centerfold is printed inside with blue-green ink: on the left is the cuisine; on the right, the wines and tobacco.

Occasion:	Banquet to honor Alrik Hammar, Pharmacist of U.S.S. Olympia, Admiral Dewey's Flagship
Sponsor:	Pharmacists of New York and vicinity
Place:	Drug Trade Club, New York City, NY
Date:	Saturday Evening, September 30, 1899

Embossed acorn, oak, and laurel branches appear in green and gold along with embossed red, white, and blue flags and lithographic images of Admiral Dewey and his flagship, the U.S.S. Olympia, on this menu cover. The occasion, however, is not naval; it is a banquet in honor of Alrik Hammar, the ship pharmacist, whose own image is reproduced from a photograph on the first inner page. The centerfolded inner sheet of the menu is printed on both sides in black-green ink.

Occasion:	Dinner to Percy Sanderson, H.B.M.C.G.
Sponsor:	President of St. Georges Society
Place:	Delmonico's, New York City, NY
Date:	December 11, 1894

The highly decorative cover of this 1894 menu is ablaze with rich color, most of it handpainted with watercolors. The lettering in mauve and blue-grey is the result of silkscreening. The seal of the St. Georges Society is a perfect gold-embossed rendition of St. George upon his horse in the act of slaying the dragon. Two green grosgrain ribbons join the cover sheet to the menu sheet, which is printed in dark blue ink.

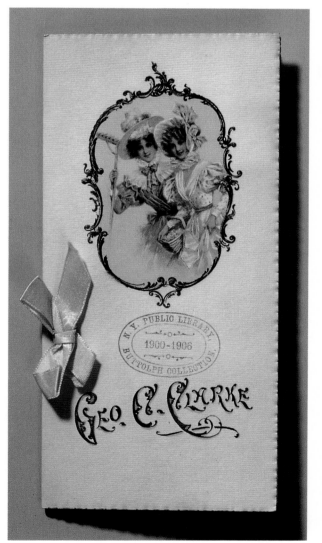

Occasion:	Dinner to Honor the President of the Colonial Club of New York—L. Lafler Kellogg named to the Board of Trustees
Sponsor:	The Colonial Club of New York
Place:	George C. Clarke, New York City, NY
Date:	Thursday, November 23, 1899

A sheet of cardboard centerfolded to 3"x7 1/2" houses an inner sheet of thick white paper, also centerfolded. The cover paper is decorated at the front with a lithotint cameo of two young women in hues of green, gold, grey, white and pink. This image is encircled by an embossed gold frame. The lettering below is also gold-embossed, but is lightly handpainted in pink as well. A pink satin bow connects the cover to the inner sheet, which is printed in blue ink.

Occasion: 25th Anniversary Dinner of
               the Bohemian Club

Sponsor: The Bohemian Club

Place: The Green Room, The
               Bohemian Club, San
               Francisco, CA

Date: April 17, 1897

One piece of 4″x5″ coated cardboard
is the "king" card of the Bohemian
Club's 25th anniversary menu. The
Club's owl logo is used both on the
front and back sides of the card; the
front is a blue-on-white mezzotint,
and the back is printed gold on
white.

Occasion: Induction of New Officers

Sponsor: The Gridiron Club

Place: The Arlington Hotel

Date: January 30, 1897

This menu's five-card design is based
on the ace, queen, king, jack and ten
cards in a playing deck. The first and
last cards (ace and ten) are printed
both sides, black on white. The three
inner face cards are tricolor designs
in red, gold and black, each
presenting a different part of the
menu. The white satin ribbon that
connects the five card "hand" is
printed with the club's gridiron logo.

Occasion:	Annual Dinner
Sponsor:	New England Society in the City of New York
Place:	Sherry's, New York City, NY
Date:	December 22, 1894

Two white grosgrain ribbons bind the three sheets of thick white cardboard which form this menu, designed by Tiffany & Co. On the front cover is a handpainted cherry blossom design. Underneath it is one-piece, ribbon-script lettering etched in brown ink and attached to the seal of the Society. The two inner pages are devoted to the menu and the toasts, respectively. Both are printed on one-side only in black ink.

Occasion:	Dinner to honor Brig. Gen. Edward F. Winslow
Sponsor:	Union League Club of the St. Louis San Francisco Railway Co.
Place:	Union League Club, New York City, NY
Date:	September 17, 1889

Three different paper stocks were used in this menu: the kraft front cover lies over two pieces of cardboard, the first of which is wrapped in a centerfolded sheet of thin, translucent stock. The thin sheet is used exclusively for protection of the fine combination stipple-and-line engraving of the event's honored guest. The menu contains many autographs of those in attendance, including Winslow. The front cover is a Victorian aquatinted etching in pink, yellow, grey, purple and green. Featured is the seal of the St. Louis San Francisco Railway Company in red wax.

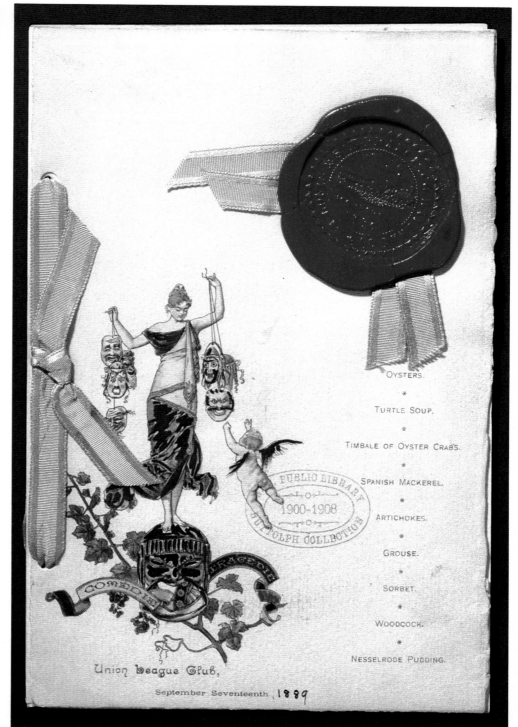

Occasion: Complimentary Dinner for
               Allan Forman

Sponsor: New York Press Club

Place: New York Press Club, New
               York City, NY

Date: October 13, 1894

This Victorian-flavor menu is printed on both sides of a centerfolded sheet of textured, coated stock and dye-cut at the edges. The inside is printed entirely in black ink while the front cover depicts a rural scene in stippled aquatint colors: burgundy, peach, gold, and light blue. The navy blue lettering refers humorously to the honored guest, Allan Forman, reading: "And he will talk, ye gods, how he will talk!"

Occasion: 27th Anniversary Banquet

Sponsor: Silk Association of America

Place: Delmonico's, New York
               City, NY

Date: Thursday, February 2, 1898

A band of 7"x8" white silk ribbon was the natural choice of medium for this anniversary banquet of the Silk Association of America. Printed entirely in purple ink, this menu presents the organization's lithograph logo at top, left; and entertains the guest with course-matched Shakespearean quotes such as "To give satiety a fresh appetite" alongside the sherbet. The closing quote smacks of lighthearted truth: "We can afford no more at such a price." The back of the ribbon is printed in navy blue and features the lyrics to *America* and *The Star Spangled Banner*.

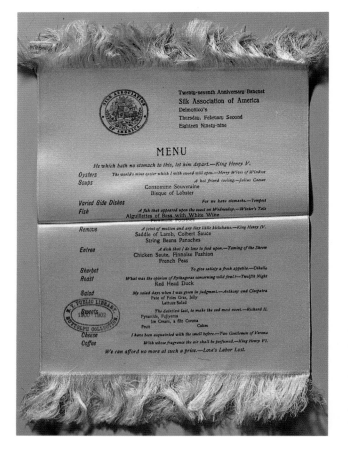

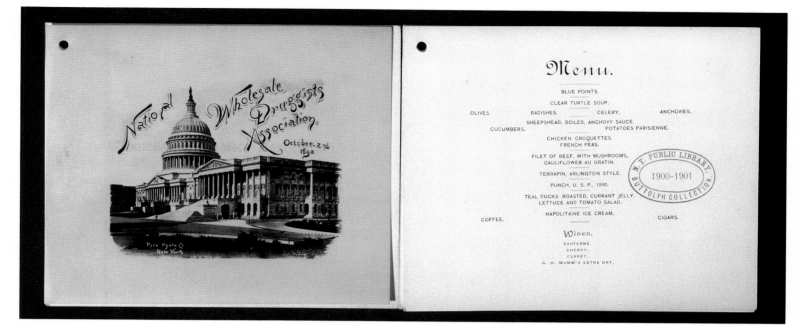

Occasion: National Druggist
            Wholesale Association
            Dinner

Sponsor: National Druggist
            Wholesale Association

Place: Arlington Hotel,
            Washington, DC

Date: October 2, 1890

The photo-engraved isinglass covers of this menu show the Capitol Buildings (House and Senate) on the front, and the Lincoln Memorial Monument on the back. The inner six cardboard sheets are printed on one side only, all in black ink. The menu card, however, is also printed in red to highlight the wines. These pieces were ring bound at the top left corner.

Occasion: Bunting Club Dinner

Sponsor: Bunting Club

Place: Clark's Tavern, Boston, MA

Date: January 28, 1892

Thick linen centerfolded paper and edged with a crimped cut is the basis of this 4 1/2"x7" menu. The cover's center is an embossed design of mated birds upon a branch in gold, with "menu" lettering embossed in a flower-entwined arrangement below, and Victorian detailed lettering in green-black ink above. The same ink is used to list the fare inside, which is simple and features only one course with wine.

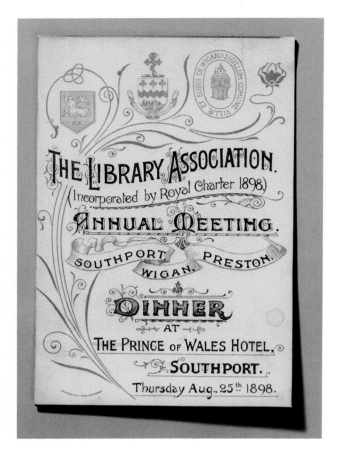

Occasion: Dinner—Annual Meeting

Sponsor: The Library Association

Place: The Prince of Wales Hotel,
Southport, England

Date: Thursday, August 25, 1898

Black and red lithography in Victorian embellishment is the design format for this 1898 menu cover. Printed in Southport, England, this menu is made of centerfolded cardboard, printed on two sides, and bevel-edged in gold. Inside, the red ink is of a more orange variety, and is used to highlight the menu courses and those honored with toasts.

Occasion: Banquet in honor of the
Tennessee Press Association

Sponsor: Citizens of Memphis

Place: Peabody Hotel, Memphis,
TN

Date: April 20, 1888

A "southern belle" of a menu, this 1888 design is composed of an outer cardboard centerfold and an inner letter-paper centerfold. The cover decoration consists of the light-blue dyecut cardboard fringed in matching blue silk fringe; a fancy silk cord with tassels ties the menu at the right. A gold-embossed caption card with gold-beveled edges is mounted on a decorative diagonal slant across the front. The interior centerfold is printed on both sides in deep blue ink, accented and lithographed in peach. A single handsewn thread forms the binding.

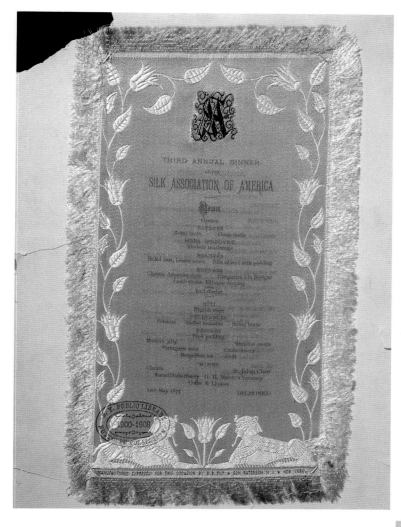

Occasion:	Third Annual Dinner
Sponsor:	Silk Association of America
Place:	Delmonico's, New York City, NY
Date:	May 12, 1875

Mounted on 8 1/2"x11 1/2" cardboard, this silk tapestry menu of 1875 was made especially for the occasion by B.B. Tilt & Son of Paterson, NJ and New York--a natural choice of media for the Silk Association of America. Along with white fringed edges, this menu also showcases the Association's monogram embroidered in blue and red. The light lavender fabric is printed with purple ink. Two white sphinxes at the bottom and flowered borders are unique additions.

Occasion:	167th Annual Banquet
Sponsor:	The Thirteen Club (the original 13 colonies)
Place:	Shore House, Bergen Point, NJ
Date:	August 13, 1898

One 2 1/4"x3 3/4" card is the smaller cover to the other two larger cards (3x5 1/2) of this 3-piece green paper menu. The 167th Annual Banquet of the Thirteen club of Northeastern New Jersey was the occasion of this summer event ("the thirteen" is believed to be in reference to the 13 original colonies of pre-revolutionary times). Printed in black ink, this menu also contains strange red-ink block prints of skeletal human figures.

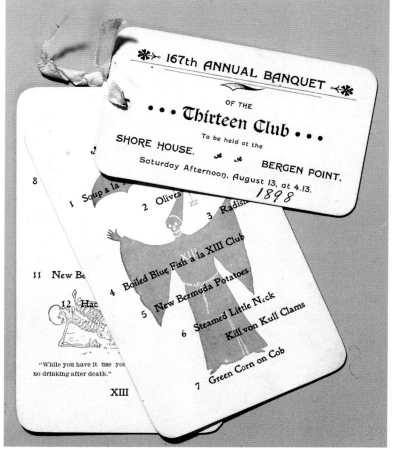

Occasion: Eleventh Annual Dinner

Sponsor: Officers' Union, Mercantile
Library Association

Place: Delmonico's, New York
City, NY

Date: November 9, 1876

Two young courtiers, a boy and girl,
appear on this menu's front cover in
full-color stipple aquatint. Like the
back cover, which is printed in blue,
the front cover design is framed with
two fine-line gold borders. This
framing is embellished to full
Victorian style on the centerfolded
menu inside, where the menu
heading and borders are ornately
rendered in pink and gold to
complement purple lettering.

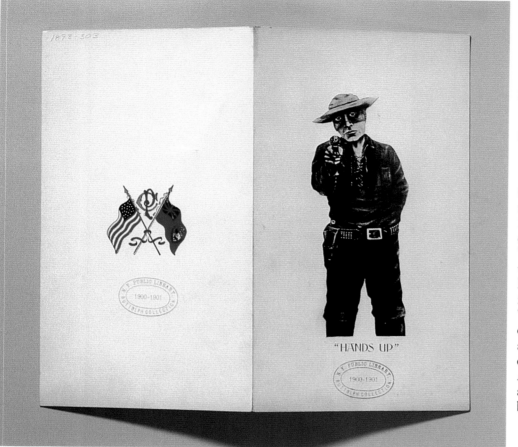

Occasion: 5th Annual Banquet

Sponsor: National Association of
             Chiefs of Police of United
             States and Canada

Place: Hotel Pfister, Milwaukee,
             WI

Date: May 12, 1898

Centerfolded thick white cardboard is the covering paper for this 5 1/4"x9 1/2" menu. The cover sports a comical halftone reproduction of a "Lone Ranger" type of character whose gun points out at the menu's holder. The caption, like most of the menu, is printed in black and reads: "Hands Up." On the menu portion of the inner pages, wines and cigars are contrasted in red ink. The back cover is ornamented with the Association's emblem—an American and Canadian flag—in stenciled red, blue and gold.

Occasion: Induction Dinner,
             Dartmouth Dragon Club '99

Sponsor: Dragon '99

Place: Philadelphia, PA

Date: June 8, 1898

Engraved multi-tint lithography, pen-and-ink, and embossing are all used on this Dartmouth Club menu cover whereon a "party girl" pops from an uncorked bottle of Mumm champagne. The bottle, Dartmouth scholars, and girl are all created with painstaking detail. All three of the centerfolded sheets used for this menu are gold-embossed, the inner pages printed in black. Two satin ribbons, one white and one green (the school colors of Dartmouth College), bind the menu pages.

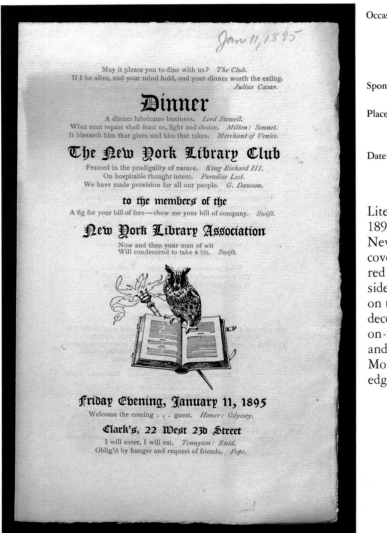

Occasion: The New York Library Club
              Dinner for Members of the
              New York Library
              Association

Sponsor: New York Library Club

Place: Clark's, 22 West 23 Street,
              New York City, NY

Date: January 11, 1895

Literary quotations abound on this 1895 menu used for the dinner of the New York Library Club. The front cover highlights these quotations in red ink, while the rest of this two-sided menu is printed in black. Also on the front is the menu's only decorative piece—a symbolic black-on-white lithograph of an owl, book, and torch. The stock is white Moroccan paper with unfinished edges.

Occasion: Dinner—59th Anniversary

Sponsor: National Lancers

Place: Faneuil Hall, Boston, MA

Date: Monday Evening, June 15,
              1896

Measuring 5 1/2"x5 1/2", this octagonal menu is both beautiful and simple in its design format. The front cover hosts an engraved bald eagle illustration, which is affixed to a base mat of the same thick cardboard. The back cover contains the National Lancer's logo engraved with the same careful attention to detail. The two thick covers are joined to the two thin paper sheets of the menu interior with a red silk bow.

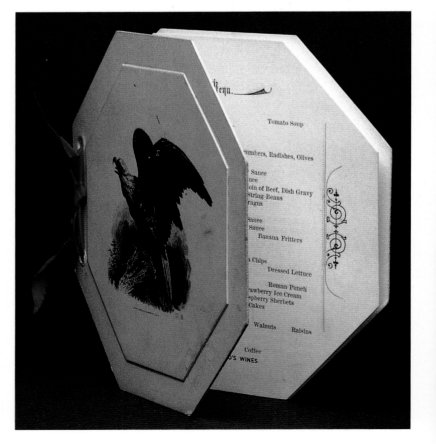

Menu (left, black and white):

Ode to the suckling Pig.
—by R. B. Esq.

"Of all the delicacies in the whole mundus edibles, I will maintain it to be the most delicate princeps obsonium."

"I speak not of your grown porkers—things between pig & pork, those hobbidehoys—under a moon old, guiltless as yet of the sty—with no original speck of the amor immunditiæ, the hereditary falling of the first parent, yet manifest—his voice as yet not broken, but something between a childish treble & a grumble, the mild forerunner or præludium of a grunt."

"He must be roasted or baked—I am ignorant that our ancestors ate them seethed or boiled, but what a sacrifice of the exterior tegument. There is no flavor comparable I will contend, to that of the crispy, tawny, well watched, not over roasted, crackling, as it is well called—the very teeth are invited to their share of the pleasure at this banquet in over coming the coy brittle resistance, with the adhesive oleaginous—O call it not fat! but an indefinable sweetness growing up to it—the tender blossoming of fat—fat cropped in the bud, taken in the shoot in the first innocence—the cream & quintessence of the child's pig's yet pure food: the lean no lean, but a kind of animal mana, or rather fat & lean (if it must be so) so blended & running into each other that both together make but one ambrosian result or common substance."

"Wilt please you taste of what is here?"

ye Bylle of Fare.
GRACE BEFORE MEAT.

ye Goodlie Companye assembled on ys occasyon wille haven setten before them for ys delectacyoun and comfort inne due & proper order, ye necessary's as next folweth, yt is to sai:

ye Fyrste Course
ye delicate Cape Cod Oysters from ye brynie deepe

ye Seconde Course
ye toothsome Anchovie toast, Olives & Celery offe Kalamazoo

ye Thyrde Course
ye Soupp, made from ye timid Texan Steer, clere, with the fruyt of the fyry hen

ye Fourth Course
ye ryhte royalle, succulent, rostyed sucklin Pig, servyd wythe ye sauce offe Apple. ye addyc-tion offe Potatoes called in ye foreyn tounge Chateau, together wythe ye tastie offe Cauliflower, mayde fitte for ye sustenance offe "Wise Men" beye baking a la Polonaise

ye Desserte........
Dyvers Cheese offe Gallic to-gether with ye Salad offe Season as maye bee found obtaynable Coffy from ye Island offe Java—who willt be dark as night, hot as hades, and sweet as love

ye Wynes........
offe Spain and France, also rare Rhyne and Moselle from Germania

ye Servyce of ye Dynere wille be after ye manere of ye pearsons offe dystynction inne Russia.
ye Guestys are bydden to eate after ye American man-nere.
"A dinner lubricates business."—L.A.F.

Saturday
Round Table Luncheon,
Century Club,
November 13, Anno Domini, 1897.
Cleveland Ohio.

Occasion: Round Table Club Luncheon

Sponsor: Round Table Club

Place: Century Club, Cleveland, OH

Date: November 13, 1897

The main (fourth) course on this 1897 menu is also the most important, as is pointed out in "Ode to the Suckling Pig," a comedic verse in honor of this "kind of animal mana" at the right margin. The actual menu is printed in the prose and font style of Middle English—much as one would find in the original works of Chaucer—to carry the Club's theme of "olde England." The blue and green inks are used in a woodcut design.

Occasion: Dinner

Sponsor: Le Bureau de la Direction de la Banque Hocheaga

Place: Montreal, Canada

Date: November 24, 1898

A brilliant red silk ribbon is the binding and beautifying final touch to this Canadian menu of 1898. The front page is a blue-and-brown ink combination of engraved design. The top half, in blue ink, contains an extremely fine engraving of the Canadian seal in microscopic detail. The bottom half, in brown ink, is a reproduced image of Montreal in 1770. The second sheet of this menu is printed one side only in red and brown.

Occasion: Dinner

Sponsor: Free Trade League

Place: U.S. Hotel, Boston, MA

Date: Monday, January 24, 1898

This menu is one sheet of dye-cut, centerfolded coated paper, printed on both sides in black ink. The front cover hosts a mezzotint design of a bow-tied green ribbon interlaced with realistically fresh-looking lily-of-the-valley. Subtle use of grey, blue and yellow in the mezzotint process is the reason for such a vivid representation.

Occasion: The Fourth Annual Dinner

Sponsor: Brotherhood of Commercial Travelers

Place: Metropolitan Hotel, New York City, NY

Date: Thursday, December 27, 1888

Textured kraft paper is centerfolded and bound to an inner centerfold of linen cardboard for this menu. The two sheets, both of which are handtorn at the edges, are joined by a cheerful plaid taffeta ribbon tied in a flat bow inside. The outer cover is a montage mezzotint in brown, showing the lifestyle of the commercial traveler, as well as the food, drink and social aspects of the annual dinner.

Occasion: Russian Buffet for the Committee from the Colonial Club

Sponsor: Democratic Club

Place: Democratic Club, New York City, NY

Date: February 19, 1892

Movable pieces are the design attraction of this menu and its accompanying placecard. On the placecard, three dyecut aquatint dog heads bob from insertion holes in the aquatint card, where their napkin-bibbed bodies await dinner at a table. On the menu card are three monkeys of the same design and construction and in the same type of table scene. Both are printed in black ink on coated stock.

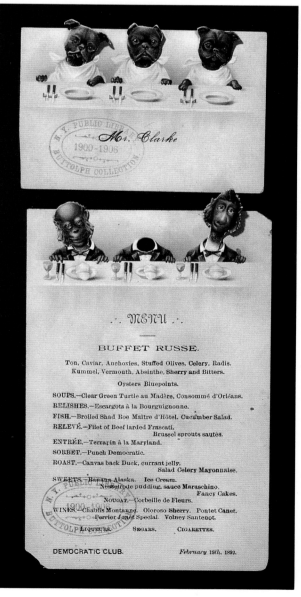

Occasion: Grand Banquet for the New Orleans Base Ball Club

Sponsor: The Rooter's Club

Place: Le Court's Hotel, West End, New Orleans, LA

Date: Thursday, June 11, 1896

The epitome of Victorian design influence, this 1896 menu of New Orleans is a spectacular layering of texture and color. On the front cover, the heavy ornate lettering of the silver-embossed "souvenir" is set above an embossed mezzotint floral arrangement in pinks, blues, greens and yellows. This dye-cut, centerfolded sheet opens with the pull of the red silk tassel (bottom, right) to reveal a thin, centerfolded sheet within, printed and decorated on both side in blue ink. The back side of the covering cardboard is mounted upon a rectangular frame of green silk cord, which is mounted upon a rectangular sheet of dye-cut cardboard, which is mounted upon a frame of blue "fleeced" ribbon, which is finally mounted on a piece of blue cardboard. This is truly Victoriana at its finest!

Occasion: Second Annual Dinner

Sponsor: Happy Jack Club

Place: Lane's Cottage, Long Beach, NJ

Date: September 9, 1890

Metallic gold, silver, copper, and pewter are textured into the vertical lines of this centerfolded cardboard menu. The lithographic orange branch, which curiously bears both blossoms and fruit, is the cover design. The inside is printed red on white.

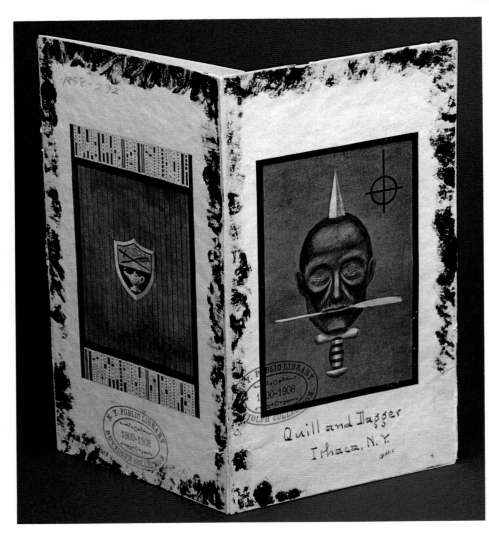

Occasion: Dinner

Sponsor: Quill & Dagger

Place: Ithaca House, Ithaca, NY

Date: May, 1898

This mystery writer's club menu uses rough artistry to create a simple, somewhat eerie cover. Photographic reproductions are used, as well as a hand-smudged border in gold dust. One sheet of thick book paper is folded into three overlapping sections. The menu is printed entirely in black.

Occasion:	Supper
Sponsor:	The Gridiron Club
Place:	The Arlington, Arlington, VA
Date:	April 8, 1899

Dye-cut thick cardboard in the shape and image of a gridiron is the design basis of this club menu. The pen-and-ink lithograph is signed by artist J. H. Cunningham and includes funny stick-figure oysters and turn-of-the-century maidens in swimwear at the beach. Black and white streamer ribbons are tied at the handle end of this one-sided menu.

Occasion:	The Triennial Meeting of The General Society of the Sons of the Revolution
Sponsor:	The Colorado Society
Place:	Palace Hotel, Denver, CO
Date:	April 19, 1899

Four differently designed "windows" surround the blue and green engraved outer surface of this 1899 menu. At the top and bottom are lithographic commemoratives of soldiers and battle of the Revolution. To the left and right are the bright, colorful emblems of the United States and Sons of the Revolution, respectively.

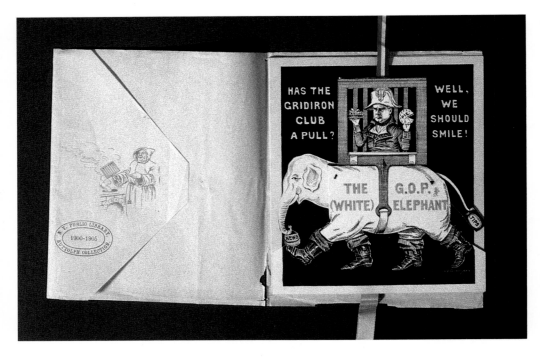

Occasion:	Club Dinner
Sponsor:	The Gridiron Club
Place:	The Arlington Hotel, Washington, DC
Date:	March 27, 1897

A parchment paper envelope with a pen-and-ink drawing of a monk and gridiron on the flap houses the thick cardboard menu of the 1897 Gridiron Club. The menu's frontside is a dye-cut design of Napoleon in a cage upon the G.O.P. elephant; when pulled, the red-white-and-blue striped ribbon atop and yellow satin ribbon below make the elephant's head and tail and Napoleon all move up or down. The entire menu is printed black on white.

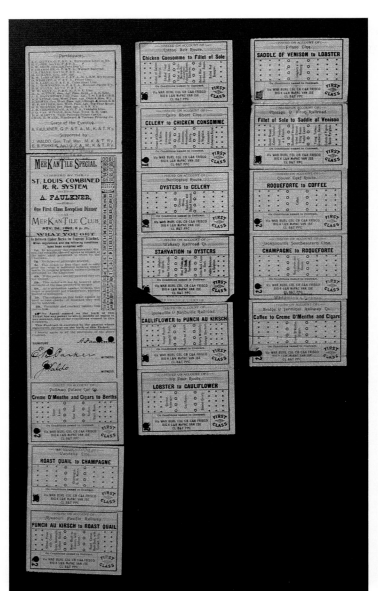

Occasion:	First Class Reception Dinner to A. Faulkner
Sponsor:	St. Louis Combined RR System
Place:	Merkantile Club, St. Louis, MO
Date:	November 3, 1892 6 P.M.

This strip of "tickets" was presented to the attendees of the dinner reception given in honor of A. Faulkner by the Merkantile Club. The courses of the dinner are represented on the individual tickets of the strip, which is printed both sides: black ink on yellow (front)/ orange (back) coated paper. The individual courses of the ticket strip are marked by perforated tear points.

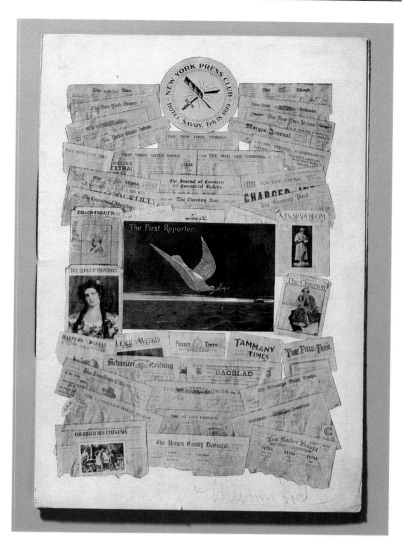

Occasion:	Annual Dinner
Sponsor:	New York Press Club
Place:	Hotel Savoy, New York City, NY
Date:	Saturday Evening 7:00 P.M., February 18, 1899

Publishing titles found in the New York metropolitan area in 1899 are the subject of this menu's cover, in an intaglio collage. Inside are 2 centerfolded sheets of matching light-green moroccan paper, both printed on 2 sides in black ink. One large handsewn stitch is used to bind the menu with a piece of thin, red silk twine. This menu was printed by The Press Club itself, located at 218 William Street, New York City.

Occasion:	8th Anniversary Dinner
Sponsor:	Clover Club
Place:	Bellevue Hotel, Philadelphia, PA
Date:	January 16, 1890

This weighty 9 3/4" diameter menu is 21 pieces long, each card (excepting the last) printed one-side only. The cover is an entirely gold-embossed medallion design, with a ram amidst clover and border lettering. The inside pages are pen and ink designs of little variance. All are printed in green with red-accented headings (for courses, greetings, etc.) and bordered with pen-and-ink clover clusters, excepting the first page and back cover. Each contains a pen-and-ink lithograph; the first page in green ink, the back cover in gold. One large blue satin bow ties the cards of the menu together.

Occasion: Dinner

Sponsor: New York Board of Trade &
               Transportation

Place: Hotel Brunswick, New York
               City, NY

Date: February 21, 1887

This menu is heavy, mainly for the reason of its multilayered kind of silver glitter. The seal of the Board of Trade and Transportation is printed in black upon the central, blue-satin surface, which is bordered with matching blue-silk cord and mounted upon a dye-cut card spangled with the glitter. Another chiseled-looking dyecut card is the menu's foundation, which is centerfolded and bound at the fold with a strip of blue satin ribbon. Inside is blue-ink printing and heavy gold embossing of the menu title. The back cover features the lithographic monogram of the Hotel Brunswick, which seems to have been the meeting place of choice for the Board.

Occasion: Dinner

Sponsor: The Camera Club of New
              York

Place: The Arena, New York City,
              NY

Date: December 4, 1897

The 10″x12″ mat of this menu, which is surface-colored in charcoal grey, overpowers its three paste-on elements: two 3″x4 1/2″ pieces of cardboard (the actual menu) printed in black; a round piece of green construction paper printed with the seal of the Camera Club in black ink; and the tiny 1 1/4″x3 1/4″ hand-signed photograph of a horserace at top, center. Each menu item is described in entertaining photographic terms; e.g., "Oysters on the half plate," "Cheese, overexposed," and "Bordeaux Intensifier,—H2O...Dilute to suit."

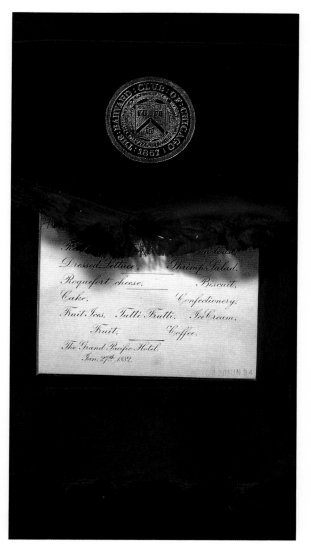

Occasion: Dinner

Sponsor: The Harvard Club of
              Chicago

Place: The Grand Pacific Hotel,
              Chicago, IL

Date: January 27, 1882

The gold-embossed emblem of the Harvard Club of Chicago shines brightly upon the deep Harvard-red satin of this menu. The five-inch wide ribbon wraps a single sheet of rectangular cardboard, bevel-edged in gold leaf. The black lettering of the menu is simply and elegantly composed in a flowing script font.

Occasion: Dinner for the New York Delegation to the Hotel Men's Mutual Benefit Association (Cleveland to New York and New York to Cleveland)

Place: Wagner Palace Car Company (dining car service) via New York Central Railway System

Date: May 10, 1891 (New York to Cleveland), May 14, 1891 (Cleveland to New York)

These two menus represent a two-way journey: New York to Cleveland on May 10, 1891 and Cleveland to New York on May 14, 1891. Both menus use 5 1/2"x6 3/4" coated paper decorated in full aquatint color. The first features a male courtier, and the second, a female courtier; excepting the last two courses, the meals were completely different. The lettering on these menus was printed on one side only in brown and mauve inks.

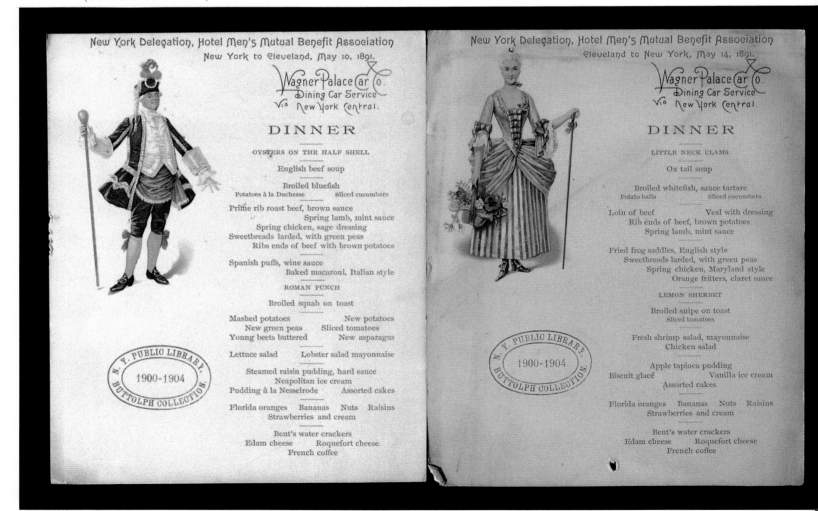

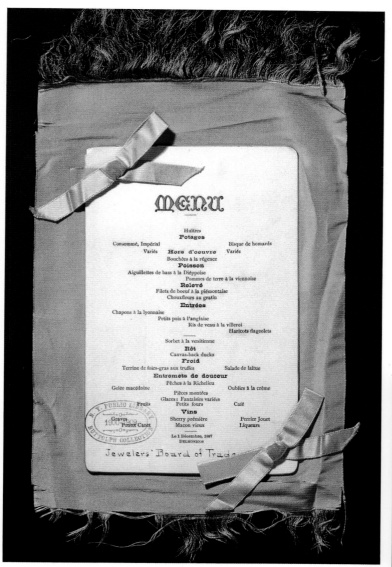

Occasion: Dinner

Sponsor: Jewelers' Board of Trade

Place: Delmonico's, New York City, NY

Date: December 1, 1887

A thick piece of white cardboard with rounded corners and edging in beveled gold is printed in black and mounted upon a 6 1/2″x9 1/2″ pink silk ribbon. The mounting itself consists only of two smaller pink satin ribbons, tied through holes in the card and bowed at opposite corners.

Occasion: 16th Annual Banquet of Merchants & Manufacturers Association of Baltimore City, MD

Sponsor: Merchants & Manufacturers Association of Maryland

Place: Hotel Rennert, Baltimore, MD

Date: Wednesday, December 30, 1896

Two strung pheasant are the hunt's reward pictured in oil colors on the front and back covers of this 1896 menu. The covers and three inner sheets are all dyecut in the pheasant design shape and are tied together at the metal-ringed pheasant eye with a silk cord of black and orange. The inner pages are printed in black; the wines accented in red.

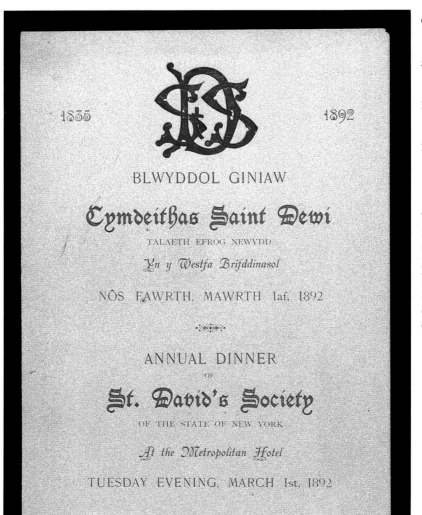

Occasion:	Annual Dinner of St. David's Society
Sponsor:	St. David's Society of the State of New York
Place:	Metropolitan Hotel, New York City, NY
Date:	Tuesday Evening, March 1, 1892

The light green coated stock of this menu is printed on both sides. Most appear to be in an ancient form of English, perhaps Gaelic. Front and back are printed in green ink; the front is also decorated with the Society insignia in a red embossed design at the top.

Occasion:	Dinner
Place:	Bergen, Norway
Date:	April 9, 1892

Featured herein is one of the smallest menus (2 3/4"x4 1/4"). This Norwegian menu of 1892 utilizes a single centerfolded sheet of coated paper. On the outer side is a silkscreen design of Egyptian art in full color with a metallic gold background. Inside is a simple menu listing in black ink.

Occasion:	Annual Dinner
Sponsor:	New England Society in the City of New York
Place:	Delmonico's, New York City, NY
Date:	December 22 or 23, 1889 (both dates appear on the menu)

This one-page 1889 menu is a lovely pen-and-brown ink collection of images relating to the New England Society and its Mayflower foundation. Shades of red, blue, brown, yellow and green are used in the final hand watercoloring. The menu itself is printed in black. Noteworthy is the incongruity of the dates used in the lithographic portion of the menu versus the printed menu portion: the former gives a "December 22nd" date, while the latter reads "Le 23 Decembre."

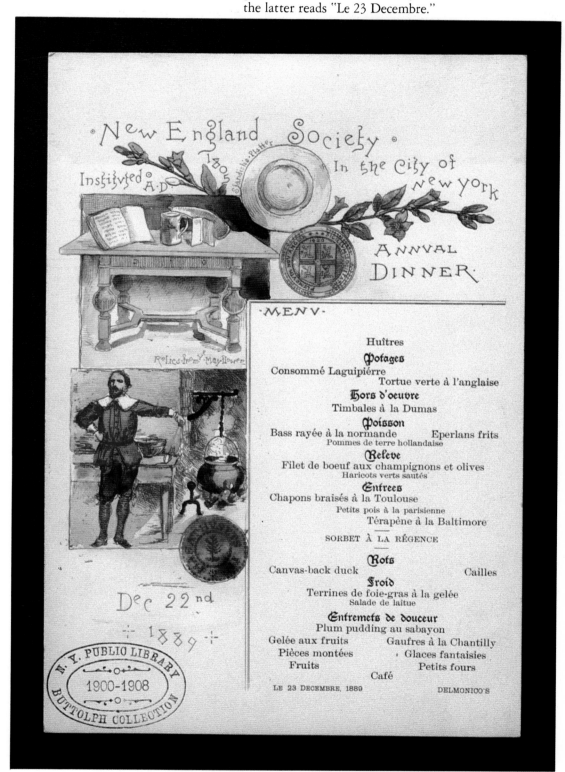

uring the 1800s, royalty was still predominant in most of Europe. Italy, Russia, Prussia, Spain, England, Holland and most of the other European countries were still ruled by monarchs.

This section of our book contains menus from various official state dinners, affairs, concerts, and coronations. King Umberto of Italy, Queen Wilhelmina of the Netherlands, Queen Victoria of England, Czar Nicholas of Russia, and Kaiser Wilhelm of Prussia have menus represented here.

VIPs AND VIP OCCASIONS

Elegant dinner parties, extravagant banquets, and huge luncheons were all showcases to honor special people. Public officials, philanthropists, military leaders, and socialites all have representations in this section.

Each menu printed for VIPs at these affairs usually contained a number of toasts to honor the person, as well as lists of accomplishments. These finely printed menus also served as keepsakes once the affair ended.

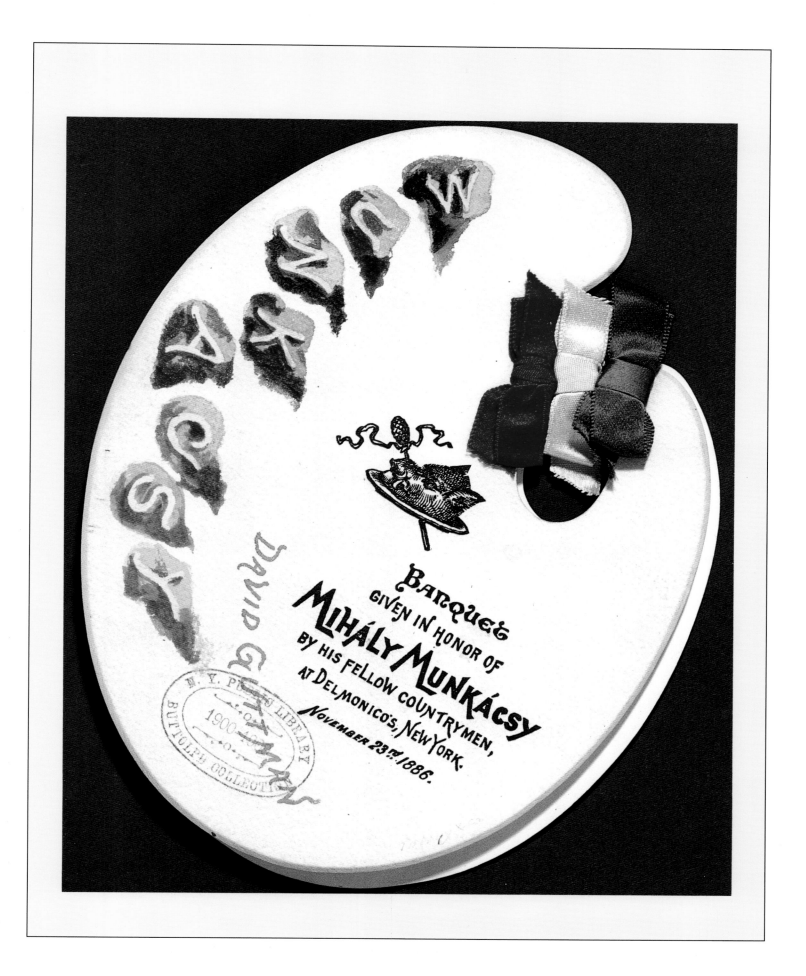

Banquet
GIVEN IN HONOR OF
MIHÁLY MUNKÁCSY
BY HIS FELLOW COUNTRYMEN,
AT DELMONICO'S, NEW YORK.
NOVEMBER 23RD 1886.

DAVID GUTMANS

Occasion: Breakfast for Admiral Dewey.

Sponsor: City of New York

Place: The Claremont Hotel, New York City, NY

Date: September 30, 1899

This breakfast menu honors Admiral Dewey. It is made up of a centerfolded piece of cardboard used for the covers, with a centerfolded piece of parchment used for the four interior pages. The cover contains a lithograph of a female representation of New York City toasting a portrait of Admiral Dewey. The entire menu is bound by a tri-colored red, white and blue ribbon. The first page contains the semaphore code for "suspend operations for breakfast"; the back cover contains a stunning gold embossing of the great seal of the City of New York.

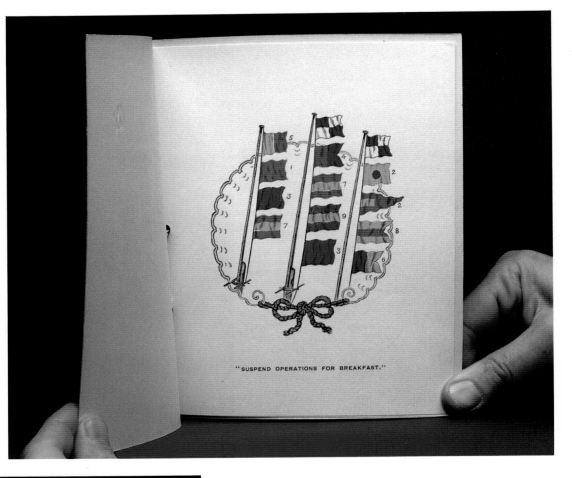

Occasion: Breakfast in Honor of Admiral Dewey

Sponsor: City of New York

Place: Hotel Claremont New York City, NY

Date: September 30, 1899

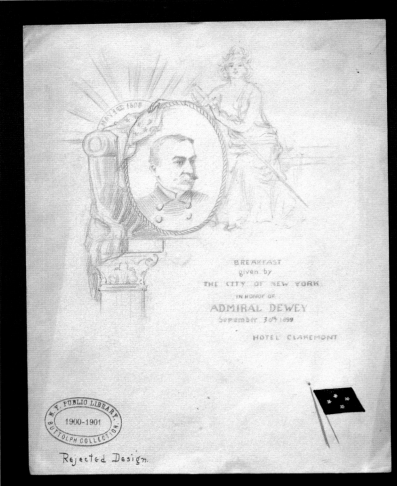

These preliminary composite sketches were rejected for the cover design for the breakfast banquet menu given by the City of New York for Admiral Dewey. The reasons why they were rejected are lost forever.

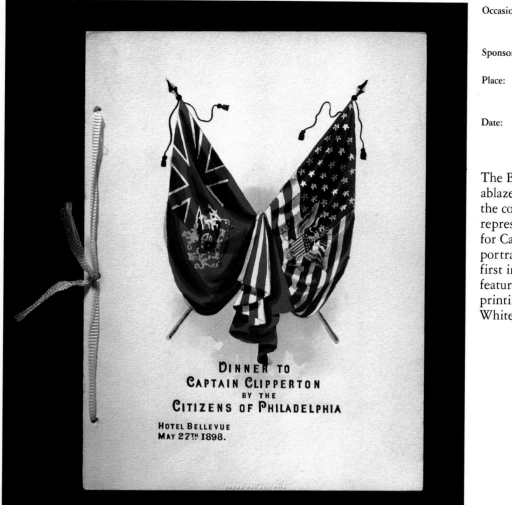

Occasion: Dinner for Captain
Clipperton

Sponsor: Citizens of Philadelphia

Place: Hotel Bellevue,
Philadelphia, PA

Date: May 27, 1898

The British and American flags are ablaze with rich silkscreened color on the cover of this 1898 menu representing a Philadelphia dinner for Captain Clipperton. Clipperton's portrait lithograph appears on the first inside page. This menu also features gold-embossed headings and printing in black with red accents. White silk ribbon serves as binding.

Occasion: Banquet Wedding

Place: Hoffman House

Date: October 12, 1887

4 1/2"x6" thick piece of cardboard is covered in white satin and trimmed with white silk cord for this wedding menu of 1887. The front side is an elegant display of the couple's initials, the date, and the place, all in silver. The menu list is printed on the other side in grey-blue.

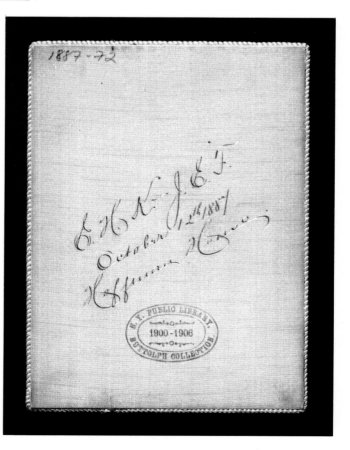

Occasion: Banquet at Guildhall

Sponsor: Hon. Alfred J. Newton,
                 Mayor

Place: London, England

Date: November 19, 1899

The front cover of this centerfolded
menu is a fine blend of aquatint color
in which cherubic babes "deck the
Guildhall." The interior pages host
intricate borders of gold surrounding
the menu and musical program, both
printed in red. An insert of blue-on-
white print contains an additional
musical program for the occasion:
Lord Mayor's Day in London,
England.

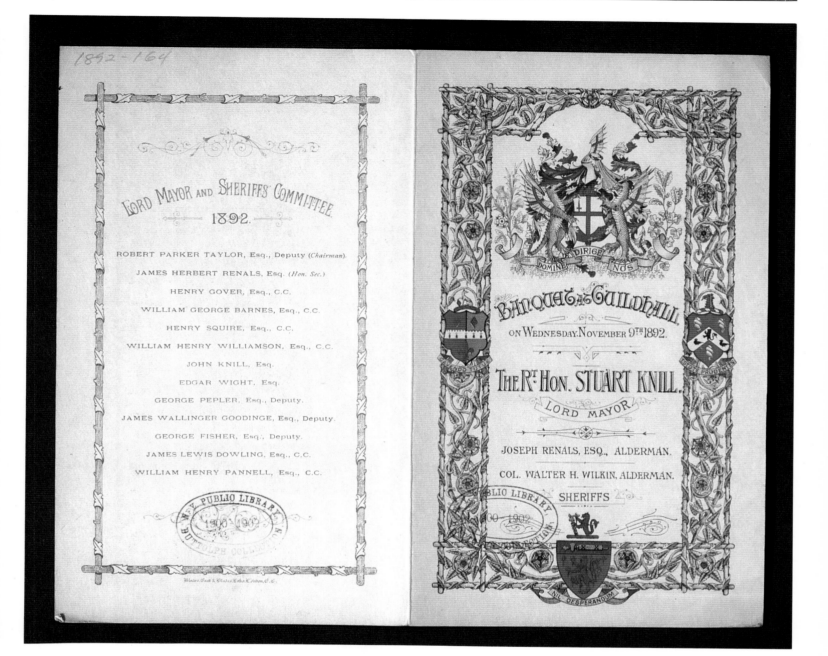

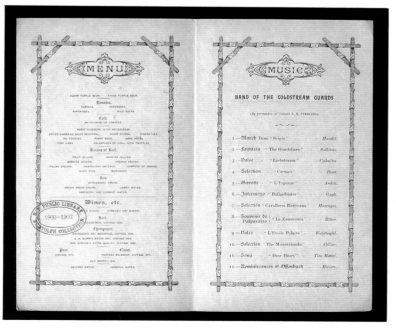

Occasion: Banquet

Sponsor: Rt. Hon. Stuart Knill, Lord Mayor and Sheriff's Committee

Place: Guildhall, London, England

Date: Wednesday, November 9, 1892

Four-color printing in red, blue, gold and brown is the format for the outer cover of this 1892 English menu. Inside, the gold is used for borders imitating those of the front cover sans the ivy and roses of that heavily ornate design. Brown ink is used consistently for lettering.

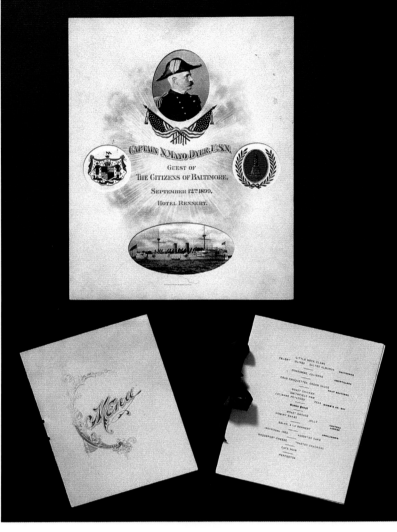

Occasion: Banquet for Captain N. Mayo Dyer, U.S.N.

Sponsor: The Citizens of Baltimore

Place: Hotel Rennert, Baltimore, MD

Date: September 12, 1899

Some menus were made to be souvenirs, as is this two-unit military theme example of 1899. The large (7 3/4″x10″) container card, which houses the menu inserted at top, is a four-windowed engraving embossed with the striking color of two American flags. The lithograph of Captain Dyer (at top) is assembled with the lithograph of a naval ship and two heavily embossed seals to the right and left. A royal-blue satin ribbon pulls out the small four-page menu, which has an intaglio cover design and contains both printed and hand-inscribed text inside.

Occasion: Banquet for Minister of the U.S.—Colonel Page Bryan

Place: Palacio da Victoria, Spain

Date: July 6, 1899

Printed in black on white, this dyecut menu is enhanced with an aquatint design at top, center, featuring a pair of Spanish maidens in cultural costume. Their image becomes the illustration for the fan design of the dyecut.

Occasion: Dinner

Place: St. Petersburg, Russia

Date: December 1, 1899

This diminutive Russian design is both placecard and menu for a St. Petersburg dinner of 1899. Dyecut centerfolded linen stock of a burnished rose color is handwritten in black ink. The cover decoration is an ornate black-and-white embossed dragon with the word "menu" in vine-laden script.

Occasion: Dinner, Judges of Philadelphia Dog Show

Sponsor: Philadelphia Dog Club

Place: Hotel Flanders, Philadelphia, PA

Date: November 22, 1899

One sheet of kraft paper is both blind embossed and embossed in green for the rustic "hunting dog" scene of this Philadelphia Dog Club menu. The menu list is printed in blue. The top, left corner lends a shot of bold color with an insert of red satin ribbon.

Occasion: Dinner in Honor of John Francis Maguire

Place: Delmonico's, New York City, NY

Date: March 14, 1867

A tiny (3″x4 1/2″) menu, this design uses coated stock with embossed borders, which are complemented inside with delicate twin bordering in purple and green inks. The cover is printed gold on pastel green in honor of the Irishman for whom the dinner was given.

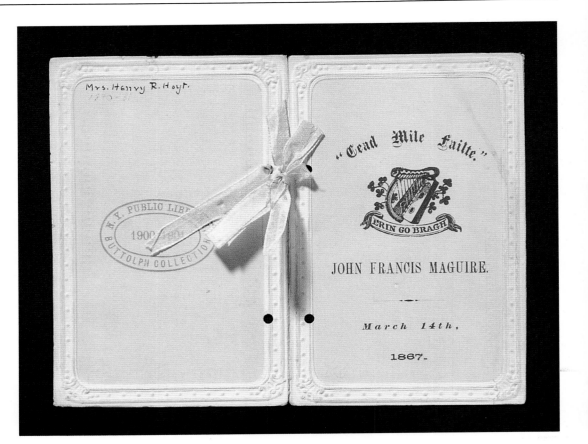

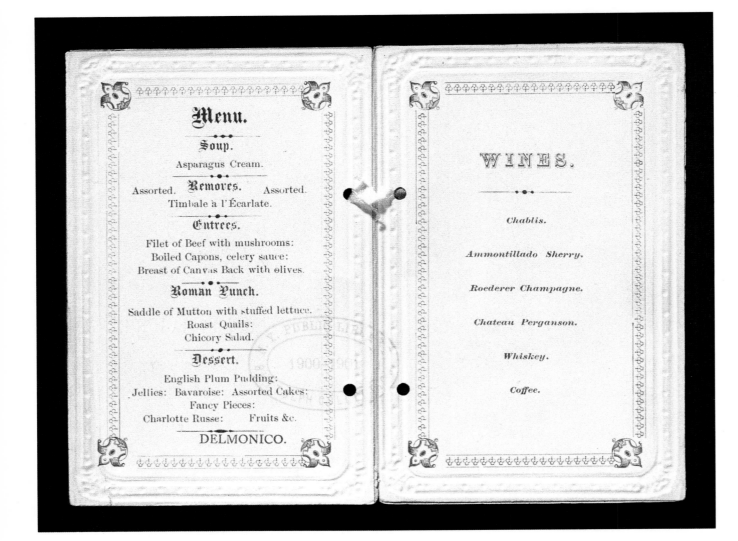

Occasion: Dinner Party (Place Card for Judge Daly)

Sponsor: William Astor

Place: The Astor Mansion on 5th Avenue, New York City, NY

Date: July 19, 1879

William W. Astor used these placecard menus for a dinner party held at his 5th Avenue mansion in 1879. The cover watercolor is handpainted and comes from Tiffany & Co. This two-piece cardboard menu opens up to reveal the dinner listing printed in lilac. The back cover contains the stylized monogram of Mr. Astor in gold ink. The two pieces are joined at the top with two white ribbons.

Occasion: Complimentary Dinner for Horace E. Deming

Sponsor: Academy of Music, Brooklyn, NY

Date: Monday, December 18, 1882

A thick piece of cardboard printed on one side only is the foundation for this menu. The illustration at the top is a pen-and-ink design of a man and maiden in a summer garden, perhaps a purposeful departure from the true season of this menu, dated "Monday, December 18, 1882."

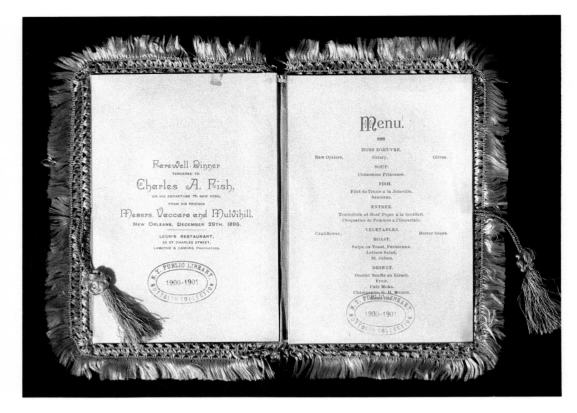

Occasion: Farewell Dinner for Charles A. Fish

Sponsor: Messrs. Vaccaro & Mulvihill

Place: Leon's Restaurant, 23rd & Charles St., New Orleans, LA

Date: December 29, 1895

French fare was the specialty of the house in which this menu was used—Leon's Restaurant of New Orleans. Two sheets of cardboard, bevel-edged in gold leaf and printed in gold ink, are wrapped in blue satin ,and trimmed in matching silk fringe—the epitome of luxe style in the Deep South during the 1890's.

Occasion: Dinner to Hon. Thomas L. James

Place: Hotel Continental, London, England

Date: September 18, 1883

This diminutive placecard cum menu (4"x4 1/2") is a mock letter, complete with a pseudo stamp (a votre Sante') and postage markings (Bon Appetit, Bon Vin, Bon Humeur). A single sheet of pink cardboard is trifolded into the shape of a small envelope. When opened, the menu is revealed printed in red with a lovely geometric gold ink border. The guest's name is handwritten in front. Unfortunately, this person's penmanship is far from legible and it leaves one wondering how the guests found their places.

Occasion:	Dinner to The Boston Transfer Exhibition Association
Sponsor:	Nathaniel Bradlee
Place:	Mr. Bradlee's house, Roxbury, MA
Date:	June 1, 1883

This placecard announces "Will't please you taste of what is here?" Standing 4"x5 3/4" tall, this placecard is made of cardboard printed with a color engraving of a begonia. Gold ink overlay forms a lovely geometric pattern. A dye-cut window allows for a piece of parchment printed with a poem and the guest's name to be inserted. A small piece of cardboard is pasted on the back to allow the place card to stand as an easel.

Occasion: ?

Place: Washington, DC

Date: March, 1887

The theme of love is realized here in an aquatint illustration of Cupid's cherubic cousins. The menu list is hand-inscribed in black ink. Gold bordering in a fine line encloses both design and text on this 4 1/2"x6 1/2" sheet of coated stock.

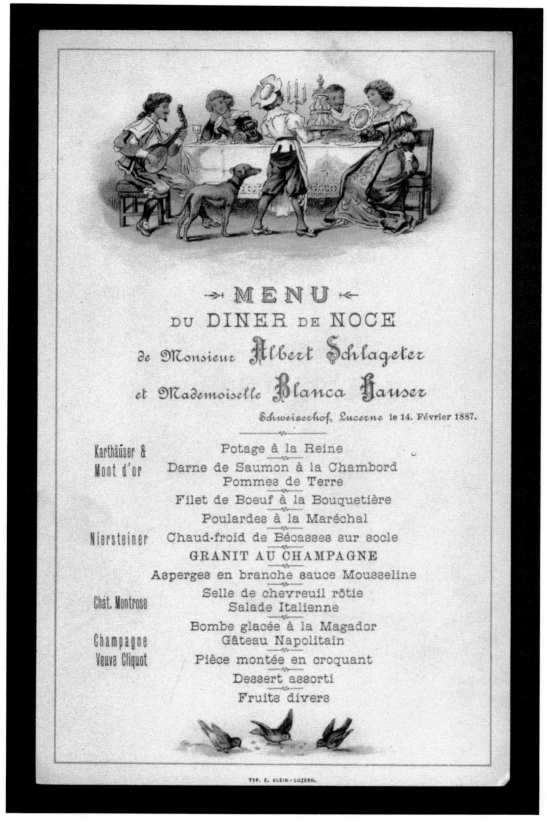

MENU
DU DINER DE NOCE
de Monsieur Albert Schlageter
et Mademoiselle Blanca Hauser

Schweizerhof, Lucerne le 14. Février 1887.

Karthäuser &
Mont d'or
Potage à la Reine
Darne de Saumon à la Chambord
Pommes de Terre
Filet de Boeuf à la Bouquetière
Poulardes à la Maréchal

Niersteiner
Chaud-froid de Bécasses sur socle
GRANIT AU CHAMPAGNE
Asperges en branche sauce Mousseline

Chât. Montrose
Selle de chevreuil rôtie
Salade Italienne

Champagne
Veuve Cliquot
Bombe glacée à la Magador
Gâteau Napolitain
Pièce montée en croquant
Dessert assorti
Fruits divers

TYP. E. KLEIN - LUZERN.

Occasion:	Wedding Dinner
Sponsor:	M. Albert Schlageter, Mlle. Blanca Hauser
Place:	Schweizerhof, Lucerne, Switzerland
Date:	February 14, 1887

The occasion was a St. Valentine's Day wedding dinner and the place was the Schweizerhof of Lucerne for this menu of 1887. An aquatint at the top commemorates the event with a subtle-hued design of the wedding table and guests. The lettering is in gold, and a fine red border frames the card.

Occasion: Banquet to Celebrate the Anniversary of the Birth of Gen. U.S. Grant

Sponsor: General W.T. Sherman, Chairman Committee of Arrangements

Place: Delmonico's Hotel, New York City, NY

Date: April 27, 1888

This table tent menu is an ingenious way to create a table decoration and incorporate a menu into it! A wide piece of pink satin ribbon is used as the base. Two isinglass sheets—one containing a photogravure of U.S. Grant and the dinner committee names; the other containing the menu. The two isinglass pieces are hole punched and tied to the pink ribbon with coordinating pink cotton cord. The overall effect is clever and beautiful.

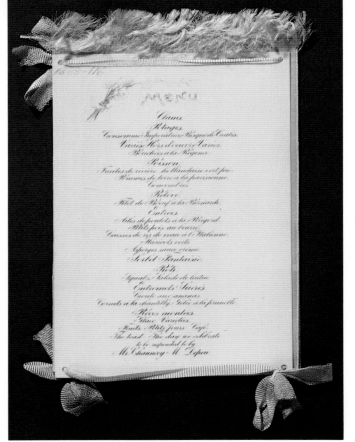

Bankett zu Ehren des

Herrn Anton Schwarz

gelegentlich des 10 jaehrigen Bestehens
der
Vereinigten Staaten Brauer-Academy

New York, December 22.

1892.

Terrace Garten.

DEMPSEY & CARROLL, NEW YORK

Occasion:	Banquet for Mr. Anton Schwarz
Sponsor:	Vereinigten Staaten Brauer
Place:	Terrace Garden, New York City, NY
Date:	December 22, 1892

This menu, entirely printed in German, is composed of a heavyweight piece of cardboard 4 1/4"x7 1/4" surrounded by a centerfolded piece of parchment serving as its cover. The parchment contains gold printing announcing the banquet in honor of Herr Anton Schwarz. The cardboard insert contains brown type printed on a beige, shell-like, geometric background. The upper lefthand corner contains an embossed lilac tinted in pink and gold. The word "menu" is also embossed and tinted pink at top center. The unit is bound by handtwisted gold silk cord.

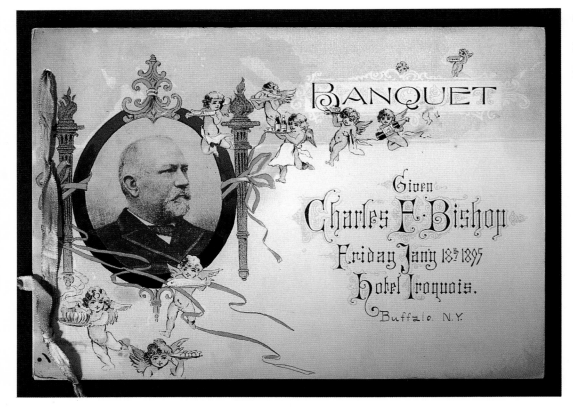

Occasion: Banquet, Charles F. Bishop

Place: Hotel Iroquois, Buffalo, NY

Date: Friday, January 18, 1895

Five pieces of 8 1/2"x6" cardboard are tied with a green silk ribbon to form this menu unit. The front cover is a curious combination of a serious photoengraving of the guest of honor paired with an over-embellished aquatint of cherubic waiters and Victorian lettering. The interior pages are all printed one-side-only in green and red.

Occasion: Banquet 74th Anniversary of the Birth of Gen. Ulysses Grant

Sponsor: Members of The Union League

Place: Philadelphia, PA

Date: April 12, 1896

The 74th Anniversary of the birth of Ulysses Grant showcased this leather and paper menu in 1896. The covers are made up of a single piece of leather. The inside pages are heavyweight kraft paper with grey ink. Lithographs highlighting the milestones of Gen. Grant's life are included in black ink. The entire unit is hole punched and bound by two rust-colored satin ribbons.

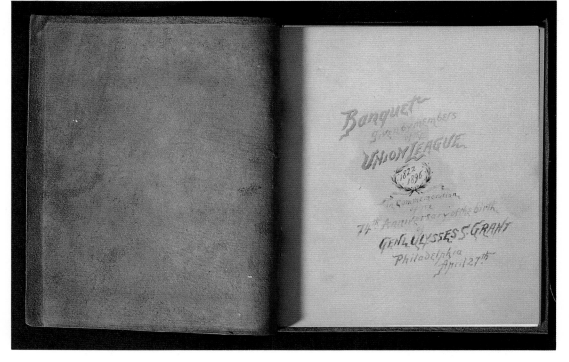

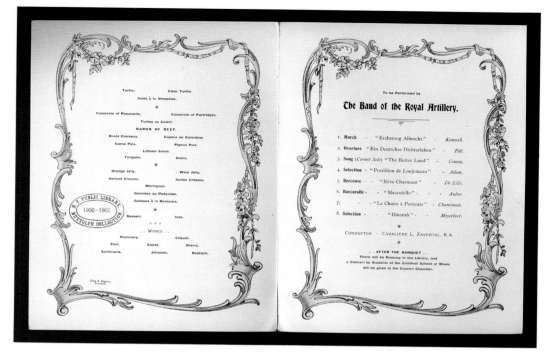

Occasion:	Banquet at Guildhall
Sponsor:	Lord Mayor Horatio David Davies & Sheriff's Committee
Place:	Guildhall, London, England
Date:	Tuesday, November 9, 1897

Victorian influence co-mingles with illustrations of the Guildhall of London on this English menu cover design of 1897. The frontal aquatint is in shades of brown, yellow, red and green; inside and on the back cover are matching border aquatints in ornate brown and yellow. This centerfolded menu is printed on both sides in black ink.

Occasion:	Dinner for Mr. Alexander Van Rensselaer
Sponsor:	Philadelphia Gun Club
Place:	Eddington, PA
Date:	January 6, 1898

Three pieces of thick 7"x9 1/2" cardboard are bound with ring and ribbon for this 1898 gun club menu of Philadelphia. A variety of design ideas were combined for this unit: on the cover are handpainted, watercolor dyecut figures; on the inside cover is a photo paste-up; embossed captions give texture to the one-color printing of the remainder.

Occasion: Dinner for Mr. Edwin S. Pierce

Place: Copley Square Hotel, Boston, MA

Date: February 16, 1898

Two wide pieces of pink satin ribbon are the print surface for this fancy *bon voyage* menu of 1898. With its thick fringes and tri-bow binding, this design required little else in decoration, making the plain black-ink printing a perfect choice. Inside, the black ink is joined by red, which for the reasons just mentioned was a glaring mistake.

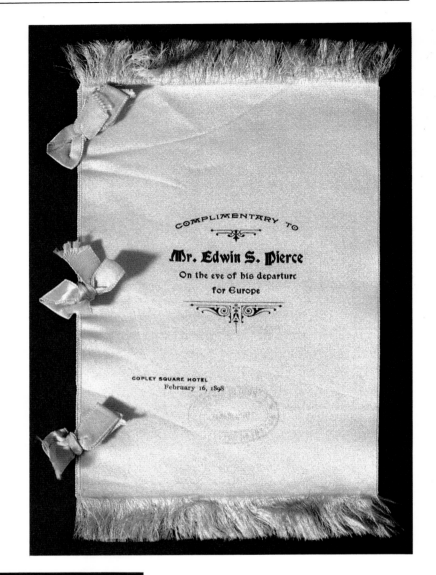

COMPLIMENTARY TO

Mr. Edwin S. Pierce

On the eve of his departure for Europe

COPLEY SQUARE HOTEL
February 16, 1898

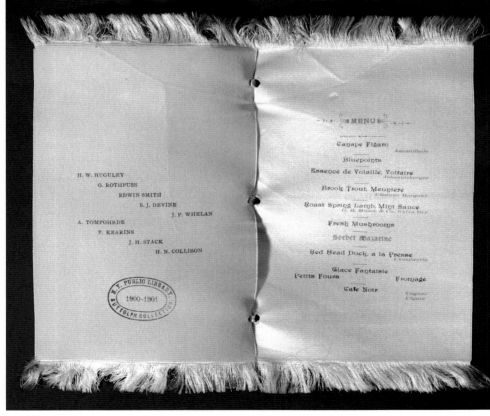

H. W. HUGULEY
G. ROTHFUSS
EDWIN SMITH
B. J. DEVINE
J. P. WHELAN
A. TOMFOHRDE
P. KEARINS
J. H. STACK
H. N. COLLISON

⋆ MENU ⋆

Canape Figaro
Amontillado

Bluepoints

Essence de Volaille, Voltaire
Johannisberger

Brook Trout, Meuniere
Chateau Margaux

Roast Spring Lamb, Mint Sauce
G. H. Mumm & Co. Extra Dry

Fresh Mushrooms

Sorbet Mazarine

Red Head Duck, a la Presse
Chambertin

Glace Fantaisie
Petits Fours   Fromage

Cafe Noir
*Cognac
Cigars*

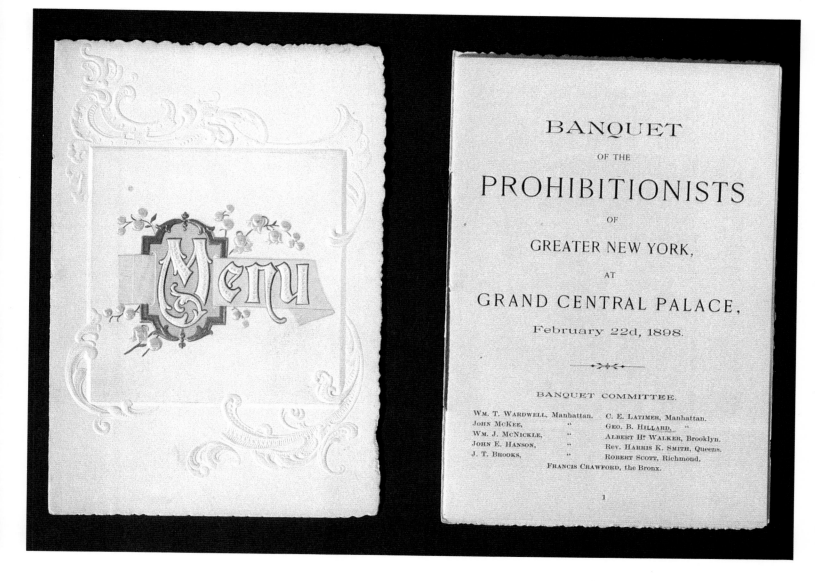

Occasion: Banquet of the Prohibitionists of Greater New York

Place: Grand Central Palace, New York City, NY

Date: February 22, 1898

Embossed kraft covers with dyecut edges are hand-bound with red silk twine to eight inner sheets of thin coated stock for this unit. The most remarkable feature of this Prohibitionists' banquet menu is the proliferation of advertisement: at least one side of nearly every page is printed with an ad. Ice cream, bicycles, insurance and pianos are all represented in this 1898 menu.

Occasion: Dinner—Concert Inauguration of the Monument of Prince Friedrich Charles of Prussia

Sponsor: Major Hiller

Place: Military Casino, Metz, Alsace-Lorraine region (then, Prussia; now, France)

Date: March 20, 1898

This extremely large Prussian menu is a fine example of German printing. The excellent military lithographs adorn the front piece of this two-part heavyweight cardboard menu. White satin ribbon binds the two pieces together. The menu inside is printed in black ink and in two languages: French and German. This is due to the fact that Alsace-Lorraine was an area constantly being claimed by either Prussia or France—depending on who was the victor.

Citizens of New York
to
Honorable Joseph F. Daly,
on Tuesday evening, January twenty-fourth, 1899.
Sherry's.

DEMPSEY & CARROLL, N.Y.

Occasion:	Dinner to Honor Joseph F. Daly	
Sponsor:	Citizens of New York	
Place:	Sherry's, New York City, NY	
Date:	Tuesday, January 24, 1899	

Judge Joseph F. Daly was honored with the dinner of this 1899 menu. Red, white and blue striped satin ribbons carry the patriotic theme of the occasion and bind the menu's inner centerfold to that of its covers. Both the front and back covers are decorated in one-color aquatint. The inside is printed in an austere format of brown on beige.

Occasion: Dinner to William A. Connor, Daniel B. Shepp, James S. McCartney and Their Friends

Sponsor: James B. Fleshman of the Morrelton Club

Place: Morrelton Club, Torresdale, PA

Date: May 17, 1899

Seven handtorn sheets of brown kraft paper make up this 4 1/4"x7 1/4" menu. A shad and spring lamb dinner was given to honor select members of the Morrelton Club; hence, the woodcut design on the cover. Each sheet is printed one side in black, containing various courses of the dinner as well as woodcuts of historical sites from Philadelphia, Pennsylvania. The menu is hole punched at the top and bound with store twine; this is a most unusual specimen.

Occasion: Dinner, Mr. Harry Furniss
            of London "Punch"

Sponsor: The Lotus Club

Place: New York

Date: April 23, 1892

Green kraft paper of sizable
dimension is the covering sheet for
this Lotus Club menu of 1892.
Printed on one side in deep green
ink, the front cover is also host to a
red seal of the Club at the upper
right corner. Inside is one smaller
page of tan kraft stock printed in
brown pen-and-ink design with an
interesting array of characters: a lion
dancing with an eagle, floating
lotuses, an Egyptian lyre-player, and
the Master of Ceremonies standing
upon a chair which is in the midst of
a body of water.

Occasion: Class of 1898 Dinner

Sponsor: Public School of
            Philadelphia

Place: The Bellevue Hotel,
            Philadelphia, PA

Date: June 6, 1898

This 5 3/4"x7 1/2" menu
commemorates the graduation of
Class of 1898 from the Public School
of Philadelphia. The covers are
composed of one piece of cardboard,
centerfolded. The interior is made up
of two sheets of linen paper
centerfolded to create four pages.
The front cover is an aquatint design
with a paste-on. The entire unit is
ribbon bound.

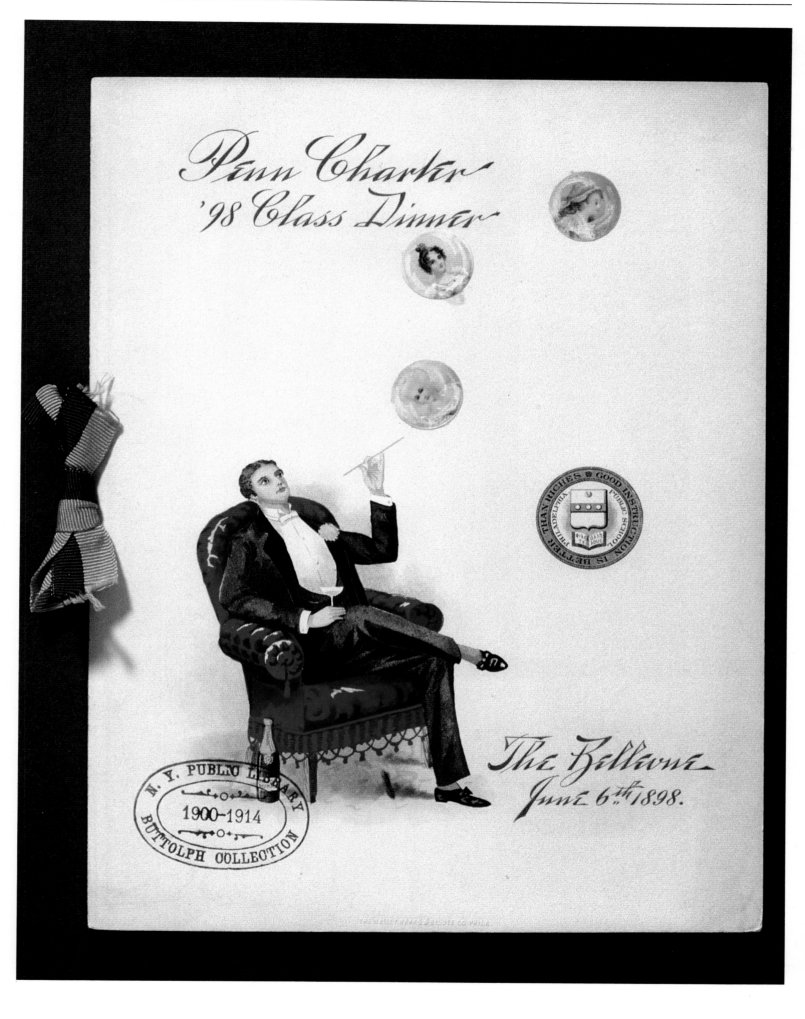

Occasion: 6th Annual Dinner in Commemoration of the Founding of New Amsterdam

Sponsor: Society of Colonial Wars

Place: Delmonico's, New York City, NY

Date: January 21, 1898

Heavyweight, centerfolded cardboard forms the covers of this menu. The front cover contains a handtinted lithograph of an Indian chief and a hand tinted embossing of a medal given to those during the Colonial Wars. The centerfolded parchment insert contains the menu printed in bright red ink. The entire piece is bound by a red satin ribbon.

Occasion: French Cooks' Ball—
Culinary Exhibition 33rd
Annual Ball

Sponsor: Societe' Culinaire
Philanthropique

Place: Madison Square Garden,
New York City, NY

Date: February 7, 1899

This rather simple design was used for an event where the importance of the food overshadows everything else: the French Cooks' Ball of New York. The cover of centerfolded coated stock, is embossed to form a frame of lithographic "wood." Blue ink was used for the cover sheet while black was used for the four-page interior. On both sides of the back cover is the well-targeted advertisement for a poultry and game purveyor.

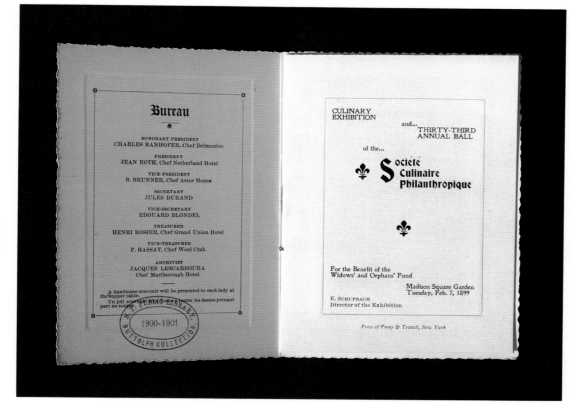

Occasion: A. Macdonald's
Transcontinental Ride

Sponsor: The Dunlop Tyre Co. Ltd.
and the Austral Cycle Club

Place: Princess's Theatre, Grand
Hotel, Melbourne, Australia

Date: September 26, 1898

This tiny 4"x3" deckle-edged souvenir menu commemorates A. Macdonald's bicycle ride from Port Darwin to Melbourne in 1898—a mere 2596 miles that took 33 days and 5 1/2 hours.

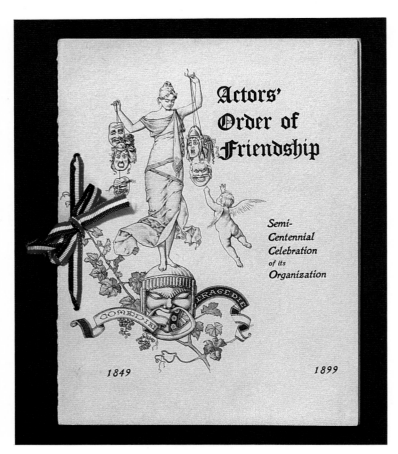

Occasion: Semi-Centennial Celebration
               of the Actor's Order of
               Friendship

Sponsor: Shakespeare Lodge No. 1,
               Edwin Forrest Lodge No. 2

Place: Delmonico's, New York
               City, NY

Date: January 15, 1899

A black pen-and-ink lithograph highlights the front cover of this 1899 Actor's Order of Friendship menu. A single, centerfolded sheet of kraft paper forms the cover. The fine lithograph of the theatre muse holding numerous masks and standing atop a comedy/tragedy mask is outstanding. The one sheet, centerfolded insert is printed black on linen stock and contains the committee's names and the menu. A tri-color red, white and blue grosgrain ribbon binds the unit—a strange addition.

Occasion: Dinner

Sponsor: Unknown

Place: Unknown

Date: March 26, 1887

This finely illustrated and handtinted menu card is on a lightweight piece of cardboard. The old men is gazing at the monogram "GM" and holds an umbrella and pipe. The menu is printed in French and a lovely shade of brown ink is used. Unfortunately, the occasion that prompted this menu is unknown; the only known fact is the date printed at the bottom, March 26, 1887.

Occasion: Fest-Bankett

Sponsor: National Verbandes Deutsch Amerikanischer Journalisten und Schriftsteller von New York

Place: Liederkranz Halle, New York City, NY

Date: May 19, 1892

Two sheets of 6″x7 1/2″ lightweight cardboard are handbound with red, white and blue ribbons to form this menu. A brown etching illustrates the front cover. The entire menu is printed in black (food) and red (wine). The only English words (everything else is in German) appear on the inside front cover— Good Night.

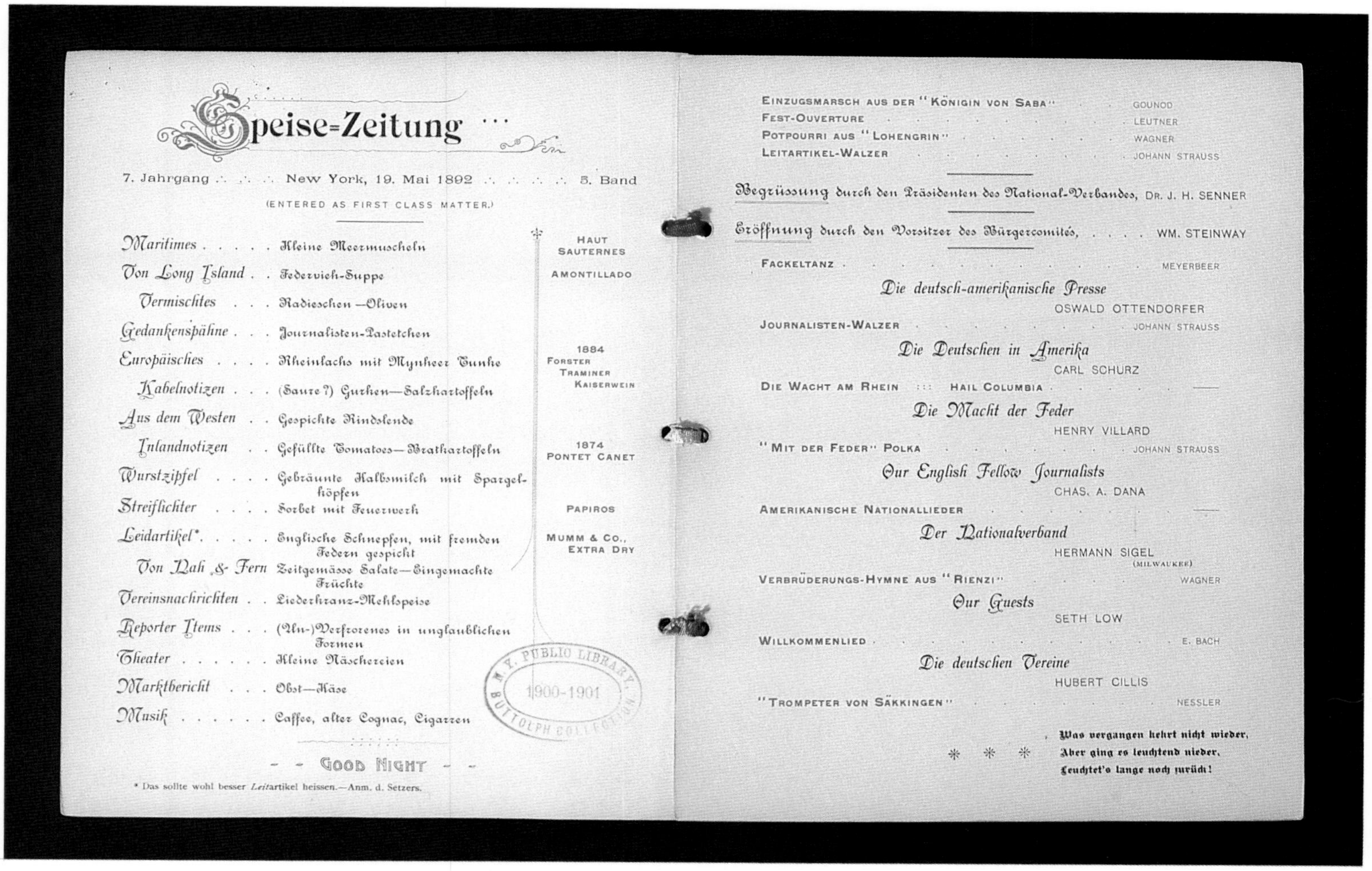

Occasion: Annual Dinner

Sponsor: Sheriff's Jury

Place: Delmonico's, New York City, NY

Date: Wednesday, January 26, 1887

Another Tiffany design is evident on the cover of this Delmonico's menu of 1887. Grapes and vines form an imaginary pedestal for the silver soup tureen of the front cover, which is a hand-colored flow of green, blue, purple and pink. The two interior pages are printed in blue with red accenting, and the back cover features a pewter-embossed "loving cup," which the dinner guests "will pass...and each one drink to all." Two light blue satin bows bind the menu.

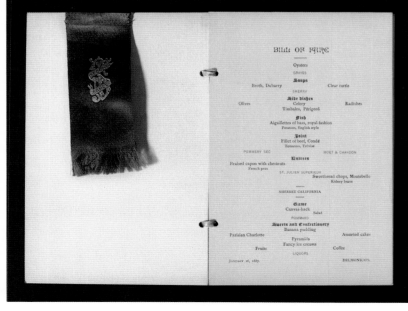

Occasion:	Banquet to honor Admiral Dewey
Sponsor:	Unknown
Place:	The Steamer Sandy Hook
Date:	September 29, 1899

This highly embossed menu is a small 4"x5 1/2". The front cover contains fine etchings of Admiral Dewey, his ship, and New York Harbor—embossed and handtinted. One centerfolded sheet of glossy paper is stapled to the lightweight cardboard covers. The inside is printed in navy blue ink.

NAVAL PARADE
and RECEPTION to
ADMIRAL DEWEY
September 29 and 30
1899

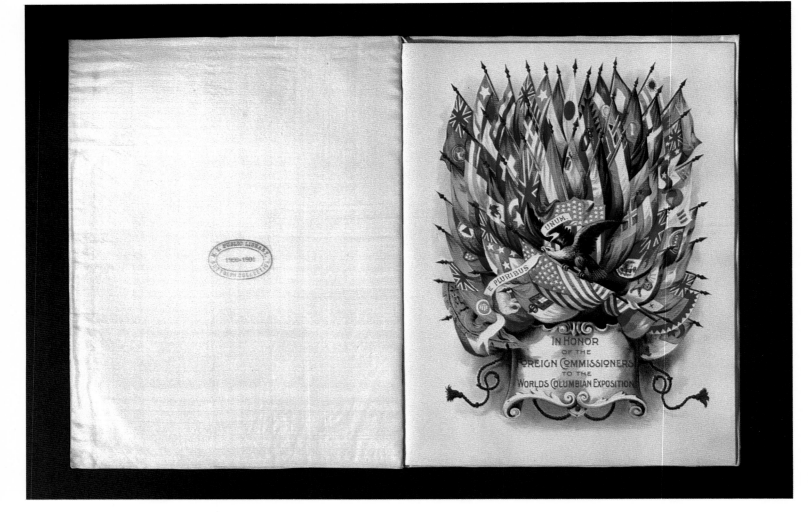

Occasion: In Honor of the Foreign
             Commissioners to the
             World Columbian
             Exposition

Sponsor: Directors of the World
             Columbian Exposition

Place: Music Hall, Packson Park,
             Chicago, IL

Date: October 11, 1893

Cream silk fabric is wrapped over
cardboard to form the covers of this
12-page commemorative menu
booklet from the world's Columbian
Exposition. A full-color lithograph
appears on page 1, while the rest of
the menu is printed in black ink. The
entire piece is bound by a beige satin
ribbon, handtied at the centerfold.

Occasion: Party Commercial Clubs of Chicago, Cincinnati and St. Louis

Sponsor: The Commercial Club of Boston

Place: Unknown

Date: June 27, 1885

A wide silk ribbon is the basis of this menu. The type is printed in black, and handpasted violets adorn opposing corners. The ribbon is mounted on a piece of cardboard with a thick white and pink tasseled silk cord. Hole punches have been used to bind the ribbon and cardboard with the cord.

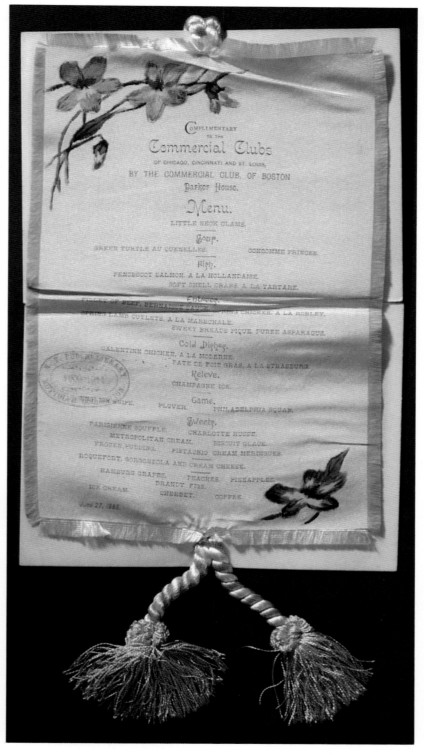

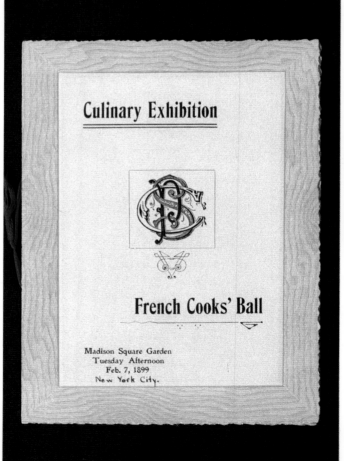

Occasion: French Cooks' Ball— Culinary Exhibition 33rd Annual Ball

Sponsor: Societe' Culinaire Philanthropique

Place: Madison Square Garden, New York City, NY

Date: February 7, 1899

This rather simple design was used for an event where the importance of the food overshadows everything else: the French Cooks' Ball of New York. The cover of centerfolded coated stock, is embossed to form a frame of lithographic "wood." Blue ink was used for the cover sheet while black was used for the four-page interior. On both sides of the back cover is the well-targeted advertisement for a poultry and game purveyor.

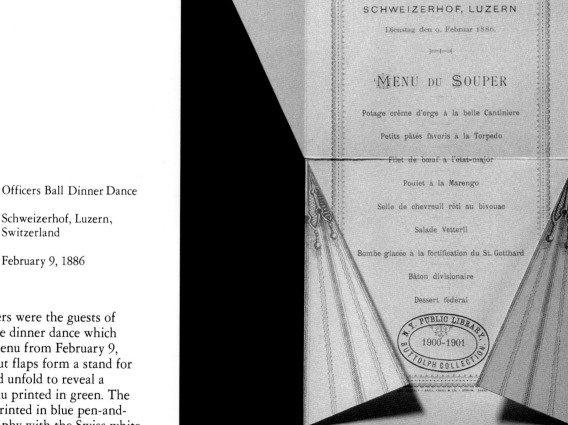

Occasion: Officers Ball Dinner Dance

Place: Schweizerhof, Luzern,
Switzerland

Date: February 9, 1886

Swiss officers were the guests of
honor at the dinner dance which
used this menu from February 9,
1886. Dyecut flaps form a stand for
the unit and unfold to reveal a
dinner menu printed in green. The
outside is printed in blue pen-and-
ink lithography with the Swiss white
cross on red shield as a focal point.

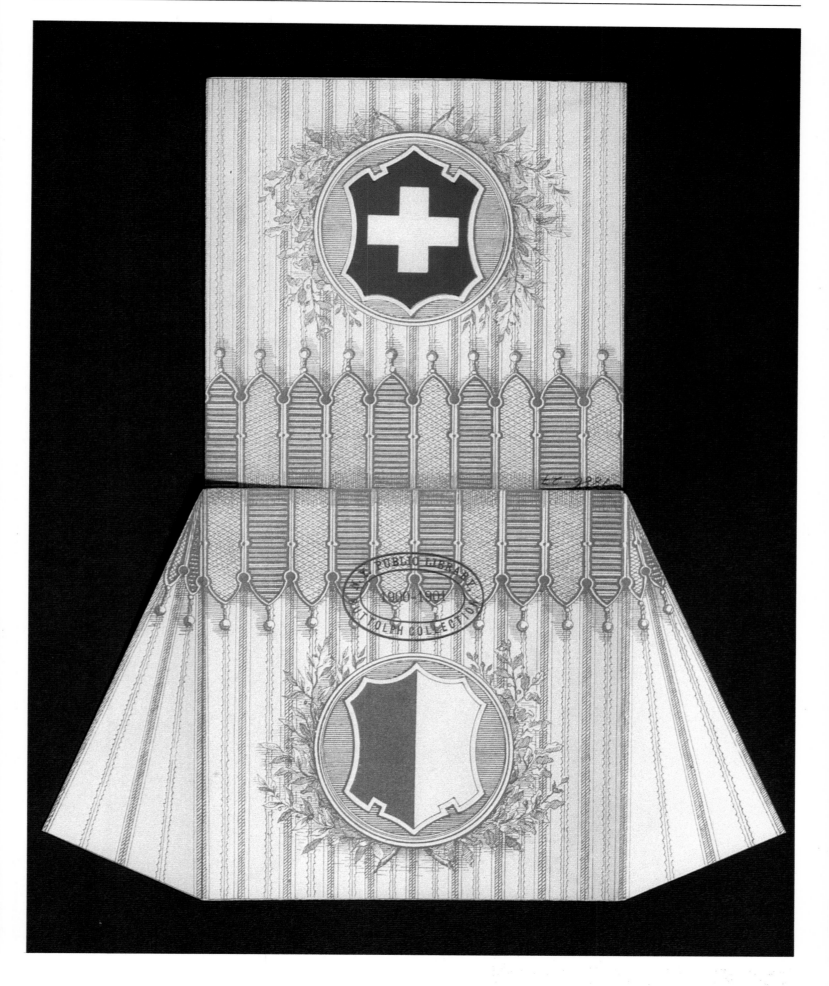

Occasion: Banquet for Henry E. Dixey

Place: Delmonico's, New York
             City, NY

Date: May 11, 1886

A profusion of design textures and
processes were used in the creation
of this personal banquet menu of
Henry E. Dixey. Blue velour-covered
wood is the two-page foundation,
upon which is mounted a silver-
embossed, grey-engraved shield
design (front), and ornately
embossed silver and blue printed
menu card (inside), a photogravure
of Henry Dixey (inside), and unusual
steel monogram of Dixey's initials
(back). The unit is tied at top with a
blue satin bow.

Occasion: Representatives of the Press
             of New York

Sponsor: Committee of the Cooks and
             Pastry Cooks Association

Place: Muschenheim's—The
             Arena, New York City, NY

Date: January 3, 1892

A simple, centerfolded piece of
cardboard is used for this menu. A
collage of all the current papers in
1892 in New York City comprise the
lithograph on the front cover.

Occasion: Luncheon for Inauguration of the New Building of the Metropolitan Museum of Art

Sponsor: The Trustees of Metropolitan Museum of Art

Place: The Waldorf Astoria, New York City, NY

Date: Monday, November 5, 1894

This menu represents the dinner to honor the new building inauguration ceremonies for the Metropolitan Museum of Art, but its hand-drawn and hand-painted cover is an artistic disappointment: much of the original pencil drawing is left uncolored and entirely visible. A bright pink satin bow binds the two menu cover sheets to a heavily engraved inner sheet of coated stock. The inside of the back cover is embossed in gold and printed in gold and red.

Occasion:	Banquet to the Delegates of the International American Conference
Sponsor:	The Spanish American Commercial Union
Place:	Delmonico's, New York City, NY
Date:	December 20, 1889

Three 10"x7 1/2" pieces of cardboard are wrapped in a large piece of green silk. An unusual watercolor illustrates the cover; each guest's name was handpainted on the cover also. The first interior cardboard insert lists the delegates in brown ink; fine-line etchings of American and Spanish symbols adorn this page. The second insert is a full-color lithograph of Central and South America; the menu is surprinted in black ink. The last insert is a full color lithograph of two hands shaking—the U.S. and South America. Finally, a large piece of parchment is tri-folded and inserted; it is the seating chart of the event.

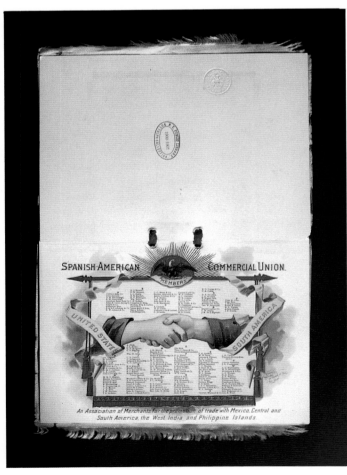

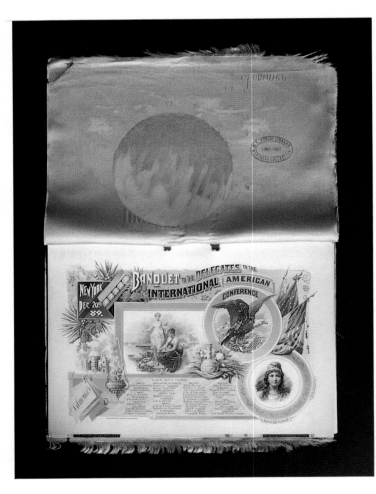

Occasion:	Lunch in honor of the Three Americas
Sponsor:	Unknown
Place:	The Schlitz Hotel, Milwaukee, WI
Date:	October 23, 1889

This extremely ornate menu hails from Milwaukee, Wisconsin—1889. The covers are two separate pieces of lightweight cardboard; the interior is composed of three sheets of glossy stock, and the entire menu is bound with a blue satin ribbon. The front cover is a full color aquatint of all the Coats of Arms of the South and Central American countries. The first interior sheet contains the menu printed in black; the second and third sheets contain photographs of the Schlitz Hotel dining room and bar room, respectively.

+ + MOONLIGHT + +

Masquerade Carnival

STEAMER GRAND REPUBLIC

SEPTEMBER 10th, 1898

—LUNCH—

Cold Squab	75
" Chicken	75
Ham Sandwiches	15
Tongue "	15
Turkey "	15
Cheese "	15

—WINES—

	QTS.	PTS.
G. H. Mumm's	4 00	2 00
Piper Heidsieck	4 00	2 00
Pommery Sec	4 00	2 00
Geo. Goulet	4 00	2 00
Mixed Drinks	25	
Plain "	15	
Pabst Milwaukee Beer	25	
Piel Bros. Beer	25	
Ruppert Beer	25	

Occasion: Moonlight Masquerade Carnival

Sponsor: Steamer Grand Republic

Place: Unknown

Date: September 10, 1898

This gold, white and black menu card is a playful souvenir of the Moonlight Masquerade Carnival. Cavorting costumed characters are silk-screened in black along the edges, highlighted with a bright gold border. It is strange to note that the meal served on the moonlight carnival is listed as lunch on the menu.

Occasion: Christmas

Sponsor: Unknown

Place: Gran Plaza de Toros

Date: December, 1893

This handwritten menu card contains an unusual lithograph of a one-legged man feeding birds. The lithograph is handcolored in grey, tan, pink, yellow and blue. The writing is in French and English, and the back of the card contains the signatures of those who attended.

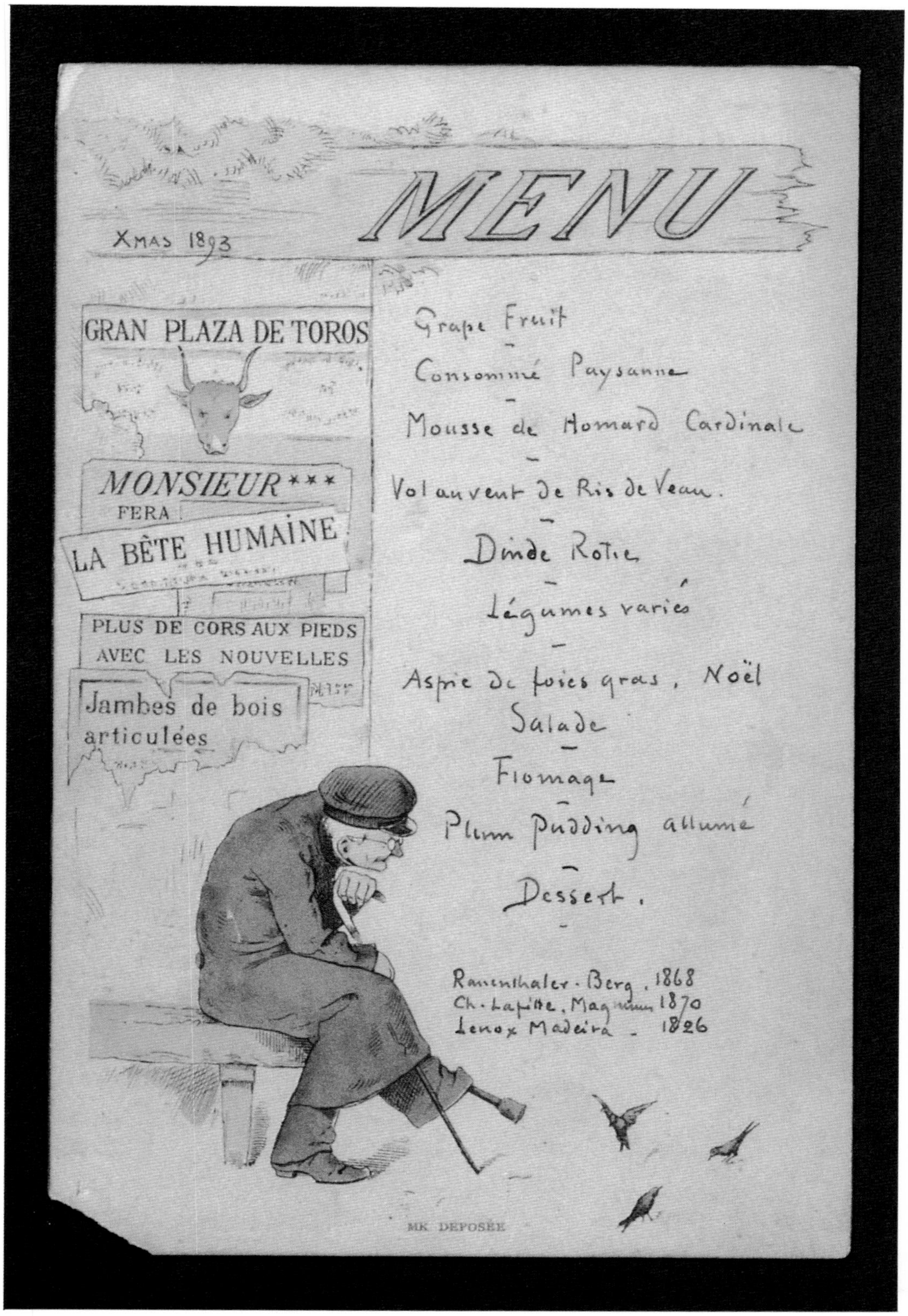

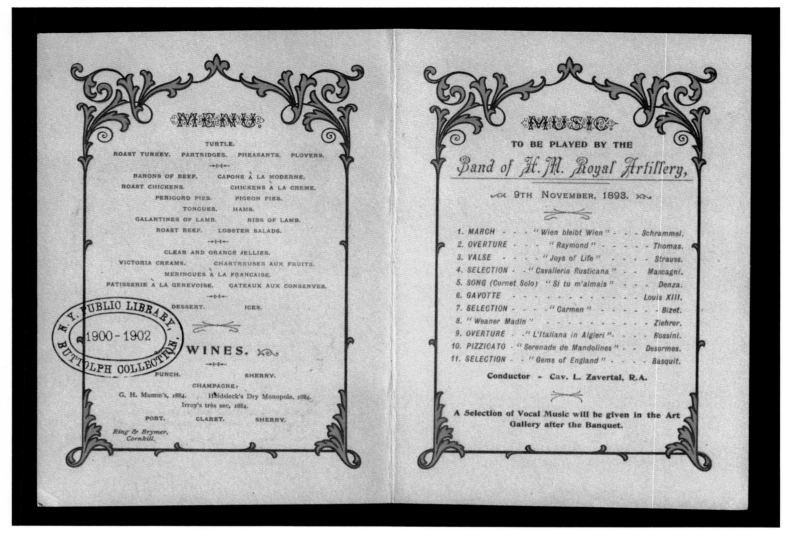

Occasion: Banquet for the Rt. Hon. George Robert Tyler, Lord Mayor

Sponsor: Lord Mayor and Sheriff's Committee

Place: Guildhall

Date: November 9, 1893

This 4"x5 1/2" menu is unusual in that the lithograph on the cover is in color, and is also handtinted. The interior contains ornate gold ink borders, handtinted in pink.

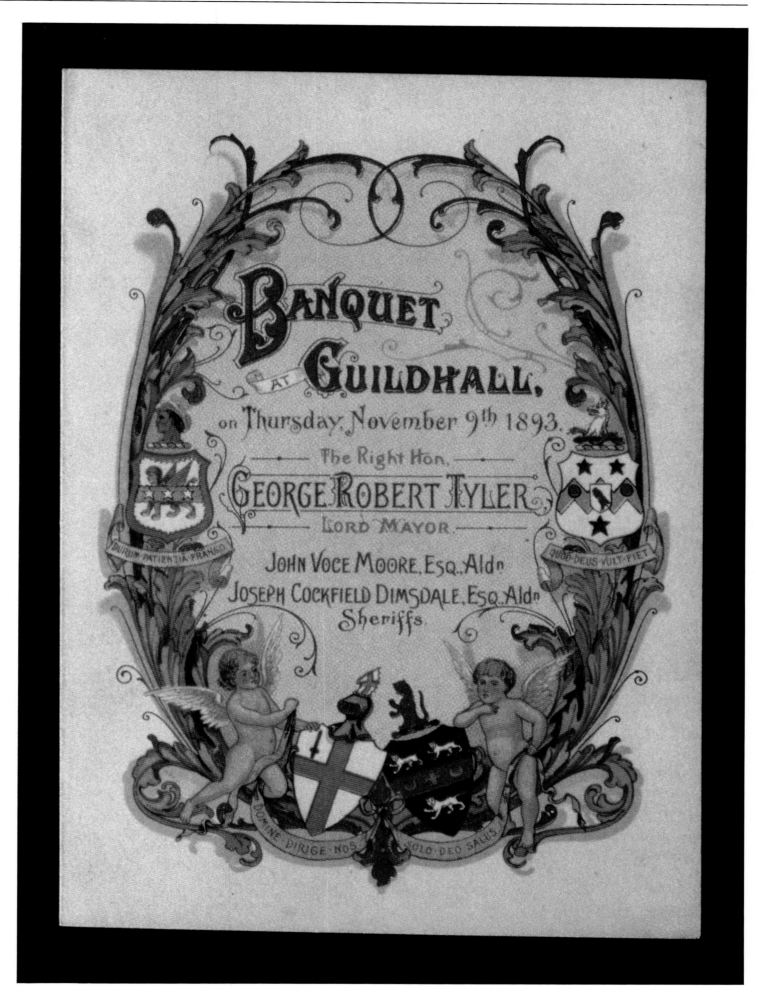

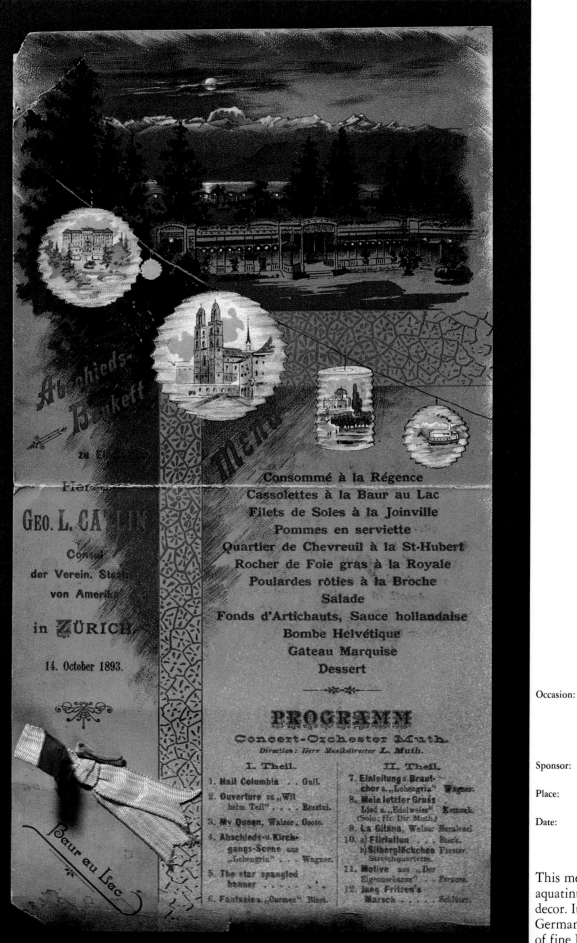

Occasion: Abschieds– Bankett zu Ehren des Herr Geo. L. Catlin Consul der Verein . Staaten von Amerika in Zurich

Sponsor: Unknown

Place: Baur au Lac

Date: October 14, 1893

This menu card contains a full-color aquatint illustration with ribbon decor. It is printed entirely in German and remains as an example of fine European printing from the late 19th century.

Occasion: Dinner—to celebrate 30 years of membership in the Union League of Philadelphia

Sponsor: Edwin N. Benson

Place: Unknown

Date: May 31, 1893

This blue silk-covered booklet is gold stamped on the cover with the insignia of the Union League. The interior consists of two sheets of kraft paper, centerfolded and bound to the cover with a gold silk cord. The interior contains two watercolors, and the menu is printed in black and red (black for food, red for wines). The majority of the menu contains blank sheets exclusively for autographs.

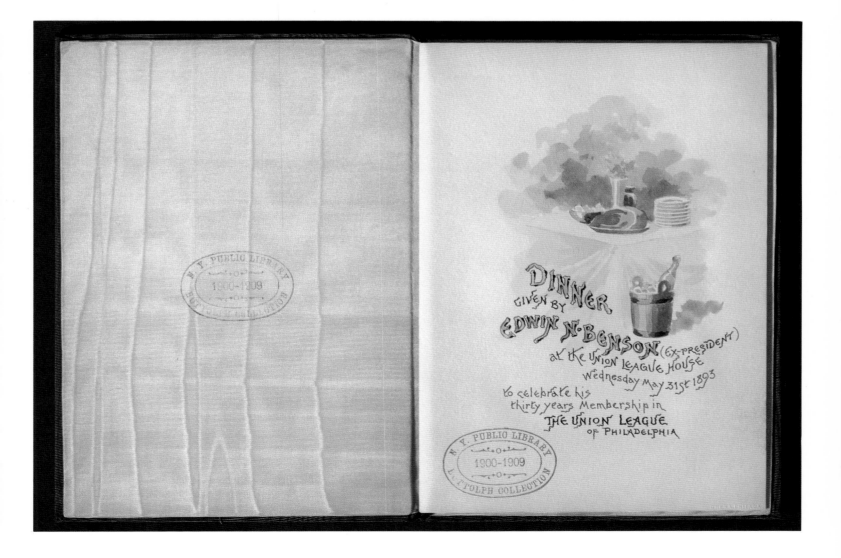

Occasion: American Centennial
                 Dinner

Sponsor: American Embassy (seal of
                 American Government)

Place: Westminster Palace Hotel,
                 London, England

Date: July 4, 1876

This 3 3/4″x5″ menu was sponsored
by the American Embassy in London,
England. The pen and ink design on
the front cover is a fine lithograph.
The centerfolded, linen paper insert
showcases the menu printed in black
and red. The unit is ribbon bound.

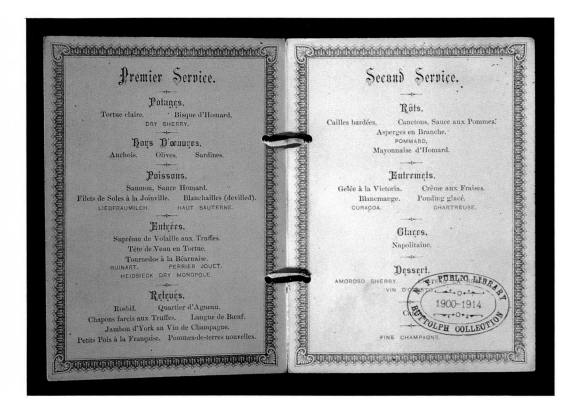

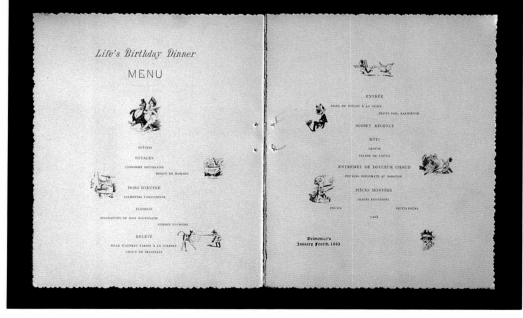

Occasion: Life's Tenth Birthday Party

Sponsor: Life Weekly Publications

Place: Delmonico's, New York City, NY

Date: January 4, 1893

This deckle-edged menu was to celebrate Life Magazine's 10th Anniversary. The cover contains a mezzotint pen-and-ink lithograph of a woman holding a quill and laurel crown. A winged cherub is at her feet writing with a quill. The interior is printed in blue ink, and the menu was bound with a white satin ribbon that, unfortunately, rotted with age.

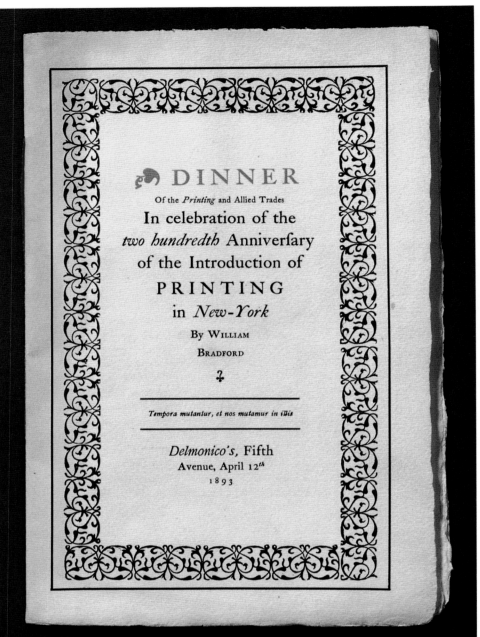

Occasion: Dinner for the 200th Anniversary of Introduction of Printing in New York

Sponsor: Printing and Allied Arts

Place: Delmonico's, New York City, NY

Date: April 12, 1893

Because this menu represented the 200th anniversary of printing in New York, it contains many interesting reproductions of the first printed materials of the area. Four centerfolded sheets of raw-edged kraft paper were printed entirely in black and red for this design. Its borders and illustrations are clean and simple.

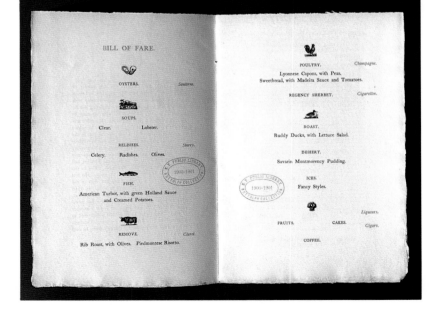

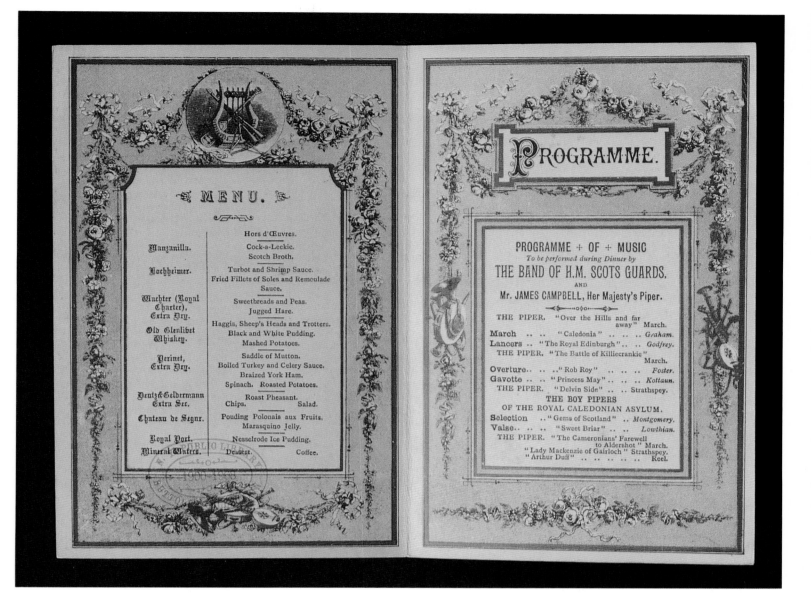

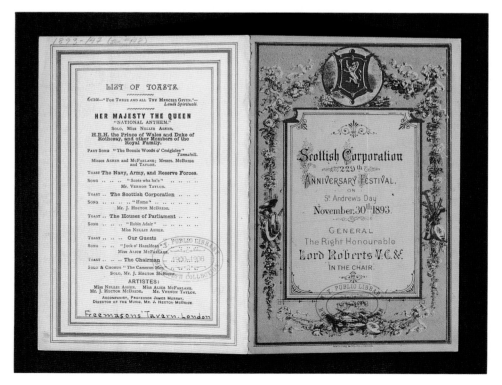

Occasion: 229th Scottish Corporation Anniversary Festival on St. Andrews Day

Sponsor: Gen. Rt . Hon. Lord Roberts V.C.

Place: Freemasons' Tavern, London, England

Date: November 30, 1893

This ornate 4 1/2"x6 3/4" menu contains excellent examples of lithography. The cover is printed in gold ink on top of a purple ink lithograph. The borders are composed of flowers, branches, leaves, musical instruments, and ribbons. The crest of the Scottish Corporation takes the place of honor at the top.

Occasion: 34th Annual Dinner St.
            Andrew's Day

Sponsor: St. Andrew's Society

Place: Palace Hotel, San Francisco,
            CA

Date: November 30, 1896

Red cotton twine joins the coated
cover sheet of this menu to the thin
paper sheet inside. Both are dyecut
in a shape that accommodates a map
of the Scottish Isles; this full-color
lithograph appears on the front
cover. Each interior page is printed
in blue ink, the back cover contains
the verse to Auld Lang Syne.

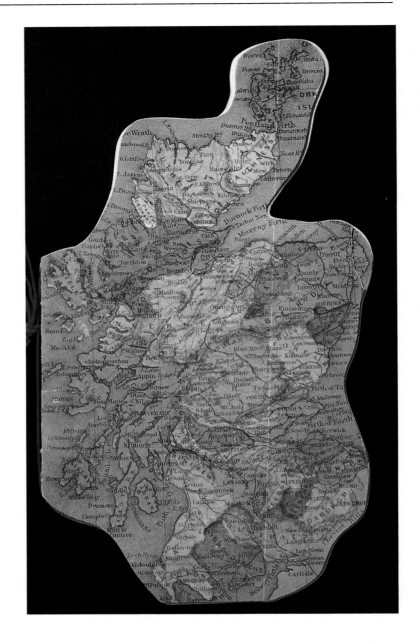

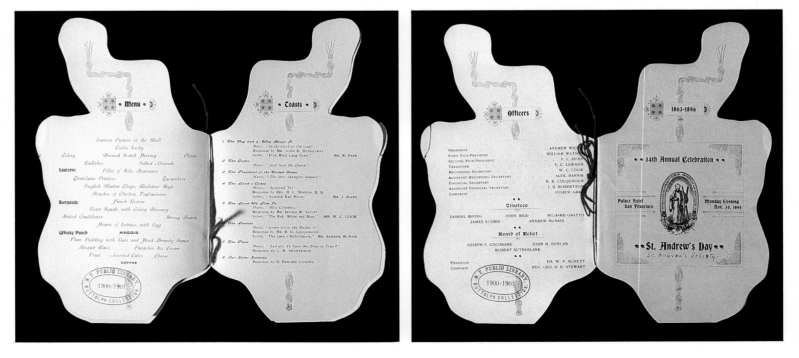

Occasion: Dinner—15th Annual Festival

Sponsor: Syrian Temple

Place: Syrian Temple, Cincinnati, OH

Date: February 28, 1896

This 5″x10 1/2″ menu is a four-panel fold-out unit. One side is printed in full-color aquatint, the other in a two-color process. This menu was used for the 15th Annual Festival Dinner of the Syrian Temple of Cincinnati.

Occasion: Annual Banquet 1896

Sponsor: The Sons of Delaware in Philadelphia

Place: Union League, Philadelphia, PA

Date: December 7, 1896

This dye-cut "D" menu was for the annual banquet of the Sons of Delaware. The cover is a mauve lithograph with gold-embossing. The four dye-cut pieces are made of cardboard and bound with a blue and gold ribbon—the Club's colors. The back cover contains the words of the Club's song "Our Delaware" sung to the tune of "My Maryland."

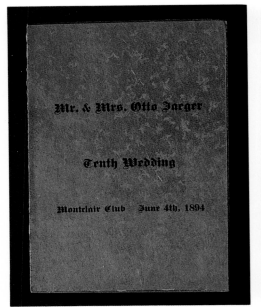

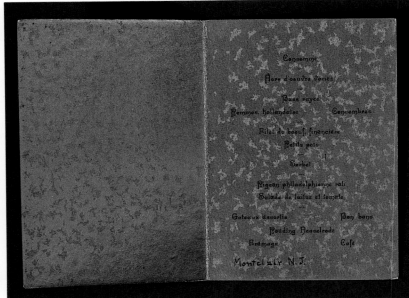

Occasion: 10th Wedding Anniversary

Sponsor: Mr. & Mrs. Otto Jaeger

Place: Montclair Club, Montclair,
            NJ

Date: June 4, 1894

This tenth anniversary dinner for
Mr. & Mrs. Otto Jaeger of Montclair,
NJ featured a 3 1/2"x5" silver
cardboard patterned menu, with
printing done in navy ink.

Occasion: Philippine Night

Sponsor: Aldine Association

Place: Unknown

Date: October 19, 1899

The Aldine Association used this
menu for its Philippine Night in
1899. The front cover contains a
photograph, reproduced in brown
ink and framed by a cameo border, of
a Philippine girl. The menu is
printed in brown ink on the inside
back cover and features French
cuisine. The back cover contains a
picture of an anchor with a serpent
entwined around it. The initials
"AL" appear to the left, "DVS" to
the right.

Menu

Toasts

THE BOARD OF EDUCATION
HON. GEORGE M. VAN HOESEN

PEACE AND WAR
CHAPLAIN J. P. CHIDWICK, U. S. N.

THE AMERICAN NAVY
HON. WILLIAM McADOO

AMERICAN POETRY
ANDREW McLEAN

THE CITY COLLEGE
EDWARD LAUTERBACH

THE PUBLIC SCHOOL: THE SAFEGUARD
OF THE NATION
JOHN W. KELLER

Occasion:	Dinner
Place:	Hotel Savoy, New York City, NY
Date:	April 15, 1899

The 2 1/2″x4″ design is a matching menu and envelope ensemble in which crimson and gold become the elements of emphasis. A gold-embossed owl and moon appear on the menu's front cover with matching embossed edges. Gold is also used to print the inner sheet, which is bound to the cover with a red silk ribbon.

Occasion: Concert and Dinner

Sponsor: The Criterion Picadilly
            Circus

Place: Winchester House, London,
            England

Date: June 11, 1887

This simple menu contains a fine
line etching on the front cover in
blue-black ink with a decorative
border. The interior contains the
menu to the left and the "music
programme" to the right. The back
cover is a handtinted lithograph of
the Winchester House; it served as
an advertisement.

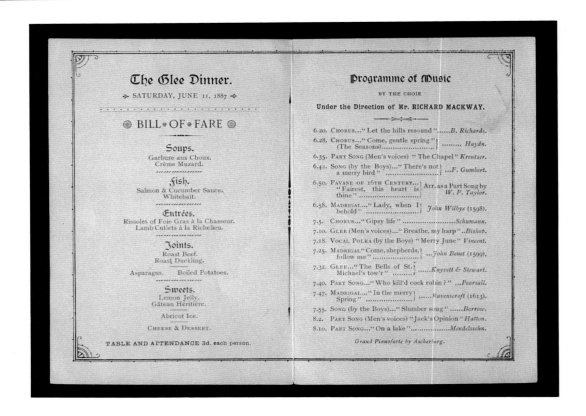

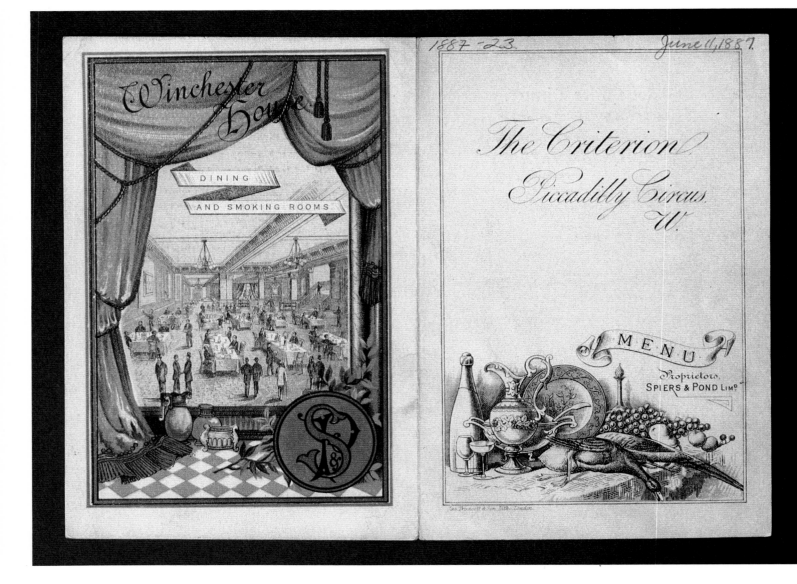

Occasion: Dinner for the Diplomats &
Officers of State

Sponsor: King Humbert I

Place: Palais du Quirinal, Rome,
Italy

Date: February 19, 1898

Nearly the entire border surface of
this royal menu is embossed, and the
color is mixed and varied. The
central flat-surface portion of the
menu is light green printed in grey-
brown ink. This menu was designed
for a dinner given by King Humbert
I of Italy to the Diplomats and
Officers of State.

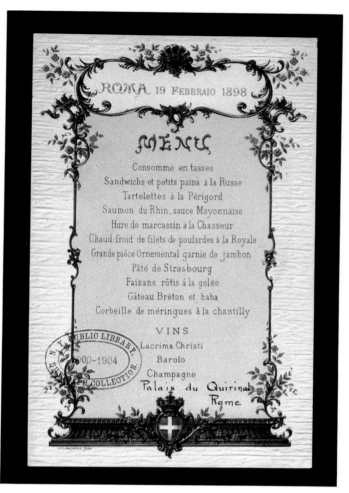

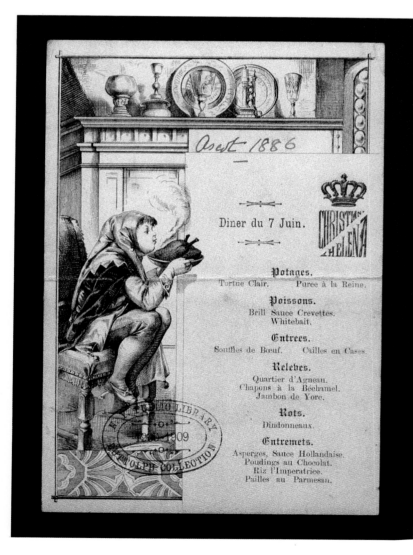

Occasion: Dinner at the Ascot Races

Sponsor: Prince Frederic-Christian of
Augustenbourg and his wife
Princess Helena of England

Date: June 7, 1886

The Ascot races of 1886 included this
dinner menu of Prince Frederic-
Christian and his wife, Princess
Helena of England, whose gold-
embossed appears at the right
margin. The rest of this one-side
card menu is simple black on white
printing, featuring pen-and-ink
illustration and lettering in French.
The back of this menu gives a
handwritten account of aristocrats in
attendance.

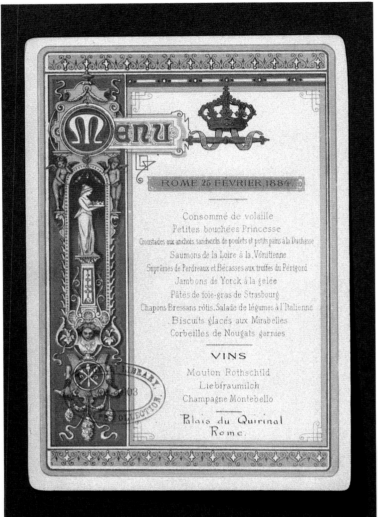

Occasion:	Royal Banquet for the Diplomat & State Offices
Sponsor:	King Umberto I of Italy
Place:	Palais du Quirinal, Rome, Italy
Date:	February 25, 1884

Red, blue and brown aquatint enhances the border design of this royal Italian menu. The one-side-printed card is 4 3/4"x6 3/4".

Occasion:	Royal Dinner
Sponsor:	King Leopold II of Belgium
Place:	Royal Palace at Laeken, Brussels, Belgium
Date:	July 1, 1899

Exquisite intricacy in the dry-embossed borders and royal seal of this menu are the spare but impressive design decorations. Printed one side only in brown and gold, this menu was used at a dinner of King Leopold II of Belgium in Brussels, 1899.

Occasion: 100th Anniversary
of Kaiser Wilhelm

Place: Hamburg, Germany (then
called Prussia)

Date: Friday, March 19th, 1897

One 13″x6″ cardboard sheet is
centerfolded lengthwise for this 1897
German menu. The front cover is
aglow with the full-color stippled
mezzotint portrait of Kaiser
Wilhelm, which is an embossed,
gold-lettered piece of dye-cut coated
stock mounted on the cardboard.
Color detail is magnificent in this
menu design. Inside, the menu and
music program are printed in deep
blue-green.

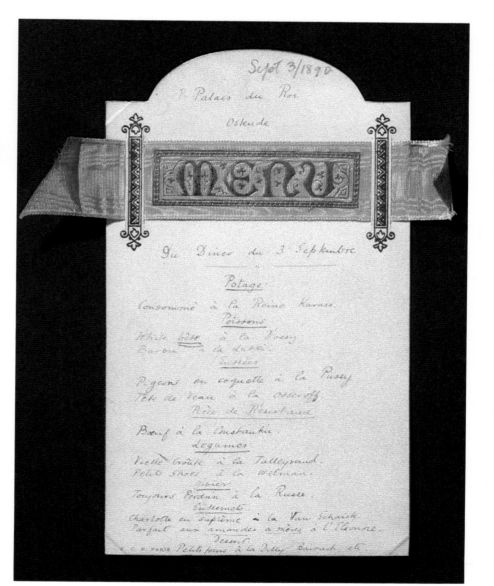

Occasion: Dinner

Date: September 3, 1890

The dye-cut edges of this royal menu
of 1890 are slightly beveled and
almost imperceptibly gilded as the
cardboard itself is rather thin. A
light-green ribbon embossed with
gold is drawn through two hand-cut
slits at either side; the slits, too, are
decoratively stenciled in gold. The
remainder of the lettering of this
menu is hand-inscribed in regal
purple ink.

Occasion: Concert Dinner to Kaiser Wilhelm of Germany (Prussia)

Sponsor: King Humbert of Italy

Place: King Humbert's Yacht "de Lutke," Naples, Italy

Date: October 17, 1888

This menu of the dinner given in honor of Kaiser Wilhelm by King Humbert is a masterful combination of German-Italian Design. The cover, of Italian design and print is a gold-laden array of royal coats of arms and opulent artistry in colorful aquatint. Inside are the menu and musical list, rendered in metallic red and gold. This portion of the design was printed by a German printhouse in Naples: "Richter & Company."

Occasion: Dinner Ball in honor of His Royal Highness, The Prince of Wales

Place: Delmonico's Hotel, New York City, NY

Date: October 12, 1860

One wide band (4 1/4"x6 1/4") of white silk ribbon was the medium for this gold-printed menu. Austere in design, the Victorian details of this menu are very minimal. The New York City dinner was held in conjunction with a ball in honor of the Prince of Wales in 1860.

DINER
DU 9 NOVEMBRE 1894.

Potages:
Tortue Clair
Crème de Concombres frais
Petits Pâtés
Sterlet à la Moscovite
Selle d'Agneau à la Richelieu
Suprême de Gélinottes aux petits Pois
Foie gras truffé garni de Mauviettes
Punch glacé
Dindonneaux à la broche
Salade
Asperges d'Argenteuil S^{ce} Hollandaise
Mazarin aux fruits
Bombe Napolitaine
Dessert.

Occasion: Dinner for the Crowned Heads of Europe who came to the Funeral of the Father of Czar Nicholas II (Czar Nicholas I)

Sponsor: Czar Nicholas II

Place: Moscow, Russia

Date: November 9, 1894

Excruciating detail is masterfully rendered in the handpainted embossed seal of this funeral dinner menu. Mere specks of color are applied with pinpoint accuracy to a menu otherwise devoid of decorative elements. The menu items are printed black on white; fittingly solemn but regal for the occasion of a Russian Czar's death.

Occasion: Dinner

Sponsor: Abdul-Hamid Khan, Sultan of Turkey

Place: Constantinople, Turkey

Date: June 29, 1893

A one-side printed piece of dye-cut white cardboard, this menu is dry-embossed at the edges for framing and gold-embossed with the Turkish seal at the top. It is printed in gold in two languages: in French at the left, and in Arabic at the right.

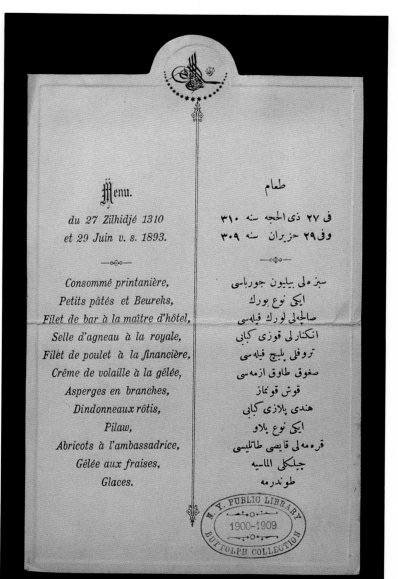

Occasion: Court Dinner for
               Protestants & Romanists

Sponsor: King Friedrich August II of
               Saxony

Place: Palais Royal, Dresden,
               Saxony

Date: July 1, 1842

One of the oldest menus of this
collection, this menu represents the
court dinner of King Friedrich
August II of Saxony for Protestants
and Romanists, given at the Royal
Palace in Dresden, July 1842.
Excepting the Gothic script at the
top, this menu is entirely
handwritten on white stationery
paper and mounted upon a thick
piece of charcoal-colored cardboard.
The menu items appear here in two
languages; an English translation
(not shown) was also provided for
this dinner.

Occasion: Coronation Dinner of King
               Wilhelm I of Prussia and
               Queen Augusta

Place: Koenigsberg, Prussia

Date: October 18, 1861

A gothic archway is created in the
black-on-white lithography of this
coronation day menu. Imbued with
the emblems and symbols of
Prussian royalty, this border design
is a frame to the menu items listed
within.

Occasion: Dinner for Senor Romero, Mexican Envoy

Place: Delmonico's Hotel, New York City, NY

Date: March 29, 1864

The electric-blue surface of this thick cardboard menu is printed in gold, making a striking statement of color. This menu was created for a dinner at Delmonico's, New York City, given to the Mexican Envoy, "Senior Romero," in 1864.

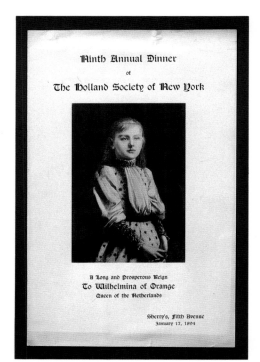

Occasion: 9th Annual Dinner

Sponsor: Holland Society of New York

Place: Sherry's, Fifth Avenue, New York City, NY

Date: January 17, 1894

This large (7"x10 1/4") menu is of one centerfolded sheet printed on two sides in black. One the front cover is an aquatint black-and-white portrait of Queen Wilhelmina of Orange, Queen of the Netherlands in 1894. On the menu's backside is a pen-and-ink drawing of country life in the Dutch Old World—an environ quite opposite that of the dinner, which was held at Sherry's on Fifth Avenue, New York City.

he only means of travel to Europe, South America, and other distant lands was the ocean liner. These "floating hotels" were luxurious and offered many amenities: private dining rooms, gymnasiums, game rooms, smoking parlours, ballrooms, shuffleboard courts, tennis courts, and so on. A person could choose to travel first class, second class, third class, or steerage.

First class passengers had their own dining room that offered sumptuous meals, fine wines and champagnes, and live orchestras.

The menus showcased in this section are all from first class accommodations. White Star Line, Olympia Line, and others are represented. Unfortunately, first class menus survived probably due to the fact that they were much more elaborate and ornate than their second and third class counterparts.

RAILROADS

The "iron horse" provided a link from New York to California that proved invaluable .

The railroad provided a faster means of transporting goods and passengers. Unfortunately, the train took approximately two weeks to get across the country, so dining services had to be provided. The menus were usually elaborate and highlighted a specific holiday or event.

HOTELS/RESTAURANTS

Restaurant menus, or bills of fare, were fairly plain in the 1800s. Special dishes and prices were the predominant items listed. Graphics and fancy type were hardly used, and the menus were usually hand lettered and disposed of at the end of the day.

Hotel menus were much more elaborate than restaurant menus. A hotel menu was usually printed and presented in a study form (leather, fabric, heavy cardboard) to present an air of grandeur, and to withstand the excessive handling by many guests.

Hotels usually contained the best restaurants in town, and in the smaller villages, the only restaurant in town. Hotels were the perfect spots for banquets, luncheons, and dinners, due to their grand size and their fine reputations.

Hotels usually offered special menus for each major holiday: Christmas, New Year's Day, Easter, Thanksgiving, and the Fourth of July. Many of these menus served as souvenirs of these special holidays and many elaborate and exotic designs and materials were utilized to enhance their "save" appeal.

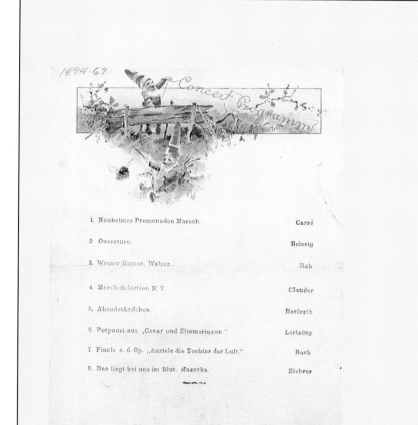

Concert Programm

1. Nauheimer Promenaden Marsch.   Carré

2 Ouverture.   Beissig

3. Wiener Humor. Walzer.   Rab

4. March-Selection N: 7.   Clauder

5. Abendständchen.   Herfurth

6. Potpouri aus „Czaar und Zimmermann."   Lortzing

7. Finale a. d. Op. „Auriele die Tochter der Luft."   Bach

8. Das liegt bei uns im Blut. Mazurka.   Ziehrer

MÜHLMEISTER & JOHLER, HAMBURG & BREMEN.

Occasion: Dinner

Place: The Brunswick, Boston MA

Date: April 25, 1880

The handcolored etching on this 3 3/ 4"x6 1/2" menu is unusually ornate. The flowers overpower the main subject of the illustration—the boat.

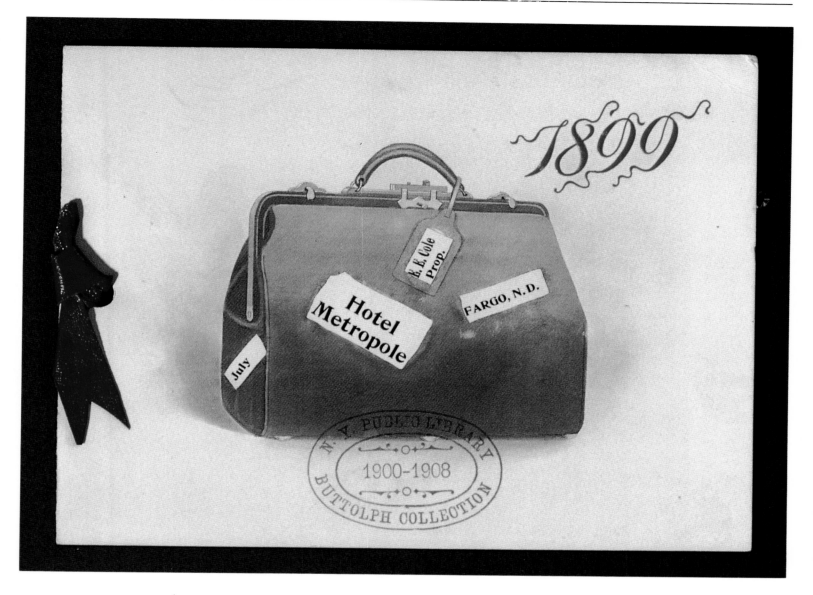

Occasion:	Dinner
Sponsor:	Hotel Metropole
Place:	Fargo, ND
Date:	July 30, 1899

Glossy thick stock, 5 1/2"x4" was printed in a two-color process and ornamented with the photograph and lithography which appears on the cover. Inside are two pages printed in one color. The unit is bound with leather ribbon.

Occasion: Dinner

Sponsor: King Humberto of Italy

Place: Rome, Italy

Date: January 24, 1893

This menu card showcases a lovely lithograph of a handtinted angel and a highly stylized monogram of King Humberto of Italy.

Occasion: Dinner

Place: Delmonico's, New York City, NY

Date: May 23, 1899

This Delmonico's menu card utilizes handcolored lithographs of dancing girls and ringleaders.

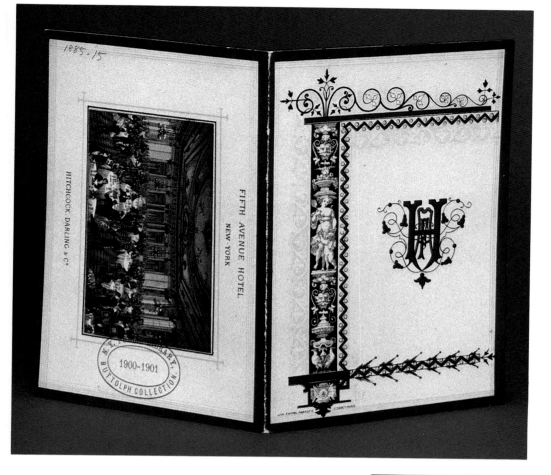

Occasion: Dinner

Place: Fifth Avenue Hotel, New York City, NY

Date: August 8, 1885

Lithographic design in heavy Victorian style is the basis for this New York menu of August 8, 1885. Contrasting the excess of decoration on its gold-laden covers, the black-bordered interior is a refreshingly plain display of the day's cuisine.

Occasion: Luncheon

Place: Grand Hotel

Date: November 11, 1899

This 3 1/4"x4 3/4", centerfolded, linen paper menu is small, yet sophisticated. Bright orange is used as a spot color with the brown lithograph of the riding helmet and crop. Navy blue is used to accent the ornate border.

Occasion: Dinner

Place: Buck & Langer, Rochester, NY

Date: July 16, 1884

This comical pen-and-ink handcolored cover is a nice touch on this 6″x9 1/2″ menu. The illustration is a cartoon look at how the Powers Hotel cares for its clients. Note that the clock reads 1 o'clock and the man is still serving dinner.

Occasion: Dinner

Place: Hotel Kaiserhof, Nordeney, Germany

Date: July 14, 1899

This menu uses a brown-black ink woodcut. Fine detailing is evident, and the use of red on the seal of the hotel, draws the viewer's eye.

Occasion: Dinner

Place: Casino Union, Manila, Philippines

Date: New Year's Eve, 1899

This textured paper, 3 1/4"x5 3/4" menu card is printed in beige, gold and green inks. The etching of Manila is extremely rough compared to its European contemporaries.

Occasion: Dinner

Place: Delmonico's, New York
               City, NY

Date: June 11, 1898

This silk ribbon menu uses blue ink
and a gold monogram of the guests'
initials. Blue design elements were
hand painted in oils to highlight the
gold-embossed monogram.

Occasion: Dinner

Sponsor: Grand Hotel—W.H.
               Burgess, Manager

Place: Melbourne, Australia

Date: October 13, 1899

Frame-within-a-frame dyecutting is
just a part of this sweet little
Australian menu. A single, white,
rectangular sheet, aquatinted in a
delicate floral print and lettered in
blue and gold, is mounted upon the
dyecut frame pieces. The trimming
designs are all in gold.

Occasion: Dinner

Place: Horse Shoe Hotel

Date: June 28, 1887

This full-color lithograph shows the Horse Shoe Hotel in beautiful detail and stresses its Old English Dinner by using Queen Victoria's portrait twice—as a young woman in 1837, and as she looked when this menu was printed in 1887.

Occasion: Dinner Menu

Place: Grand Union Hotel, Saratoga Springs, NY

Date: June 27, 1894

This centerfolded, 5 1/4"x6 3/4" full-color lithograph menu shows in great detail the Grand Union Hotel in Saratoga Springs, New York.

Occasion: Dinner

Sponsor: Hotel Marlbourgh

Place: Hotel Marlbourgh, New York City, NY

Date: February 22, 1893

Two-color (black and green) lithography is used for the cover of this raw-edged menu. The interior centerfold, printed in blue, is bound to this thick-stock cover sheet with a silk cord of gold, yellow and white fibers.

Occasion: Dinner

Place: Delmonico's, 12 East 70th Street, New York City, NY

Date: December 19, 1895

This 3 1/2″x6 1/2″ dye-cut border menu is extremely elegant—from the gold, silver and purple embossed edges to the paste-on mother-of-pearl portrait.

Huîtres
Potages
Consommé de volaille   Bisque d'écrevisses
Hors d'oeuvre
Mousseline, Isabelle
Poisson
Pompano, maître d'hôtel
Concombres
Pommes de terre, Duchesse
Relevé
Selle d'antilope, Athalie
Céleri braisé
Entrées
Artichauts à la Hollandaise

Terrapène à la Newberg

Sorbet, Montmorency
Rôt
Canards canvas-back
Tomates au céleri et laitues, mayonnaise
Fromage
Entremets de douceur
Pommes, Baron de Brisse
Glaces fantaisies
Fruits   Petits fours
Bonbons   Devises
Café

Jeudi le dix neuf Décembre, mil huit cent
quatre vingt quinz.
12 Est 70 Rue.
DELMONICOS

Occasion:	Dinner—Session of 1892—Trenton Sunday Press
Sponsor:	Trenton Sunday Press
Place:	Trent House, Trenton, NJ
Date:	March 9, 1892

Pen-and-ink tom foolery abounds on the cover of this newspaperman's dinner menu of 1892. The interior centerfold, comprising four pages, is printed in black on white. The grand finale of this design is the back cover drawing of the dinner's attendees—all "under the table" (which is littered with empty bottles). The caption reads: "No newspapers issued to-morrow."

MESSAGE FROM THE COOK.

Mr. President—A message from the Cook.
Mr. Katzenbach.
The Cook desires me to inform the Club and its guests that he has approved the following bills, and asks the concurrence of the company therein :

BILL WON—An act to propagate Blue Point Oysters, with Sauterne amendments.

BILL CHEW—An act for the better destruction of Irish Turtles and the eradication of red-head Radishes.

BILL THOMPSON—An act for the better removal of bones from Shad, with Claret amendments.

BILL 4-2-8—An act for the better encouragement of Confectioners and Bakers, with Mr. Mumm's bottled amendment.

BILL COONS—An act to protect Chickens after dark, particularly Coquetting Chicken.

CONCURRENT RESOLUTION—That it shall be unlawful for Terrapin to have diamonds on their backs when out in company, excepting those Sherry-fed.

BILL MULDOON—An act making Roman Punching the only legitimate sport for State symposium.

JOINT RESOLUTION—That the Game laws of this State be not enforced on this occasion, for Quail washed down with G. H. Mumm & Co.'s Extra Dry is enough to make Governors and Judges break the laws.

BILL HARRIGAN—All persons pocketing Cakes or Brie Cheese will be taken before the bar of the house for judgment.

BILLET DOUX—Coupes and messenger boys.

THE GAS METRE.

When the flow of gas registers ten minutes, the warning is given by a shrill cuckoo.

GOVERNOR ABBETT,
Any subject except Reporters.

PRESIDENT ADRAIN,
"Punch a la Sea Girt."

SPEAKER BERGEN,
"Pages."

GEN. SEWELL,
"The President's Duck."

JUDGE HENRY,
"Grown-up Girls."

SENATOR BARRETT,
"His War Record."

SENATOR MARSH,
"What is Elizabeth's last name?"

SENATOR HUDSPETH,
"Water."

Occasion:	Thanksgiving Dinner
Place:	Hotel Savoy, New York City, NY
Date:	November 30, 1899

This 6 1/2"x9 1/2" textured paper menu is one-side printed in brown. The brown woodcut of Thanksgiving is eerie (notice the large butcher knife in the foreground pointing at the turkey!)

Occasion: Dinner

Place: Delmonico's, New York
              City, NY

Date: March 31, 1881

A 4″x5″ piece of cardboard is mounted on large pink ribbon for this menu. All print is in black and a gilt, beveled edge was used on the cardboard to give a sophisticated feel to the menu.

Occasion: Dinner

Place: Menzies' Hotel, Melbourne,
              Australia

Date: July 29, 1899

This single-sheet menu contains a lovely, handcolored lithograph of seventeenth century noblemen eating dinner. The unusual centering of the type comprising the menu portion gives this menu an unusual graphic appeal.

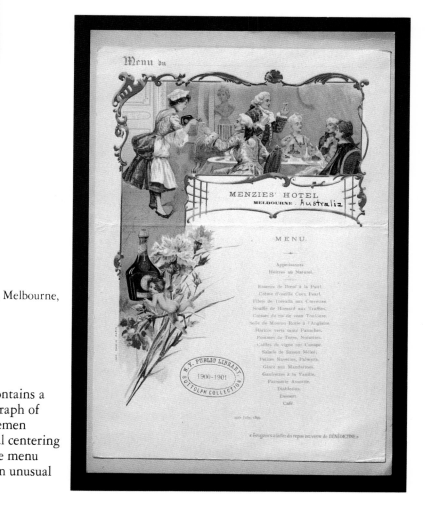

Occasion: Christmas Dinner

Sponsor: Lakota Hotel

Place: Chicago, IL

Date: Christmas 1897

Printed and copyrighted in Boston by L. Prang & Company, this 1898 Chicago Christmas menu also contains a calendar for the patron's use in 1899. "Pansies" is the color lithographic theme that is carried throughout the five-page unit. Each page is printed on one side with menu-related text, on the other with the calendar art. Beige satin ribbon serves as binding.

Marseilles   1894

MENU

16. VIII.

Dîner.

St. Germain

Merlan Ste Colbert

Pièce de bœuf braisée
                    Napolitaine

Volaille Demidoff

Fond d'Artichauts au
                    velouté

Pintadon rôti
                    Salade

Ponding Diplomate

Deserts

PLAN·GUIDE
DES
MONUMENTS
DE
MARSEILLE·

1 Station Saint-Charles	9 Palais de Longchamp	17 Église du Chapître
2 Grand Hôtel Louvre et Paix	10 Château-d'If	18 Docks
3 Bourse	11 Nouvelle Cathédrale	19 Temple Protestant
4 Mairie	12 Grand-Théâtre	20 English Church
5 Préfecture	13 Notre-Dame de la Garde	21 Hôtel-Dieu
6 Poste Centrale	14 Castellane	22 Palais de Justice
7 Abbaye de Saint-Victor	15 Château Borely	23 Faculté de Médecine
8 Bibliothèque	16 Porte d'Aix	24 Route de la Corniche
	25 Allées du Prado	

Occasion: Dinner

Place: Grand Hotel du Louvre & de la
             Paix, Marseille, France

Date: 1894

This blue-ink, fine-line engraving is
magnificent. Detail is apparent in
the buildings, the oceans, and the
scenes. Note that the engraving of
the hotel takes prominence by being
placed at a diagonal in the center of
the other four illustrations. The
inside back cover contains a detailed
map showing points of interest and
monuments in Marseille, circa 1894.

1894.37

GRAND HOTEL DU LOUVRE & DE LA PAIX

Le seul des grands Hôtels de Marseille sur la Cannebière, situé en plein Midi, avec la Lumière Électrique dans toutes les chambres.

Maison de tout premier ordre, se recommandant par son excellente Cuisine, la renommée de sa Cave qui ont fait depuis longtemps sa grande réputation, entièrement justifiée.

***

SUPERBE SALLE A MANGER

Restaurant - Fumoir - Salles de Bains

JARDIN D'HIVER

Téléphone - Ascenseur Hydraulique

ON PARLE TOUTES LES LANGUES

Renseignements complets sur les Départs & Arrivées des Bateaux de toutes les Compagnies.

OMNIBUS A TOUS LES TRAINS

1894

GRAND·HÔTEL DU LOUVRE & PAIX

V. NEUSCHWANDER, Marseille

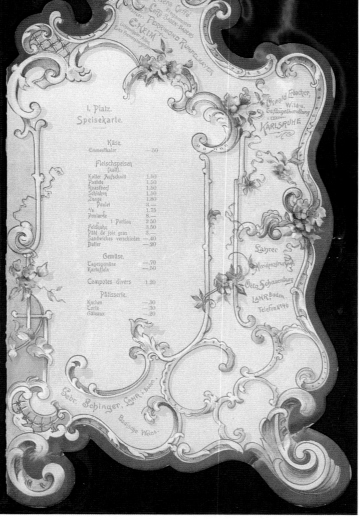

Occasion:	Dinner
Sponsor:	Riviera Caffee
Place:	Augustapratz, Germany
Date:	1897

Hardly a centimeter of this 1897 German menu remains uncolored or undecorated. Apparently used during the August horseracing season, this design starts with irregular-shaped dyecut paper printed in elaborate shades of wide-ranging aquatint color. Victorian borders are infused with entwined flowers and gold-leaf accents, and the free-flowing text is dispersed across the menu pages into unlikely areas of space. This menu is very large, measuring 11 3/4"x7".

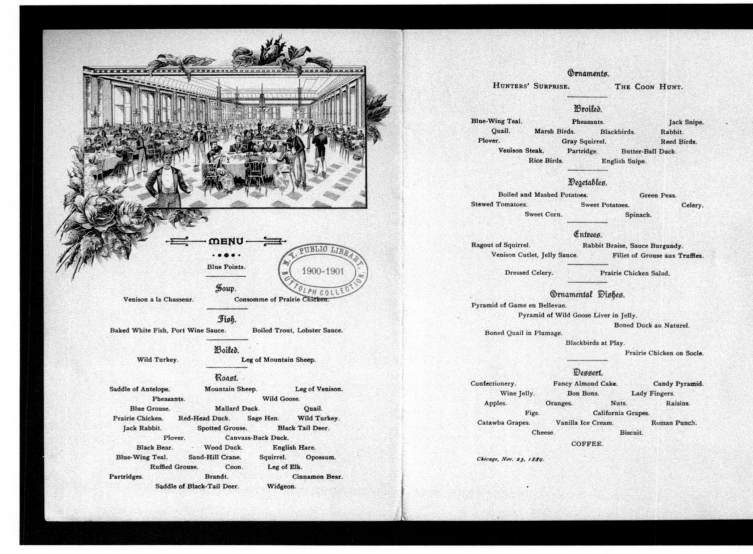

Ornaments.
HUNTERS' SURPRISE.   THE COON HUNT.

Broiled.
Blue-Wing Teal.   Pheasants.   Jack Snipe.
     Quail.   Marsh Birds.   Blackbirds.   Rabbit.
Plover.   Gray Squirrel.   Reed Birds.
     Venison Steak.   Partridge.   Butter-Ball Duck.
          Rice Birds.   English Snipe.

Vegetables.
     Boiled and Mashed Potatoes.   Green Peas.
Stewed Tomatoes.   Sweet Potatoes.   Celery.
          Sweet Corn.   Spinach.

Entrees.
Ragout of Squirrel.   Rabbit Braise, Sauce Burgundy.
     Venison Cutlet, Jelly Sauce.   Fillet of Grouse aux Truffles.

     Dressed Celery.   Prairie Chicken Salad.

Ornamental Dishes.
Pyramid of Game en Bellevue.
          Pyramid of Wild Goose Liver in Jelly.
                    Boned Duck au Naturel.
     Boned Quail in Plumage.
               Blackbirds at Play.
                    Prairie Chicken on Socle.

Dessert.
Confectionery.   Fancy Almond Cake.   Candy Pyramid.
     Wine Jelly.   Bon Bons.   Lady Fingers.
     Apples.   Oranges.   Nuts.   Raisins.
          Figs.   California Grapes.
Catawba Grapes.   Vanilla Ice Cream.   Roman Punch.
          Cheese.   Biscuit.
                    COFFEE.

Chicago, Nov. 23, 1889.

MENU
· · · ·
Blue Points.

Soup.
Venison a la Chasseur.   Consomme of Prairie Chicken.

Fish.
Baked White Fish, Port Wine Sauce.   Boiled Trout, Lobster Sauce.

Boiled.
Wild Turkey.   Leg of Mountain Sheep.

Roast.
Saddle of Antelope.   Mountain Sheep.   Leg of Venison.
          Pheasants.   Wild Goose.
     Blue Grouse.   Mallard Duck.   Quail.
Prairie Chicken.   Red-Head Duck.   Sage Hen.   Wild Turkey.
     Jack Rabbit.   Spotted Grouse.   Black Tail Deer.
          Plover.   Canvass-Back Duck.
     Black Bear.   Wood Duck.   English Hare.
Blue-Wing Teal.   Sand-Hill Crane.   Squirrel.   Opossum.
          Ruffled Grouse.   Coon.   Leg of Elk.
Partridges.   Brandt.   Cinnamon Bear.
     Saddle of Black-Tail Deer.   Widgeon.

Occasion:	Dinner—34th Annual Game Dinner
Sponsor:	The Grand Pacific Hotel
Place:	The Grand Pacific Hotel, Chicago, IL
Date:	November 23, 1889

One large sheet of coated stock is centerfolded to form this 1889 menu. The cover is a combination of a charcoal drawing of flowers and birds and a lithographic illustration of the Grand Pacific Hotel in Chicago; inside is the restaurant's main dining room. The back cover contains a humorous charcoal drawing of a group of bears taking revenge on a hunter and his dog.

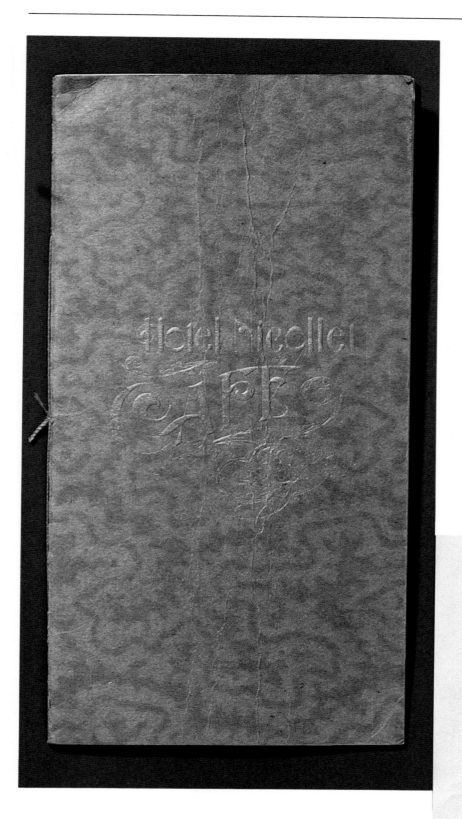

Occasion: Dinner

Sponsor: Hotel Nicollet Cafe—
Shattuck & Wood,
Proprietors

Place: Minneapolis, MN

Date: April 1894

The texture of the paper used for
this menu is a Victorian pattern in
two shades of green. Gold embossing
and printing appear on the front.
The white inner pages are printed in
black and accented in red, but their
most unusual aspect is that they are
cut at the right margin to form
labeled tabs.

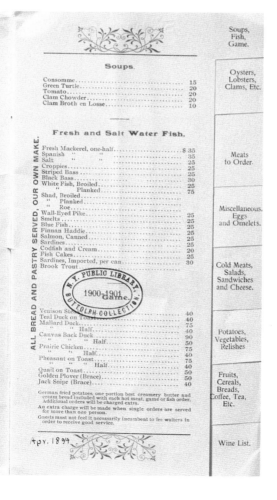

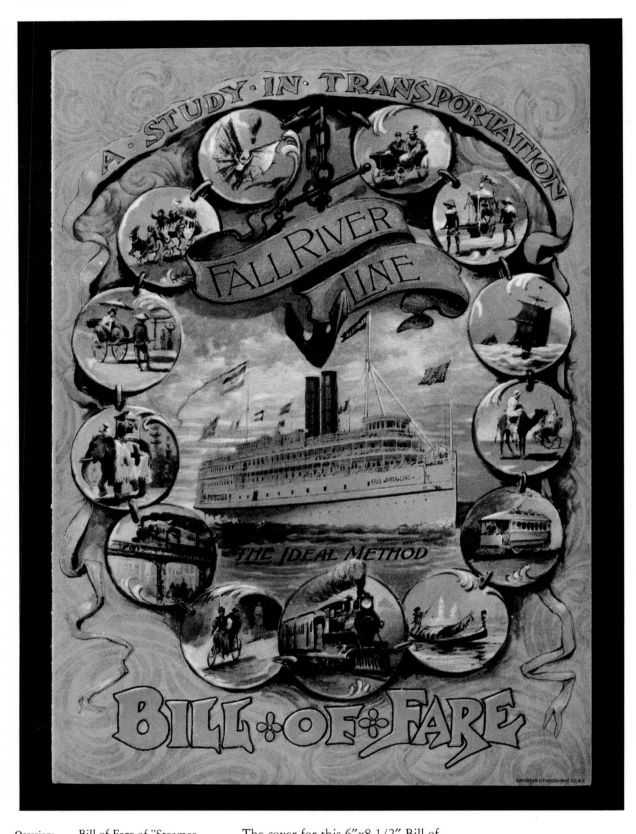

Occasion:	Bill of Fare of "Steamer Priscilla"
Sponsor:	Fall River Line
Date:	1899

The cover for this 6"x8 1/2" Bill of Fare for the Steamer Priscilla offers us "A Study in Transportation." The Fall River Line presents a montage of diverse methods of transportation shown in a beautifully detailed full-color watercolor on coated paper.

Occasion: Bill of Fare aboard "La Gascogne"

Sponsor: Compagnie Generale Transatlantique

Date: March 5, 1887

The cover for this 1887 menu for the La Gascogne is a colorful aquatint reproduction of the ship. The 4 3/4" x7 1/4" menu is printed on heavyweight paper with the cover side in full color and the second side in two-color printing.

Occasion: Dinner Aboard the Ship
            "Princesse Clementine"

Sponsor: A. Stracke

Date: August 21, 1897

This 1897 dinner menu for the
Princesse Clementine is printed on
heavyweight centerfolded 3"x5 1/2"
stock. The cover design is a
classically inspired three-color
lithograph.

MENU
DU
Déjeûner-Dînatoire
servi à bord du bateau
PRINCESSE CLÉMENTINE
le 21 Août 1897.

POTAGE.
Bouillon à la Princesse (en tasses)

RELEVÉ DE POISSON,
Filets de Soles d'Ostende à la Joinville
Pommes de terre nouvelles

RELEVÉ DE BOUCHERIE.
Cœur de Filet de Bœuf à la Lucullus

ENTRÉE.
Noisette de Chevreuil à la Perigueux
Chaud-froid de Volaille à la Russe

LÉGUMES.
Petits Pois à la Léopold II

ROTIS.
Cailles d'Italie sur Canapé
Homards de Norwège en Belle Vue,
sauce Ravigote

ENTREMETS.
Pouding à la Diplomate sce Sabayon
au Champagne

FRUITS.
Raisins, Pêches, Poires, Brugnons,
Reines-Claude, etc., etc.

PATISSERIE VARIÉ.

DESSERTS ASSORTIS.

A. Stracké, traiteur de la Cour de Sa Majesté
le Roi de Wurtemberg et de S. A. R. le Duc
Alfred de Saxe-Cobourg-Gotha; Restaurateur
des Paquebots-Poste de l'État belge entre
Ostende-Douvres.

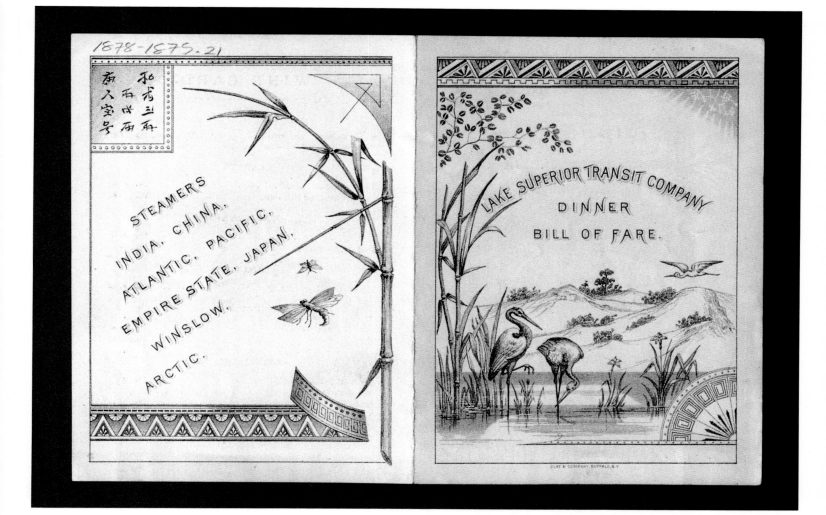

1878-1875.21

和光三雨
西咸雨
南入客号

STEAMERS
INDIA, CHINA,
ATLANTIC, PACIFIC,
EMPIRE STATE, JAPAN,
WINSLOW,
ARCTIC.

LAKE SUPERIOR TRANSIT COMPANY
DINNER
BILL OF FARE.

CLAY & COMPANY, BUFFALO, N.Y.

Occasion: Bill of Fare aboard the
             Steamer "China"

Sponsor: Lake Superior Transit
             Company

Date: June 21, 1879

The Bill of Fare aboard the Steamer
China reflects the oriental theme
with designs of Chinese characters
and an ornamental fan accenting the
cover designs. The 3 1/2"x4 3/4"
menu is printed in single color on
colored lightweight stock.

Occasion: Banquet for the Sailors &
             Marines of the "U.S.S.
             Olympia"

Sponsor: Randolph Guggenheimer,
             Chairman

Place: The Waldorf-Astoria Hotel,
             New York City, NY

Date: 1899

This program for the banquet to
honor the sailors and marines of the
U.S.S. Olympia looks very patriotic
with its two-color printing in red
and blue on 6 1/2"x12" white
cardboard stock.

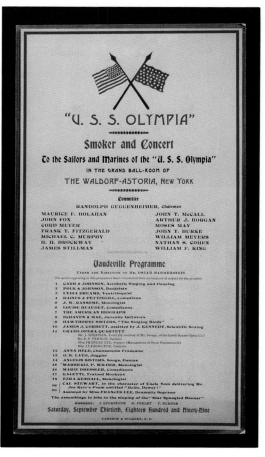

"U. S. S. OLYMPIA"
Smoker and Concert
To the Sailors and Marines of the "U. S. S. Olympia"
IN THE GRAND BALL-ROOM OF
THE WALDORF-ASTORIA, NEW YORK

Committee
RANDOLPH GUGGENHEIMER, Chairman

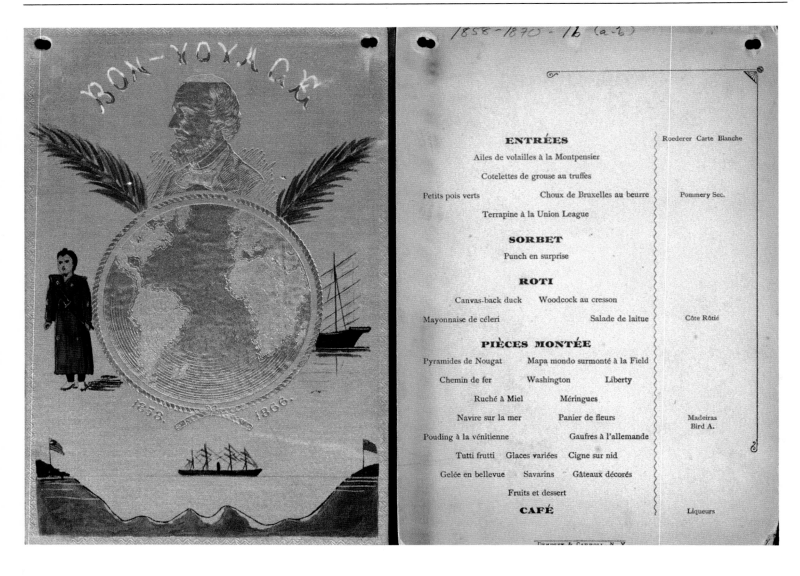

Occasion: Bon Voyage Party Dinner
            for Cyrus W. Field

Sponsor: A few of his personal
            friends

Place: Union League Club

Date: October 26, 1880

A *bon voyage* party for Cyrus W. Field was the occasion for this striking menu. It is satin covered 0.3″ cardboard with a handpainted design surrounding a lithograph printed in gold on the front with single color printing (black) on the back.

Occasion: Bill of Fare aboard "S.S. Waesland"

Sponsor: Red Star Line

Date: June 9, 1892

This 1892 centerfolded menu from the S.S. Waesland has a richly colored aquatint design on the cover. The 4 1/4"x7" menu was printed on heavyweight paper with full-color on the front and back covers and two-color printing inside—black and red.

Occasion: Bill of Fare aboard "S.S.
                Fulda"

Sponsor: Norddeutscher Lloyd
                Bremen Ship Lines

Date: September 23, 1894

This Bill of Fare for the S.S. Fulda's
1894 Bremen to New York crossing
is a three page two-sided menu
printed on heavyweight 5 1/4"x7 1/
2" linen paper. Its cover is a colorful
lithograph of a shipboard scene with
an inset of the ship.

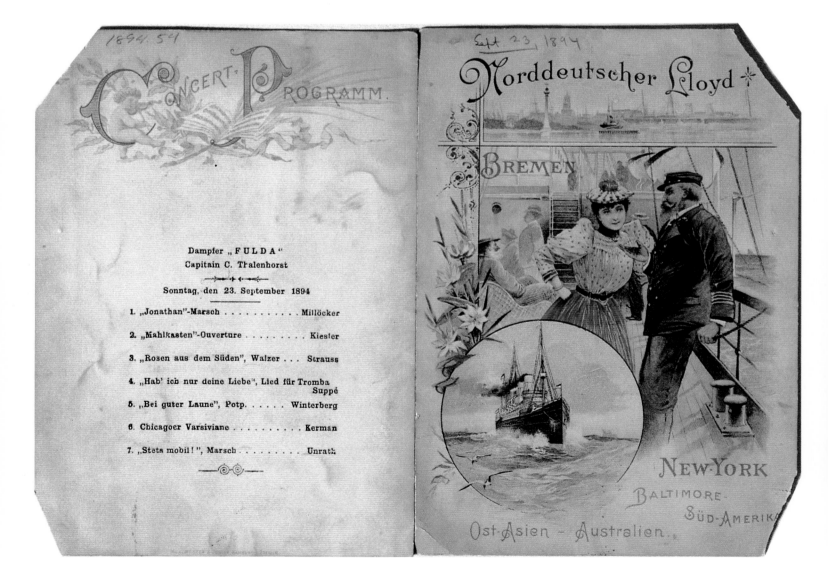

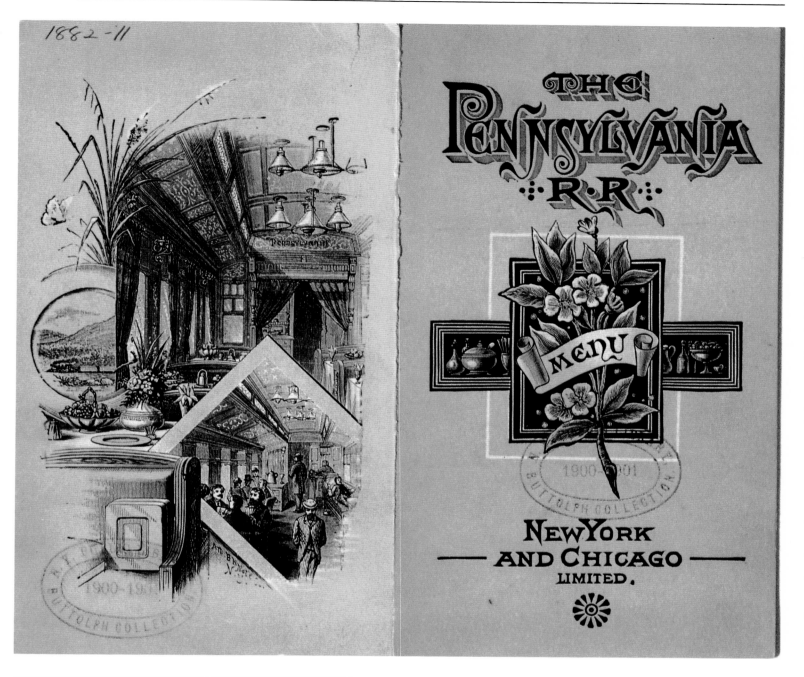

Occasion: The New York and Chicago Limited

Sponsor: The Pennsylvania Railroad Menu

Place: Dining Car

Date: Autumn 1882

The Pennsylvania Railroad's menu for its New York and Chicago Limited is printed in black and white on brown stock. The 3 1/2"x6" menu features a two-color lithograph on the covers with engraved borders of vines and branches in a faint white on the inside.

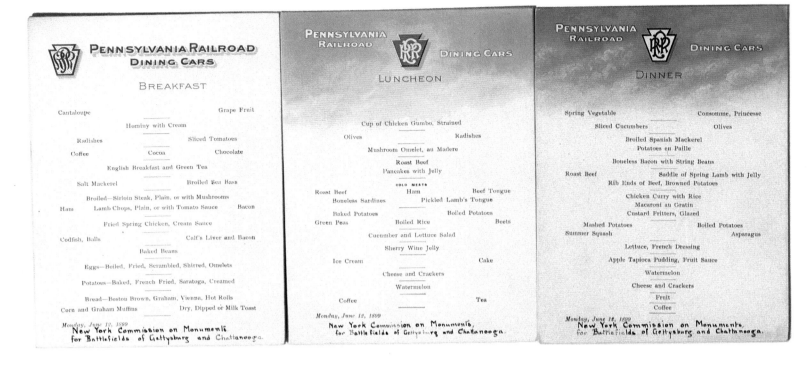

Cantaloupe   Grape Fruit

Hominy with Cream

Radishes   Sliced Tomatoes

Coffee   Cocoa   Chocolate

English Breakfast and Green Tea

Salt Mackerel   Broiled Sea Bass

Broiled—Sirloin Steak, Plain, or with Mushrooms

Ham   Lamb Chops, Plain, or with Tomato Sauce   Bacon

Fried Spring Chicken, Cream Sauce

Codfish, Balls   Calf's Liver and Bacon

Baked Beans

Eggs—Boiled, Fried, Scrambled, Shirred, Omelets

Potatoes—Baked, French Fried, Saratoga, Creamed

Bread—Boston Brown, Graham, Vienna, Hot Rolls

Corn and Graham Muffins   Dry, Dipped or Milk Toast

Monday, June 12, 1899
New York Commission on Monuments
for Battlefields of Gettysburg and Chattanooga.

PENNSYLVANIA RAILROAD   DINING CARS

LUNCHEON

Cup of Chicken Gumbo, Strained

Olives   Radishes

Mushroom Omelet, au Madere

Roast Beef

Pancakes with Jelly

COLD MEATS

Roast Beef   Ham   Beef Tongue
Boneless Sardines   Pickled Lamb's Tongue

Baked Potatoes   Boiled Potatoes
Green Peas   Boiled Rice   Beets

Cucumber and Lettuce Salad

Sherry Wine Jelly

Ice Cream   Cake

Cheese and Crackers

Watermelon

Coffee   Tea

Monday, June 12, 1899
New York Commission on Monuments,
for Battlefields of Gettysburg and Chattanooga.

PENNSYLVANIA RAILROAD   DINING CARS

DINNER

Spring Vegetable   Consomme, Princesse

Sliced Cucumbers   Olives

Broiled Spanish Mackerel
Potatoes en Paille

Boneless Bacon with String Beans

Roast Beef   Saddle of Spring Lamb with Jelly
Rib Ends of Beef, Browned Potatoes

Chicken Curry with Rice
Macaroni au Gratin
Custard Fritters, Glazed

Mashed Potatoes   Boiled Potatoes
Summer Squash   Asparagus

Lettuce, French Dressing

Apple Tapioca Pudding, Fruit Sauce

Watermelon

Cheese and Crackers

Fruit

Coffee

Monday, June 12, 1899
New York Commission on Monuments,
for Battlefields of Gettysburg and Chattanooga.

Occasion: Luncheon/Dinner/Breakfast

Sponsor: New York Commission on Monuments for Battlefields of Gettysburg and Chattanooga

Place: Pennsylvania Railroad Dining Cars

Date: June 12, 1899

These three menus from the Pennsylvania Railroad Dining Cars for June 12, 1899 are printed in two colors on 4 3/4"x6 1/2" heavy stock and all feature the embossed logo of the Pennsylvania Railroad. The breakfast menu is printed on plain white paper, while on the lunch menu there is a rose-tinted design at the top of the page; on the dinner menu, the design is in blue.

Occasion: Unknown

Sponsor: The Bass Rock

Place: Gloucester, MA

Date: August 15, 1888

This 3 3/4"x5" menu printed on glossy stock is decorated with an oil painting of a richly colored, realistic still life.

Occasion:	Dinner Menu
Sponsor:	The Van Nuys Restaurant
Place:	Los Angeles, CA
Date:	April 24, 1897

This 1897 menu for the Van Nuys Restaurant has delicate hand-painted violets and silver embossed lettering on its cover. It is bound with a purple satin ribbon, and the inside text in both French and English is printed in purple.

Occasion:	Daily Menu
Sponsor:	Cafeteria
Place:	Cafeteria, 57 Broad Street, New York, NY
Date:	December 29, 1899, December 26, 1899, December 28, 1899

This 5 1/2″x9 1/2″ menu printed on heavy glossy stock in a single color looks like a typical cafeteria menu. However, when turned over, the back is filled with handwritten specials and large pen and ink caricatures.

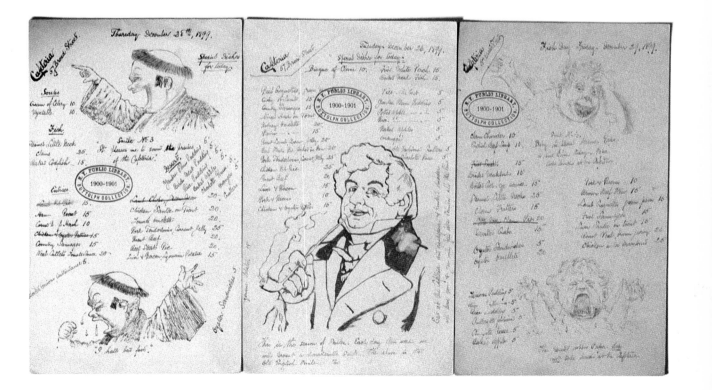

CHAPTER 7 Miscellaneous

oreign menus and menus from special occasions (weddings, showers, etc.) are displayed in this chapter.

Exotic feathers, fine fabrics, hand-tooled leathers, and handpainted artwork are represented. Many of these menus are unusually large or extremely diminutive and served as keepsakes after the occasion for which they were used ended.

GÂTEAU A LA VICTORIA.

Ant´ hr tn á ānu rҳī

ҳt áu tn hr īī m ta r t´r

f hr māᵉn nt báa n

p-t mropu hr ut´-ur

ámmā árī tn hāu qau

ámmā snb tn ámmā ānҳ

tn nt´m mā qtau nt´m naī

nu ta.

Salut à vous! ô scribes et savants!
qui êtes venus de toute la terre
par chemin de fer ou par mer.
Que votre vie soit d'une longue durée,
que vous soyez en bonne santé,
que votre sort soit doux, comme doux sont nos gâteaux!

Hiéroglyphique.

J. LIEBLEIN.

Occasion: Dinner

Sponsor: 8th International Congress of Orientalists

Place: Stockholm, Sweden

Date: September 1, 1889

This 5 1/4"x9" menu is in booklet form, and served as a menu/souvenir for the 8th International Congress of Orientalists held in Stockholm in 1889. The cover is a beautifully detailed, colorful lithograph with an unusual oriental design. This menu was printed in over 22 languages including: Akkadia, Japanese, Persian, and Hieroglyphics.

POTAGE A LA SUÉDOISE.

瑞典羹詩

皆 漢 駝 李 伊 彭
豈 章 蹄 德 尹 鏗
及 帝 羹 羹 烹 斟
瑞 龍 一 直 鵠 雄
羹 羹 甌 三 鳥 帝
之 絕 千 百 之 何
艮 香 兩 縆 羹 饗

Phing-kien servait un potage «aux faisans», et l'Empereur (Yao) le dégustait;
I-yin bouillait un potage de «cygnes»;
Le potage de *Li-Tih-jou* coûtait 300,000 sapèques;
Et un plat de potage «aux pieds de Chameaux» coûtait mille onces d'argent;
Le potage »aux Dragons" de l'empereur *Tchang* de la dynastie de *Han* était odorant;
Mais peuvent-ils être comparés à l'excellence du potage suédois!

Chinois.

GUSTAVE SCHLEGEL.

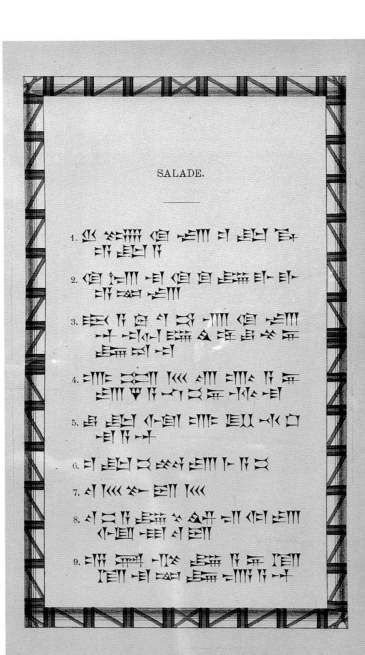

SALADE.

1. cuneiform text
2. cuneiform text
3. cuneiform text
4. cuneiform text
5. cuneiform text
6. cuneiform text
7. cuneiform text
8. cuneiform text
9. cuneiform text

DESSERT INTERNATIONAL.

Classisches Japanisch.

Dr. ISUBOI.

VIN DE BORDEAUX.

Langue de Babel.   PAUL HAUPT.

REMERCÎMENT POUR LE REPAS.

خوان سپاس

(۱)

كاعست كه پاس وسپاس آريم

زين بزم ستبرك هنرمندان

واميست كذار كه بگزاريم

اين وام همى زين دندان

(۲)

بزميست همايون وشاعانه

دروى زهنر ورو فرزانه

چندان كه ندانيم بديانه

در بزمكه خرد يونان

(۳)

بنكر بسخن سنجان بنكر

اين جشن برايكان مشمر

زين كوند سخن سنجان ايدر

سود آنچه توان بستد بستان

(۴)

جشنى بين برده زمينورنك

ياران همه با فرو با فرهنك

جانها پاكى دلها بى زنك

زين به جشنى ديكر نتوان

Occasion: Dinner

Sponsor: 8th International Congress
             of Orientalists

Place: Stockholm, Sweden

Date: September 1, 1889

This 5 1/4"x9" menu is in booklet
form, and served as a menu/souvenir
for the 8th International Congress of
Orientalists held in Stockholm in
1889. The cover is a beautifully
detailed, colorful lithograph with an
unusual oriental design. This menu
was printed in over 22 languages
including: Akkadia, Japanese,
Persian, and Hieroglyphics.

Occasion: Coronation of Czar Nicholas Alexandrovich and Czarina Alexandra Feodorovna

Place: St. Petersburg, Russia

Date: May 14, 1896

This breathtaking, full-color lithographed menu is an impressive 11 1/2"x36 1/2". It commemorates the coronation of Czar Nicholas Alexandrovich and Czarina Alexandra Feodorovna, the last Czar and Czarina of Russia.

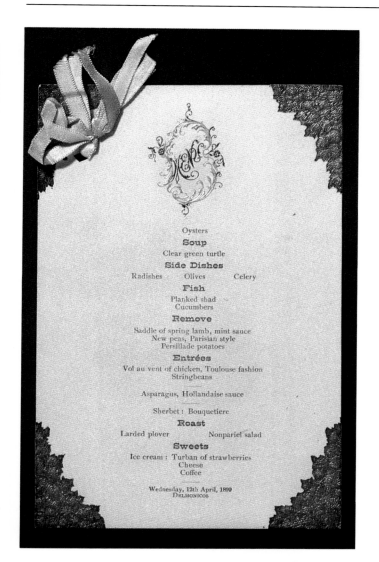

Occasion: Wedding Menu

Sponsor: Unknown

Place: Delmonico's, New York City, NY

Date: April 12, 1899

This elegant wedding banquet menu is printed one-side in gold; the corners are also embossed in gold. The caption "menu" is gold-embossed with a stylized silver-embossed "D" around it. The upper lefthand corner is hole punched and blue and white ribbons are pulled through and tied into a decorative bow.

Occasion: Banquet for J.L. and S.E.L.

Sponsor: Unknown

Place: Delmonico's, Madison Square, New York City, NY

Date: April 18, 1899

This 1899 Delmonico's menu is striking in the detailed, full-color lithograph on its front cover. The masked harlequin is dancing with two finely-dressed ladies. The inside of this 4″x5 1/2″ cardboard, centerfolded menu is printed in black ink.

Occasion:	Dinner for Mr. Lawrence Barrett
Sponsor:	Mr. Wilson Barrett
Place:	Langham Hotel, London, England
Date:	April 2, 1884

This 3 1/2"x5 1/2" menu is dye-cut into the shape of a Japanese room screen. The Japanese design is printed on the covers in brown, gold and dark pink. The interior is printed gold, green and blue.

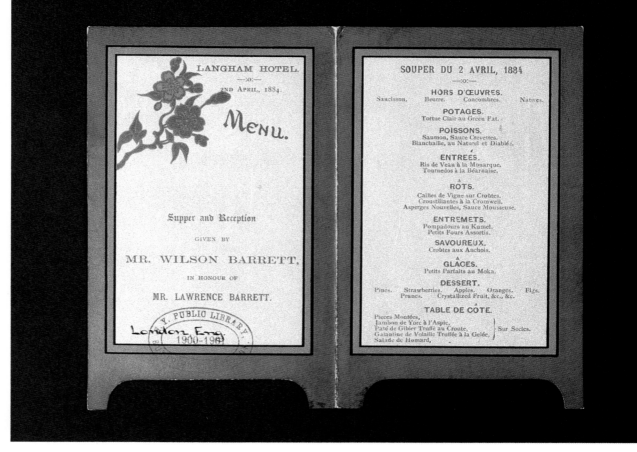

Occasion: Dinner

Sponsor: A. M. Palmer

Place: Unknown

Date: March 10, 1886

This dye-cut palette shaped menu is completely hand-lettered; the lithograph of the boy and girl fishing are handcolored. A crimson satin ribbon is tied through the dye cut hole for decoration.

Occasion: Dinner

Date: Valid 1882-1901

A strip of tickets is a clever way to highlight a dinner. The tickets are lightweight cardboard (green (front)/orange (back)) and are joined in a strip. Note that each ticket is not perforated but folded. The type is printed in black ink.

'Now good digestion wait on
appetite
and health on both!"
Shaks.

February 9, 1899

Menu

Oysters on half shell

Soup
Green Turtle Melée

Fish
Filet of Bass à la Joinville
Potatoes Parisienne
Olives   Salt Almonds

Entree
Patés à la Financiére
Filet Mignon saute à la Perigeux
French Peas   Potatoes Duchesse
Sorbet au Kirsch

Game
English Partridge
Salad

Dessert
Ices in Fancy Forms
Assorted Cakes   Petits Fours

Coffee

Occasion:	Dinner
Sponsor:	Architectural League
Place:	Unknown
Date:	February 9, 1899

This 6″x9″ handpainted water color menu is unusual in that the menu portion is gold ink printed, while everything else is hand done on this cardboard piece. The young gentleman is sitting on a pile of books, while at his feet lies 2 urns and a bowl of fruit. The quote from Shakespeare may allude that the gentleman could be Hamlet, or another character from one of Shakespeare's plays.

Occasion: Dinner—Union League Club

Sponsor: Union League Club

Place: Philadelphia, PA

Date: May 9, 1879

This Japanese design menu is from the 1879 Union League Club Annual Dinner. The beautiful Japanese, full-color lithograph is by Tiffany & Co. The reverse side of this 5 1/2″x8 3/4″ single sheet menu is printed solely in red ink and contains the name of the sponsor and the date in a decorative border.

Occasion: Funerary Dinner

Sponsor: Troy House--L. Collins, Proprietor

Place: Troy, NY

Date: July 28, 1885

This black cardboard menu was specifically printed for a funerary dinner. All of the print is in silver ink.

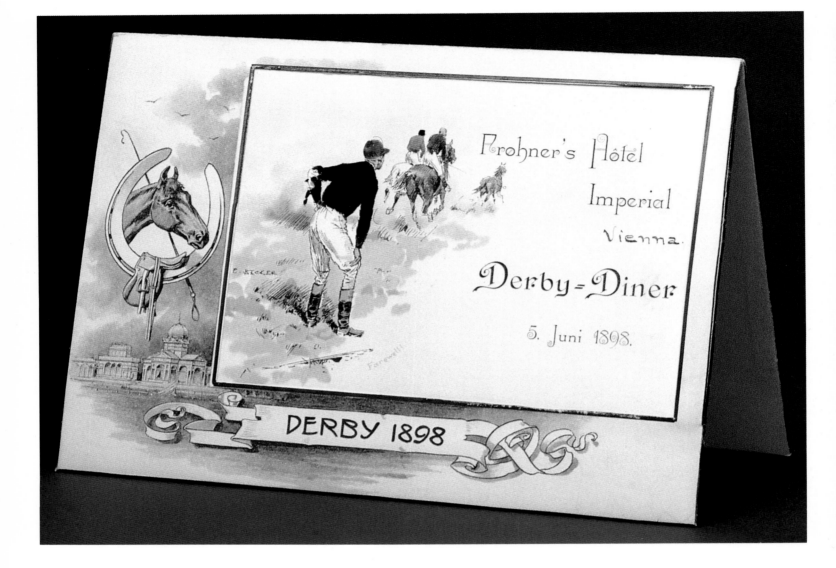

Occasion: Derby Dinner

Place: Frohner's Hotel Imperial—
Vienna, Austria

Date: June 5, 1898

This menu card is to commemorate the Derby of 1898. The cover is a lithograph with a dye-cut window to showcase an insert with the occasion and hotel name on it. Notice the handcolored etching on the insert.

Occasion: Farewell Subscription Banquet

Sponsor: Boston-Franklin Exhibition

Place: Quincy House, Boston, MA

Date: January 17, 1884

This centerfolded, kraft paper menu contains pen-and-ink lithographs printed in green ink! The menu is printed on the inside in light grey ink and is almost impossible to read. The illustrations are very bizarre and include beggars, a naked nymph, a funerary urn, various cameras, a lion's head, a drunk nobleman, a brawl with a Chinese gentleman lying in the foreground, and a doctor.

Occasion: Cafeteria Lunch Restaurant

Place: 57 Broad Street, New York
               City, NY

Date: December 16, 1899

This restaurant menu is one sheet of
cardboard. One side is printed in
black and contains the regular menu.
The back of the menu contains an
ink drawing with the specials of the
day.

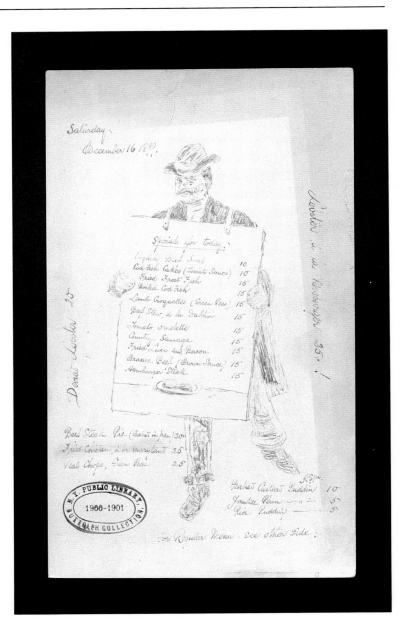

Occasion: Unknown

Sponsor: Unknown

Place: Hotel Savoy, New York
               City, NY

Date: April 19, 1899

This 2 3/4"x6 1/2" parchment
paper menu is unusual, with its
partially dye-cut edges, embossed in
silver. The caption "menu" is silver
embossed, while the listings are
printed in light green ink.

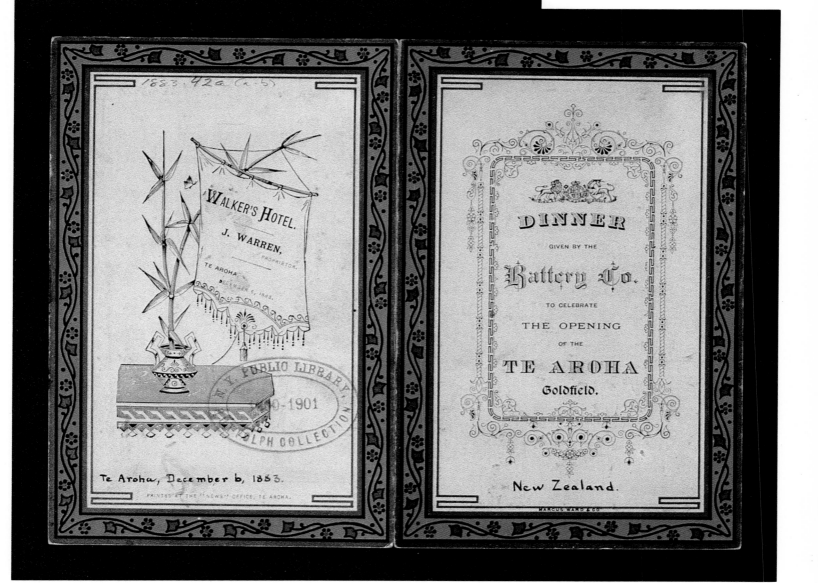

MENU.

POTAGES.
White Oyster. | Kidney.

ENTREMETS.
Lobster Patties.
Fricassee of Chicken.
Lamb Cutlets and Peas.
Stewed Duck and Olives.

REMOVES.
Canterbury Hams.
Boiled Turkeys, Celery Sauce.
Roast Sucking Pigs.
Spring Lamb and Mint Sauce.
Ox Tongues.
Roast Chickens.
Roast Geese.
Sirloins of Beef.

ENTREMETS.
Gateaux a la "Butler's Spur."
Lemon Jelly a la "Premier."
Blancmange a la "New Find."
"Colonist" Puddings.
"Waiorongamai" Tartlets.
"Mata Mata" Cheese-cakes.
"Waihou" Plum Puddings.
Fanchonettes a la "Inverness."

Bonne Bouches a la "Dividends."

Celery and Cheese. | Dessert in Season.

TOASTS.

1. The Queen.

2. His Excellency the Governor.

3. The General Assembly.

4. The Te Aroha Goldfield.

5. The Piako County Council.

6. The Captains of Industry.

Occasion: Dinner—The Opening of the Te Aroha Goldfield

Sponsor: Battery Co.

Place: Walker's Hotel, Te Aroha, New Zealand

Date: December 6, 1883

This 3 1/2"x5" menu is black and gold ink printed on centerfolded, green cardboard. The back cover contains a pen-and-ink lithograph in black of bamboo shoots in a vase.

WALKER'S HOTEL.
J. WARREN,
PROPRIETOR.

TE AROHA
DECEMBER 6, 1883.

Te Aroha, December 6, 1883.

PRINTED AT THE "NEWS" OFFICE, TE AROHA.

DINNER

GIVEN BY THE

Battery Co.

TO CELEBRATE

THE OPENING

OF THE

TE AROHA
Goldfield.

New Zealand.

MARCUS WARD & CO.

Occasion: Unknown

Sponsor: Unknown

Place: Dresden, Germany

Date: February 27, 1897

This simple menu card is a full-color, handtinted lithograph. The type is a stylized script and in German. The edges are printed in gold ink.

Occasion: Restaurant Menu

Sponsor: The Pure Food Cafe

Place: Stewart Bldg. NW corner Washington and State Streets, Washington, DC

Date: November 16, 1898

This 4 3/4"x7" menu is made up of trifolded green construction paper. The items are listed in red ink, the prices in green ink. The cover contains the name of the restaurant in red ink and a decorative border in green ink.

Menu
den 27. Februar 1897.

Austern.

Suppe.

Lachsforelle.

Filet mit Gänseleber.
Frische Rinderbrust.

Langusten.

Junge Enten.

Cardis mit Mark.
Frische Bohnen.

Eis.

Special
Table
d'Hote
Dinner

5 to 8 P. M.—35cts.

Table d'Hote

35 CENTS

Split Green Pea Soup or Mock Oyster Soup

Cereal Veal Cutlet, with cream horseradish
and mashed turnips
or
Vegetable Croquette a la Jardiniere, mashed potatoes

Salads

Celery   String Bean   Lettuce   Pea

Sago-Custard
or
Apple Cobbler

Coffee, Tea, Caramel-cereal, Cocoa Milk or Buttermilk

THURSDAY, NOVEMBER 16, 1899

A la Carte

Minimum Charge 15c.

Soup
Split Green Pea Soup 10   Puree of Tomato 10
Mock Oyster Soup 10

Entremets
Cereal Veal Cutlet, cream horseradish, mashed turnips 20
Vegetable Croquettes a la Jardinere 20
Poached Egg, with cheese and cream 25
Omelette, with tomato 25
Our Baked Beans 10   Spaghetti a la Mortimer 10

Eggs
Shirred 20   Scrambled 20   Poached 20   Poached on Toast 25
Fried 20   with Nut Brown Butter 25
The Sirdar's Favorite 25
Bread and Butter Included

Omelettes
Omelette, plain 20   Spanish 25   Italian 25   Jelly Omelette 30
Vegetable Omelette 25   Parsley 25
Bread and Butter Included

Salads
Protose en Mayonnaise 10
Lima Bean 10   Banana en Mayonnaise 10
Lettuce en Mayonnaise 10   Celery Salad 10   Pea Salad 10
Mortimer Full Lunch Salad 25   Cucumber Salad 10
Special Vegetable Salad 10   Plain Celery 10

Sandwiches
Cheese 10 Lettuce 10 Calcutta 10 Hungarian 10 Lima Bean 10
Peas 10   Mortimer Cream Cheese 15
Hot Egg Sandwich 15
Tell waitress when sandwich is to be made of
Entire Wheat Bread

Vegetables
Baked Hubbard Squash in Shell 10
Succotash 5   Squash 5
Peas 5   Boiled Onions 10   Lima Beans 5
Potatoes
Broiled Sweet Potatoes 10   Mashed Potatoes 10
Shoestring Potatoes 10   Baked White Potatoes 10
Saratoga Chips 10   Saute 5   Lyonnaise 5   Hashed Browned 10

Relishes, Cheese, Etc.
Roquefort 25   Brie 20   Camembert 20   Neufchatel 15
Imported Swiss 15   New York Fancy Cream 15
California Ripe Olives 10   Queen Olives 10   Pim Olas 15
Stuffed Bar Mango 10   Piccalilli 10   Horseradish 5
Sweet Pickles 10   Dill Pickles 5
Manitou Ginger Champagne, (non alcoholic) 10

Peach Roll, with whipped cream 15

Sweet Cider 5

A la Carte

Dessert, Etc.
Sago-Custard 5
Apple Cobbler 5
Apple 5   Mince 5   Pumpkin 5   Cocoanut 5
Wheat or Buckwheat Cakes, with Maple Syrup or Honey 15
Baked Apple Dumpling, with hard sauce or wine sauce 10
Granose Biscuit, with fruit sauce and cream 15
Shredded Wheat Biscuit, fruit sauce and cream 15
Rice with Honey 10 Fruit Salad 10 Baked Apple and Cream 10
Mortimer Dream 15   Rice with Cream 15   Milk Toast 15
Rice with Milk 10   Assorted Cake15   Palace Wafers 15
Macaroons 15   Plain Loaf Cake 10   Nut Loaf Cake 15
Old Fashioned Raised Doughnuts [without shortening 5
New England Doughnuts, with shortening 5

Fruits
Sliced Oranges 10   Assorted Fruit 15   Grapes 10   Bananas 10
Apples 10

Ice Creams
Ice Cream with Siberian Crab-apple Jelly 20
Ice Cream with Choice of Preserves 20
Vanilla Ice Cream with Preserve Figs 20
Pie a la Mode 10   Assorted Cake 15
Vanilla 10   Strawberry 10   Lemon Ice 15

Preserves
Preserved Figs, with cream 15
Damson 10   Tomato 10   Strawberry 10   Peach 10   Cherry 10
Blackberry 10   Red Raspberry 10   Black Raspberry 10
Siberian Crab-apple Jelly 10   Home-made Quince 10

Tea, Coffee, Etc.
Pure Food Champagne (non alcholic) 10   Tiffin 5   Lemonade 5
Tea 5   Coffee 5   Milk 5   Buttermilk 5
Caramel-Cereal 5 Manitou Ginger Ale (non alcholic)10 Cocoa 5
Grape Juice 10   Grape Juice with Seltzer 10
Minimum Charge for single Drink 10c.

Crackers Served with Soup   Bread and Butter 5
Battle Creek Sanitarium

Health Foods
Granola with Milk 10   Granose with Milk 10
Granola with Cream 15   Granose with Cream 15
Granose Biscuit Toast 10   Zwieback 5   Caramel-Cereal
Fruit Coco 10   Malted Nuts 10
Ambrosia 15   Fig Ambrosia 15
Bromose 15   Fig Bromose 10   Coco Bromose 10
Sliced Nuttose 15   Nut Butter 5   Nuttolene 15
Protose 15
BREAKFAST AFTER 6:30 A. M.
Minimum Charge 15

Occasion:	Unknown
Sponsor:	Unknown
Place:	Bergen, Norway
Date:	November 2, 1881

This beautiful menu card from Norway is a gold printed lithograph with handtinted watercolors. The young musicians serenade the lovely ladies from a balcony, while the ladies weave floral garlands. The back of the menu is printed in black ink in Norwegian.

Occasion: Dinner

Place: Bergen, Norway

Date: October 4, 1884

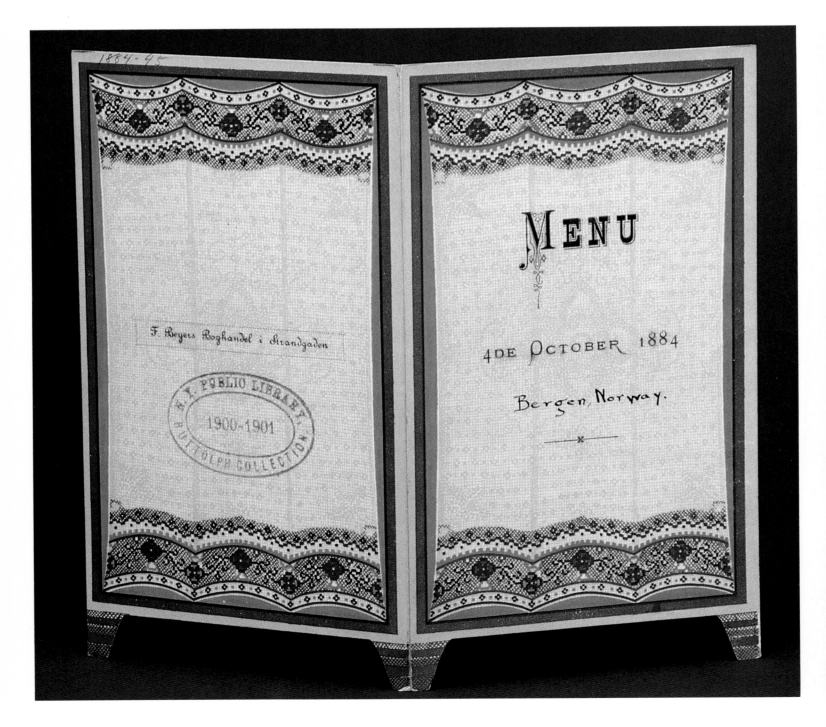

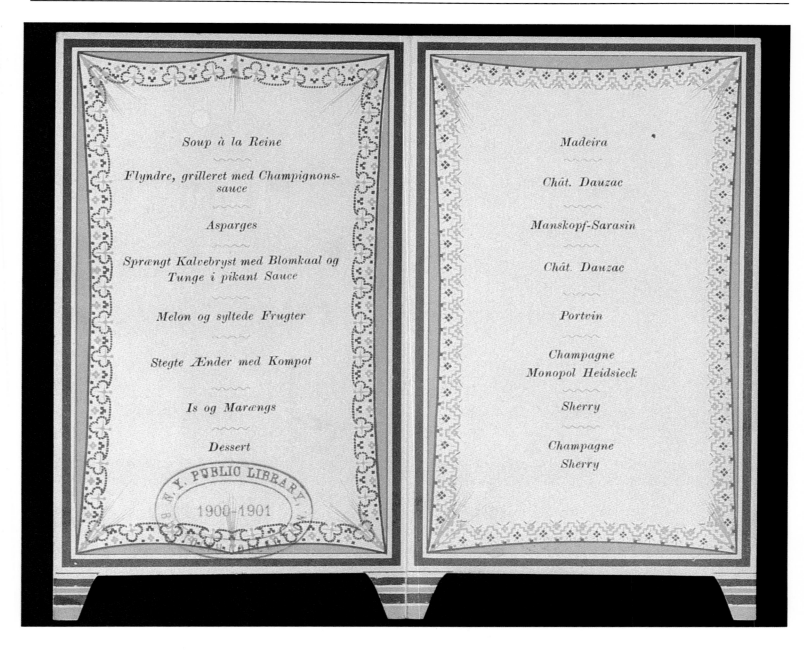

Soup à la Reine

Flyndre, grilleret med Champignons-
sauce

Asparges

Sprængt Kalvebryst med Blomkaal og
Tunge i pikant Sauce

Melon og syltede Frugter

Stegte Ænder med Kompot

Is og Marængs

Dessert

Madeira

Chât. Dauzac

Manskopf-Sarasin

Chât. Dauzac

Portvin

Champagne
Monopol Heidsieck

Sherry

Champagne
Sherry

This 3 1/4″x5 1/2″ menu is dye-cut
in the shape of a room-divider
screen. The background is finely
printed to resemble lace and
embroidery. The interior is printed
in black, gold, and pink inks, with
the fabric design carried through in a
decorative border.

Occasion: Dinner

Sponsor: American Library
             Association

Place: Fabyan House, NH

Date: September 10, 1890

This Library Association menu is deckle-edged and printed on centerfolded construction paper. The dimensions are 5"x4 1/2", and the interior is printed in black ink. The cover has a mini, eight-page booklet pasted on, containing verses from many famous authors including: Wordsworth, Shakespeare, and S. Smith. Three handpainted cattails are painted behind the booklet to add color.

Occasion: Dinner—150th Anniversary
             Thurn and Taxis Family

Sponsor: Unknown

Place: Palais Frankfurt, Frankfurt,
             Germany

Date: May 8, 1899

This dinner card is printed completely in French. The two 7 1/2"x11 1/2" pieces of heavy linen paper are ribbon bound; the cover is adorned with a fine lithograph.

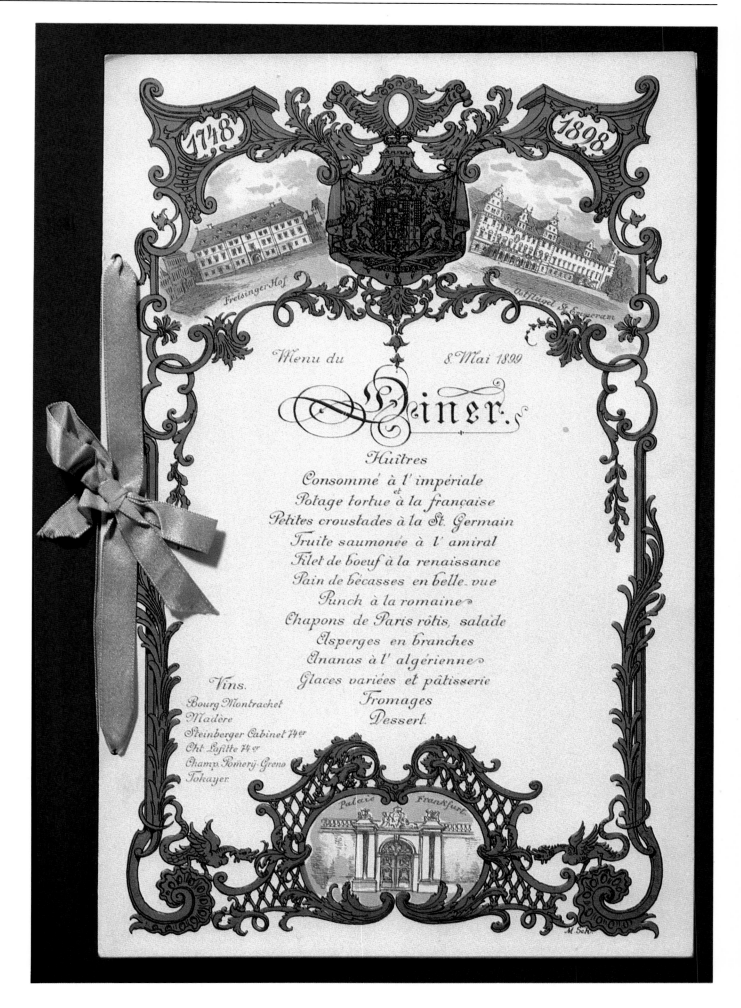

Occasion: Waldorf-Astoria Tea Room Menu

Place: Waldorf-Astoria, New York City, NY

Date: 1897

This beautiful etching is indicative of the advances in printing. The Waldorf-Astoria insignia appears in the upper left of this 4"x5 1/2" cardboard, centerfolded menu. Coffee and tea is listed as 25¢ per cup, fairly expensive for 1897.

Occasion: Dinner

Sponsor: Union League Club

Place: Philadelphia, PA

Date: March 5, 1879

An unusual multi-colored Japanese lithograph decorates the front of this Union League Club menu printed by Tiffany & Co. An unusual, diagonally positioned construction paper paste-on contains the menu in red and black ink. The back of the menu lists the sponsor in blue and red ink, with the date and a decorative border in blue ink.

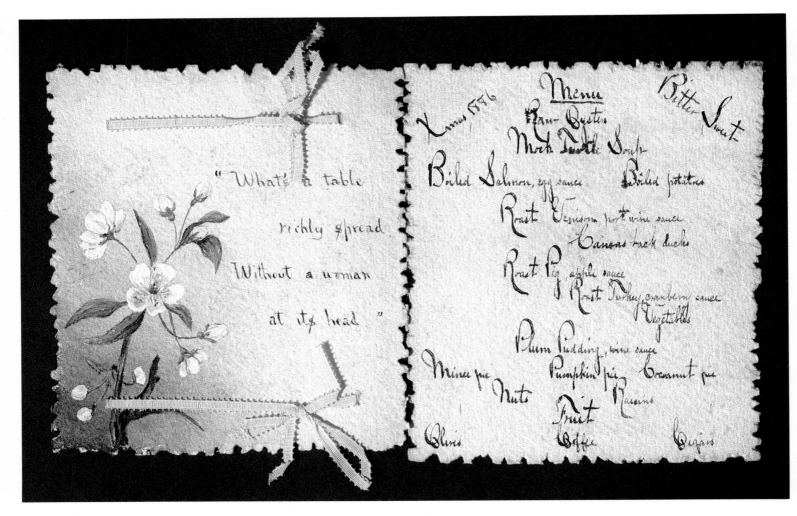

Occasion: Christmas 1886

Sponsor: Unknown

Place: Unknown

Date: December 25, 1886

This menu is completely homemade. Two pieces of construction paper were pasted together and tied with beige silk ribbon. The cover is handpainted with an apple blossom branch and contains a handwritten verse "What's a table richly spread, without a woman at its head." The menu is handwritten and dated Christmas 1886.

Occasion: Bar of Northern Berkshire Dinner

Sponsor: Mr. Fred F. Dowlin

Place: The Wilson, North Adams, MA

Date: September 13, 1898

This 4"x5 1/2" book-shaped menu has leatherette covers with a silver embossed title "Blackstone's Commentaries." The one-sheet linen paper insert is cut in the same shape as the covers and is printed in black ink. The word "menu" is silver embossed at the top of the menu page. The entire piece is bound by a hand-tied beige satin ribbon.

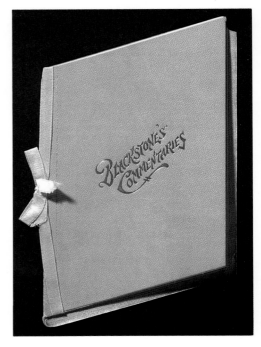

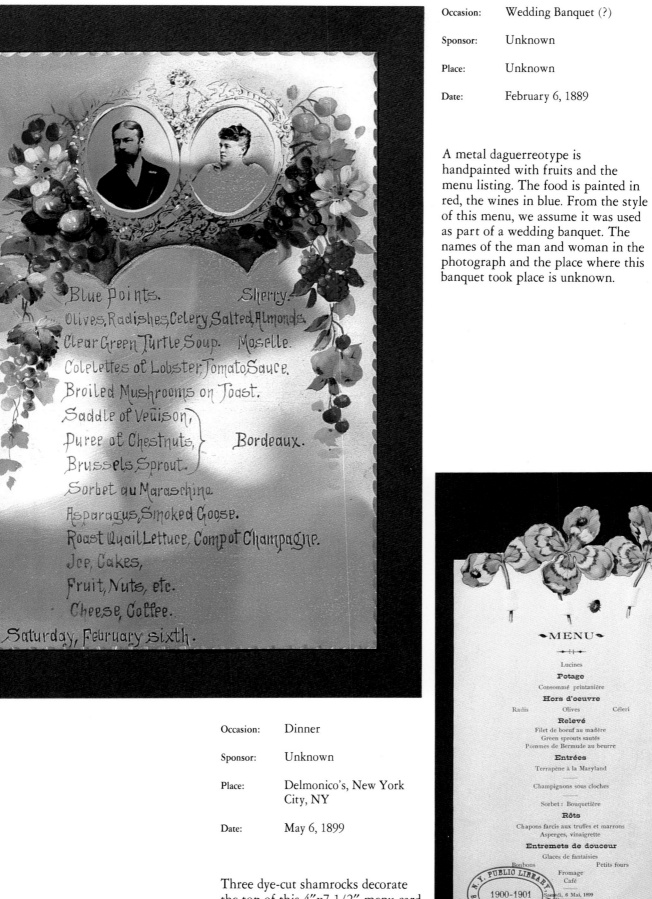

Blue Points.   Sherry.
Olives, Radishes, Celery, Salted Almonds.
Clear Green Turtle Soup.   Moselle.
Colplettes of Lobster, Tomato Sauce.
Broiled Mushrooms on Toast.
Saddle of Venison,
Puree of Chestnuts,   }   Bordeaux.
Brussels Sprout.
Sorbet au Maraschino.
Asparagus, Smoked Goose.
Roast Quail Lettuce, Compot Champagne.
Ice, Cakes,
Fruit, Nuts, etc.
Cheese, Coffee.
Saturday, February sixth.

Occasion: Wedding Banquet (?)

Sponsor: Unknown

Place: Unknown

Date: February 6, 1889

A metal daguerreotype is handpainted with fruits and the menu listing. The food is painted in red, the wines in blue. From the style of this menu, we assume it was used as part of a wedding banquet. The names of the man and woman in the photograph and the place where this banquet took place is unknown.

Occasion: Dinner

Sponsor: Unknown

Place: Delmonico's, New York City, NY

Date: May 6, 1899

Three dye-cut shamrocks decorate the top of this 4"x7 1/2" menu card. Embossed lady bugs are handtinted red, as are the shamrocks handtinted green. The menu portion is printed in black ink.

⤙MENU⤚

Lucines

Potage
Consommé printanière

Hors d'oeuvre
Radis   Olives   Céleri

Relevé
Filet de boeuf au madère
Green sprouts sautés
Pommes de Bermude au beurre

Entrées
Terrapène à la Maryland

Champignons sous cloches

Sorbet : Bouquetière

Rôts
Chapons farcis aux truffes et marrons
Asperges, vinaigrette

Entremets de douceur
Glaces de fantaisies
Bonbons   Petits fours
Fromage
Café

Samedi, 6 Mai, 1899
Delmonicos

INDEX
CLASSIC MENU
(By Date of Menu)